MOBILIZING OPPORTUNITIES

RACE, ETHNICITY, AND POLITICS
Luis Ricardo Fraga and Paula D. McClain, Editors

MOBILIZING OPPORTUNITIES

THE EVOLVING LATINO ELECTORATE
and the FUTURE OF AMERICAN POLITICS

Ricardo Ramírez

University of Virginia Press   *Charlottesville and London*

University of Virginia Press
© 2013 by the Rector and Visitors of the University of Virginia
All rights reserved
Printed in the United States of America on acid-free paper

First published 2013
First paperback edition published 2015
ISBN 978-0-8139-3811-0 (paper)

1 3 5 7 9 8 6 4 2

The Library of Congress has cataloged the hardcover edition as follows:

LIBRARY OF CONGRESS CATALOGING-IN-PUBLICATION DATA
Ramírez, Ricardo.
    Mobilizing opportunities : the evolving Latino electorate and the future of American politics / Ricardo Ramírez.
        pages   cm.—(Race, ethnicity, and politics)
    Includes bibliographical references and index.
    ISBN 978-0-8139-3510-2 (cloth : alk. paper)—ISBN 978-0-8139-3511-9 (e-book)
    1. Hispanic Americans—Politics and government. 2. Political participation—United States. 3. Elections—United States. 4. United States—Politics and government. I. Title.
    E184.S75R35 2013
    323.1168073—dc23

                                                                    2013013898

To Angélica, Mónica, Rebeca, and Érica

mis AMoREs

Contents

Acknowledgments

This book is about context and evolution in American politics. It is about Latino lives throughout the United States and the unique effect that context has on their levels of civic and political engagement. For some Latinos, the states in which they reside mobilize them into politics at faster than expected rates. For others, their incorporation into civic and political life is slower, but nonetheless steady. The degree to which we understand how and when the evolution of the Latino electorate happens is tied into institutions, place, and motivation and mobilization.

How this book became a reality is also intrinsically tied to the institutions with which I have engaged, the places where I have lived, and the sources of my motivation to see this project through. I have benefited from the financial and research support of four institutions outside of my academic home. I began my career after graduate school at the Public Policy Institute of California (PPIC). Their financial support, especially Mark Baldassare's support, allowed me the time to develop some of the early ideas for this book. I also benefited from the financial support of the National Science Foundation, which allowed me to conduct some of the data-intensive research while housed at the Institute for Social Science Research at UCLA with my sponsoring scientist, David Sears. The time and resources proved essential, but not sufficient, as I could not have obtained all of the necessary data without the willingness of the National Association of Latino Elected Officials (NALEO) and National Council of La Raza (NCLR) to grant me access to the work they do to change the lives of Latinos throughout the United States. At these institutions, I am particularly grateful for the support of Evan Bacalao, Efrain Escobedo, Marcelo Gaete, Rosalind Gold, Clarissa Martinez, Gladys Negrete, and Arturo Vargas.

The places where I have worked also greatly impacted the book, less because of their location and more because of how these places shaped my daily life. I consider myself fortunate to have had colleagues and friends who made going to work something to look forward to every day, which made conducting the research for this book seem less onerous. At the University of Southern California, they include Macarena Gomez-Barris, Ange-Marie Hancock, Pierrette Hondagnau-Sotelo, Jane Iwamura, Jane Junn, Anthony Kammas, Roberto Lint-Sagarena, Manuel Pastor, Michael Preston, Laura Pulido, Shana Redmond, Leland Saito, Michael Waterman, and Nick Weller. At the University of Notre Dame, they include Peri Arnold, Jaimie Bleck, David Campbell, Darren Davis, Cynthia Duarte, Juan Carlos Guzman, Carlos Jauregui, Tatiana Jauregui-Botero, Geoff Layman, David Nickerson, Paul Ocobock, Dianne Pinderhughes, Tim Scully, Naunihal Singh, Christina Wolbrecht, all of the faculty at the Institute for Latino Studies, and the students in my graduate seminar on ethnicity and immigration. I am also grateful to be a core member of the Rooney Center for the Study of American Democracy and for the generosity of its donors, Francis and Kathleen Rooney, who believe in the importance of Latinos for the future of American politics.

The institutional support and work environment provided the means to undertake the painstaking task of conducting research and writing. The motivation to channel these resources to produce a book on Latino politics came from other sources. In this book, I make the case that the Latino electorate is evolving and that this coincides with the dramatic evolution in the study of Latino politics since I began my doctoral work in the 1990s. At the forefront of this evolution is the work and example of the principal investigators of the 2006 Latino National Survey (LNS): Luis Fraga, John Garcia, Rodney Hero, Michael Jones-Correa, Valerie Martinez-Ebers, and Gary Segura.

If the LNS team has been at the forefront of the changes in the study of Latino politics, Adrian Felix is emblematic of the promise of tomorrow. I witnessed his evolution from my graduate student to trusted friend and colleague. He, along with others in his cohort, will help shape the future of the subfields of Latino politics and Latin American studies. I am also thankful for his great feedback on earlier drafts of the book.

Additionally, I have benefited from the insights, advice, and interactions with David Ayon, Christina Bejarano, Cristina Beltrán, Shaun Bowler, Bruce Cain, Susan Clarke, Vicky DeFrancesco Soto, Louis DeSipio, Jaime Dominguez, Jonathan Fox, Lorrie Frasure-Yokley, Alfonso Gonzales, Don Green, Zoli Hajnal, Vince Hutchings, Jonathan Fox, Taeku Lee, Ben Marquez, Natalie Masuoka, Jenn Merolla, John Mollenkopf, Celeste

Montoya-Kirk, Stephen Nuño, Ron Schmidt Sr., Simon Weffer, and Chris Zepeda-Millán.

I am most indebted to Dom Apollon, Matt Barreto, Rudy Espino, Sylvia Manzano, Adrian Pantoja, Karthick Ramakrishnan, Gabe Sanchez, and Janelle Wong. Their support and long friendship has helped sustain me and has been at the core of my own evolution as a scholar through the many stages of my academic career. Without a doubt, our many conversations about politics and academia over the years have impacted my approach to the study of American politics generally, and Latino politics in particular.

I was lucky enough to have spent some time writing in Morro Bay for a few days in the summers of 2011 and 2012. Thank you, Val Staley for letting me use your home. I could not have picked a more ideal place to finish putting the manuscript together. I would like to thank Dick Holway at the University of Virginia Press for his vision and early interest in this project, as well as the Race, Ethnicity and Politics series editors, Luis Fraga and Paula McClain. I am grateful for the excellent feedback and suggestions of the anonymous reviewers who steered me through the final big picture sections that ultimately made the book come together.

I would like to express my deepest gratitude to my family. As the son of migrant farmworkers of very modest means, I would not have had the motivation to go to college, graduate school, or the professoriate without their love and support. My mother, Guadalupe López Ramírez, instilled in me a sense of perseverance and determination that continue to be the cornerstone of my success. When I doubted myself, a simple "no te me achicopales" helped motivate me to push harder. I am thankful for the love and support of my siblings Martha, Maria, Jorge, and Pati, as well as Doña Esther and all of the Mendoza family. To my brother Domingo (1970–1981), you still inspire me to do all that I know you could have done.

Finally, I would like to thank my wife, Lupe. Thank you for believing in me and us; I love you! I dedicate this book to our daughters Angélica, Mónica, Rebeca, and Érica. You are my inspiration, and you fill me with joy every day. Each of you is so different, but all have the same effect on me. I am truly blessed because you came into my life. While other fathers might feel trepidation at the thought of how their little girls will change, I embrace your future adventures, challenges, and successes. It is because of you that I can cling to the promise of equality and a better world.

Las quiero mucho mis AMoREs!

Portions of chapter 2 were previously published in Ricardo Ramírez, "Mobilization en Español: Spanish-Language Radio and the Activation of Political Identities," in *Rallying for Immigrant Rights: The Fights for Inclusion in 21st Century America,* edited by Kim Voss and Irene Bloemraad, © 2011 by the Regents of the University of California. Published by the University of California Press.

Portions of chapter 5 appeared in Ricardo Ramírez, "Segmented Mobilization: Latino Nonpartisan Get-Out-the-Vote Efforts in the 2000 General Election," *American Politics Research* 35, no. 3 (2007): 155–75.

MOBILIZING OPPORTUNITIES

1

STATE CONTEXTS, MOBILIZATION, AND THE EVOLVING LATINO ELECTORATE

In 2008, pundits heralded Latino voters as playing a significant role in the Democratic presidential primary. Having swept up most of the sought-after endorsements of Latino elected officials long before the Iowa caucuses and New Hampshire primary, the Hillary Clinton campaign believed that Latino votes would follow suit. Latinos were seen as a key component of Clinton's campaign strategy, and it was expected that the growing bloc of Latino voters could help swing key states in February's "Super Tuesday."[1] According to Sergio Bendixen, Clinton's head of Latino outreach, February 5 "is the firewall, and the Latino vote in California is the most important part of the firewall. . . . If she can win California, no matter what happens the race is on" (Carlton 2008). Nine months later, Latinos would be seen as a bloc of voters crucial to the election of Barack Obama as president, having helped him win key swing states like Florida, New Mexico, Colorado, and even Indiana and North Carolina (Barreto, Collingwood, and Manzano 2010).

Four years later, there was renewed anticipation about the role that Latinos could play in the presidential election. In March 2012, *Time* magazine posited that "Latino voters will swing the 2012 election." This cover story focused on the growth, presence, and preferences of the Latino electorate and the resulting consequences for the presidential election. Not all pundits or analysts were as upbeat about the role of Latinos or their willingness to coalesce behind one candidate in the general election. Less than one month before the election, some state polls such as the Tampa Bay Times / Bay

News 9 / Miami Herald poll of Florida voters suggested that Latino support only slightly favored the incumbent president. Other state polls, such as the one completed by SurveyUSA, claimed that Barack Obama held only an eight-point lead over Mitt Romney among Latino voters in Nevada. The Pew Hispanic Center, through its more systematic sampling of Latinos, estimated that support for Barack Obama would likely be much higher, but indicated that Latinos were less certain about voting than non-Latinos (Lopez and Gonzalez-Barrera 2012). Unlike English-language mainstream outlets, the impreMedia/Latino Decisions tracking poll consistently estimated a more than two to one preference for Barack Obama over the challenger Mitt Romney, and their election-eve report estimated high voter turnout.

On election night, November 6, 2012, and in the days that followed, pundits trumpeted the significant role that Latinos played in the election and the role that they would play in years to come. An editorial political cartoon in the *New Yorker* highlighted the political establishment's urgent need for "binders full of Latinos."[2] While the hype about Latinos' potential impact on national elections has been a recurring theme in every presidential election since the mid–1990s, the media has only recently begun to pivot away from earlier metaphors of Latinos as a "sleeping giant" based on the disparity between the size of the Latino population and the potential but unrealized political impact of the Latino electorate. In the end, the noteworthy change in the landscape of American politics during the 2012 election was not the awakening of a Latino "sleeping giant." Instead it was the apparent wake-up call to campaign strategists about the significance and evolving nature of the Latino electorate despite many signs of this change throughout the 1990s and the first decade of the twenty-first century. Media pundits, think tanks, and campaign strategists underestimated the level of political interest in the election among Latino voters. Not only was estimated turnout higher than had been predicted, but the partisan distribution of votes cast in favor of Barack Obama's reelection also took many by surprise.[3] One of the most cited revelations had to do with the fact that Barack Obama was the preferred candidate among Latinos in Florida for a second consecutive election. The political behavior of Latino voters in Florida in 2008 and 2012 is noteworthy beyond their presidential vote choice in one or two elections. These elections reflect the consequences of growth and change in the composition of the state's Latino electorate whose partisan attachments are increasingly malleable. Moreover, it is not just in Florida where the Latino electorate is evolving. The change is taking place throughout the United States.

Existing Approaches to Understanding the (Heterogeneous) Latino Electorate

The study of Latino voters can take various forms, ranging from historical narratives and case studies to quantitative analyses of Latinos focused on understanding the extent to which Latino voters are distinct, and the consequence of this behavior on political outcomes. Three approaches characterize most studies of Latinos: the "ethnic approach," the "pivotal vote thesis," and the "demography is destiny" approach. I discuss each of these approaches before turning to my state-centered and process-driven approach.

There is much discussion of the Latino population and the Latino electorate. Characterizations of Latinos as an easily identifiable group may seem justified because the group is more concentrated than other racially defined groups. Three-quarters of all Latinos live in just ten states: California, Texas, Florida, New York, Illinois, Arizona, New Jersey, Colorado, New Mexico, and Nevada. For comparison, to reach the same threshold among other racial groups, one would have to take the top 22 states, 15 states, 16 states, and 11 states for non-Hispanic whites, African Americans, American Indian & Alaska Native, and Asian Americans respectively (*Statistical Abstract of the United States* 2012).[4] Even with concentration of Latinos in ten states, the rates of population concentration vary by individual states. While Latinos constitute 16 percent of the population nationally, and at least 16 percent in the ten states mentioned, the mean proportion of Latino population in these ten states is 27 percent. There is also within-group variation of population concentration, national origin diversity, socioeconomic status, nativity, and age, which helps make the case against a view of a singular or homogeneous Latino population.[5]

Cognizant of the dangers of thinking of Latinos as one undifferentiated group, the "ethnic" approach focuses on the heterogeneous nature of the Latino population based on national origin and the related differences with respect to citizenship, immigrant generation, and class (Oboler 1995; DeSipio 1996; Jones-Correa 1998; Beltrán 2010; Abrajano and Alvarez 2010). This approach to the study of Latino politics focuses on understanding the differences in voting behavior among and between Mexican Americans, Puerto Ricans, and Cuban Americans, the three largest national-origin groups, while also questioning the rationale for treating Latinos as a panethnic group. This ethnic approach gained traction at an earlier period because the distinct history of arrival and presence by Latinos from different parts of Latin America represented very unique patterns of social and political integration largely related to the scope and nature of each community's citizenship acquisition. Puerto Ricans, for instance, are citizens by birth regardless of whether they were born on the mainland or on the island of Puerto Rico. Cuban immigrants, as political refugees, enjoy the most favorable immigration policy of any country in the world and therefore have an expedited path to legal permanent residency and citizenship. The Mexican-origin population has a longer and more complex history in the United States, which began when Mexico ceded present-day states that comprise the southwestern United States in the Treaty of Guadalupe Hidalgo in 1848. As a result, a small segment of the population was granted U.S. citizenship, another segment immigrated legally through family reunification provisions of immigration law,[6] and yet another segment of the population gained legal permanent residency as a result of the Immigration Reform and Control Act of 1986. In addition to the large segment of second- and third-generation Mexican Americans, the remaining segment of the population consists of unauthorized immigrants, primarily from Mexico and Central American countries, who arrived after the 1980s. It therefore was sensible for earlier analyses of Latino politics to center on this ethnic approach.

In line with this research, Cristina Beltrán (2010) provides a contrarian view to the notion of a coherent, pan-ethnic Latino identity and political agenda. To make the case, she begins by exploring the Chicano and Puerto Rican movements of the 1960s and 1970s and argues that the visions of unity and pan-ethnic identity are temporal and primarily elite-driven ideas of movement leaders. She then criticizes the notion that the homogenization of Latino diversity is a necessary precondition for Latino empowerment, precisely because Latino elites "are unable to invoke the representative 'we' that sustains discussions of the 'Latino vote' and other markers of the pan-ethnic project" (16). Her critique is consistent with prior works that question the consequences of the interaction between internal heterogeneity and the salience of ethnicity (or pan-ethnic behavior) for Latinos as it relates to politics. In his seminal book *Counting on the Latino Vote,* Louis DeSipio asserts that "while the conditions for a politically salient ethnicity based on exclusion may exist, factors internal to the Latino populations may prevent them from challenging the U.S. political system in ethnic terms" (1996:10). This is not only true for Latinos, as one could both criticize and appreciate the homogenization of other groups based on race or place.

For example, political scientists have long used "the South" as a heuristic for political identity and political behavior primarily for whites living in the South. Why, after the many radical changes in the South from the

Civil War, to civil rights, to the more recent migration from northern states and of unauthorized Latino immigrants, do political scientists and pundits make reference to the South as if there were a homogenized southern identity or tangible political behavior among voters from the South? One could similarly appreciate and criticize the homogenization of black identity and behavior. In the case of African Americans, the notion of linked fate as a black utility heuristic has demonstrated consistent and enduring effects on African American political behavior (Cohen 1999; Dawson 1994). In the case of Latinos, the "ethnic model" often privileges the presence of national-origin differences. Fraga et al. (2010) provide compelling evidence that pan-ethnic similarities may be more important at present than national origin differences. Based on extensive focus groups and preliminary data from the 2006 Latino National Survey, they find a noticeable increase in pan-ethnic identity and behavior in the last ten to fifteen years, with potential consequences for politics. Beltrán's theory challenges this, but she draws on characterizations of Chicano identity from more than forty year ago that may have been replaced by new pan-ethnic identities. There is room for disagreement about the utility of a pan-ethnic focus, but my goal is not to surmise a particular intent among Latino elites to promote civic *Latinidad,* as Beltrán suggests, or to dwell on the social construction of ethnicity that accompanies the relatively new invented identity and term "Latino." Instead, *Mobilizing Opportunities* allows for the possibility that Latino identity, taken on out of convenience or under duress, can acquire its own political reality for individuals, society, and the polity that can have very real consequences for shared Latino behavior. I acknowledge the diversity within the Latino population, but make the case that the uncertainty about the salience of ethnicity for Latinos has faded as the U.S. political system has consistently engaged Latinos as one ethnic group. Distinct from southern identity or linked fate among African Americans, Latinos have reacted to the system in identifiable ways both as an ethnic group and as selective subgroups of Latinos based on nativity and state contexts where they live. The analytical framework I provide captures pan-ethnic similarities and national-origin differences by focusing on when, where, and to whom these matter. Moreover, my state-centered approach moves beyond identity to highlight how state contexts are essential to understanding the patterns in mobilization not as an event but as processes. Once we conceptualize the potential for Latino political influence as a dynamic process, we can begin to more fully understand the "how" and "why" of Latino politics in the United States today.

A second prominent approach among scholars and pundits is less concerned with the utility (or lack thereof) of theories about a singular "Latino electorate." Because it is more concerned with identifying instances when Latinos provide the margin of victory for particular races, the "pivotal vote" thesis implicitly critiques earlier approaches that privilege national-origin differences because it is premised on bloc voting and could be a demonstration of strong Latino identity. According to this approach, it is possible to determine the import of Latino voters if we can identify cases when the outcome of a particular election would have changed if no Latino had voted. Several analyses find that Latinos have limited to no effect on determining presidential elections at the state level and make the case that this largely explains their marginalization within presidential campaigns (de la Garza and DeSipio 1992, 1996, 1999, 2005). However, this approach is increasingly problematic for three reasons. First, this approach's assumed bloc voting among Latinos neglects the fact that some of this may be driven by the composition of Latino population in many states. In earlier periods, the composition of the Latino population was dominated by one national origin group or another. However, there is now greater variation of national-origin Latino subgroups than once was the case. In some states, national-origin Latino groups that once constituted a majority or plurality of the state's Latino population in 1990 witnessed a significant drop in their share by 2010. This can be attributed to some geographic dispersion and the influx of Latinos of other national origins. For example, in 1990, Puerto Ricans accounted for 49 percent of the Latino population in New York and 43 percent of New Jersey's Latino population. Twenty years later, these proportions had dropped to 31 percent and 28 percent respectively. Similarly, Cuban Americans accounted for 43 percent of Florida's Latino population in 1990, but only 29 percent in 2010. In eight of the ten states considered, the proportion of Mexican-origin population increased, but in Arizona and Texas, there was a slight increase in the non-Mexican-origin population. The increasing national-origin heterogeneity among state Latino population should not be assumed to be inconsequential. If there is similar voter behavior by this more diverse Latino electorate, why is this so? Is it because of efforts from within the community or exogenous pressures that lead to this common behavior?

The second reason why the "pivotal vote" approach is problematic is because of the unrealistic supposition that one could remove Latinos from election settings without impacting campaign dynamics. After all, candidate campaign strategies do not begin during the general election. They begin during the primary process, and the composition of the electorate helps determine which candidates decide to enter the race. One should not assume that the candidates in the general election would be the same if we hypothetically removed an entire segment of the electorate. Campaign dynamics therefore are responses that should not be assumed to hold constant when the composition of the electorate suddenly changes. Third, the "pivotal vote" approach to the study of Latino politics is static because it focuses on single election outcomes and fails to consider the many ways in which Latinos can impact the electoral calculus of campaigns, including transforming state contexts from competitive to one that advantages a particular party. The sole focus is on explaining a specific election and has nothing to do with change over time. In other words, this approach is too vested in the present by attempting to discern when Latino political behavior is salient without taking into account the process-oriented factors that explain how and why long-term political salience can be achieved.

The third approach to understanding Latino political influence, "demography is destiny," is most aptly captured by Shaun Bowler and Gary Segura (2011) in their book *The Future Is Ours: Minority Politics, Political Behavior and the Multiracial Era of American Politics*. The authors focus on the political behavior of America's racial and ethnic minorities, how this behavior manifests itself, and the likely partisan consequences. From values and beliefs to issue preferences, partisanship, and descriptive representation, the distinctiveness of American minorities, according to Segura and Bowler, is likely to have a long-term impact on national elections. "Taken together, the two critical factors of demography and the Obama electoral coalition appeared in 2008 to imply a possible Democratic realignment, as large and enduring as that which accompanied the Great Depression and New Deal and which dominated American politics for a generation" (Bowler and Segura 2011:4). The core of this approach hinges upon sheer demographic growth and Latinos *eventually* attaining particular endogenous and exogenous thresholds[7] and becoming voters who are critical to winning coalitions.

There is an apparent chasm between the rhetoric of inevitable Latino influence (combined with African Americans and Asian Americans) and the less sanguine assessment of Latinos' significance for national elections typical of the "pivotal vote" approach. The "demography is destiny" thesis focuses too much on population size as the source of eventual influence, whereas the "pivotal vote" approach relies on election outcomes and whether or not Latinos provided the margin necessary to win a particular election. In a sense, one is imprecise and future-oriented, and the other is excessively formulaic and overly concerned with the present. Neither approach is developmental by design, so neither can explain changes over time. In this work, I seek to better understand *how, when,* and *where* Latino voters have become salient and have redefined politics and partisan strategies.

New Approach to Understanding the Latino Electorate

Understanding how, when, and where Latinos have successfully shifted perceptions of their uncertain political relevance to a sense that they are redefining state politics and American democracy hinges on understanding the influx of Latino citizens and voters over the last twenty years. In delineating the process by which this change takes place, I seek to reconceptualize how we think about Latinos as an evolving electorate and their impact on politics. This evolution can best be explained by the variation in state-specific political contexts and the mobilization of new Latino voters with distinct voter preferences. When and where Latinos will become politically salient through their electoral presence or growth is contingent on the *responsive capacity* of the Latino population across state contexts. Responsive capacity refers to the interaction of factors related to elite efforts to shape the civic infrastructure and voters' ability to respond to external factors. It hinges on the incidence of two types of mobilizing opportunities: *proactive mobilization* and *reactive mobilization.*

Proactive mobilization involves a range of elite-sponsored activities targeting barriers to Latino civic and political incorporation, which consists of both electoral and nonelectoral participation.[8] As such, the barriers targeted by elite-sponsored activities do not include only concrete or easily identifiable factors such as voter turnout. Some barriers to participation, such as age requirements for voting, impact all American citizens but have a disproportionate impact on Latinos because children comprise a significant portion of the Latino citizen population. In addition to "get out the vote" (GOTV) efforts, activation into civic and political life includes empowering Latinos to voice support or opposition to policies and/or civic and political leaders, providing assistance to Legal Permanent Residents at various stages of the naturalization process,[9] and registering eligible Latinos to vote. The distinct feature of proactive mobilization is the importance of cumulative resources provided by organizations and Spanish-language media, but the concept also takes into account various forms of localized proactive mobilization by Latino elites.

It makes sense that there would be variation in proactive mobilization given the differences in organizational capacity to address the most pressing barriers, as well as distinctions in local community needs for particular service provision. For example, there is a longer history of Latino civic organizations in Colorado than in Nevada, given the legacy of Chicano civil rights leaders like Rodolfo "Corky" Gonzalez, but it is also the case that in the last ten years labor unions in Nevada have advocated on behalf of Latinos on various issues in recognition of their strong membership in these unions. The 2011 Congressional Research Service reports that only 10 percent of the overall population in Colorado was born outside the United States, whereas almost twice that proportion, or 19 percent, of Nevada's population is foreign-born (Kandel 2011). Given that about one-third of the foreign-born population in both states is already naturalized, it follows that barriers to naturalization present a more pressing concern in Nevada than Colorado. Citizenship is not the only barrier to Latino participation in Nevada, relative to Colorado. Even without the citizenship or age barrier, as of 2010 only 42 percent of the Latino citizen voting age population (CVAP) in Nevada was registered to vote, whereas 47 percent of Colorado's Latino CVAP was registered to vote. This also points to differing mobilization needs across state contexts. Moreover, proactive mobilization does not consist of a checklist of activities in which Latino elites engage; it is meant to provide an overarching compilation of the efforts to address the barriers to civic and political incorporation.

Reactive mobilization, on the other hand, is a response to real or perceived imminent political threat. This exogenous shock is the catalyst for change in established patterns of civic and political engagement. This political threat can take the form of proposed laws (through statewide initiatives, state legislatures, or Congress) that spur protest activity and/or greater rates of naturalization, voter registration, and voter turnout. Perhaps the example of reactive mobilization in the Latino community most often discussed is the case of Proposition 187 in California during the 1994 gubernatorial reelection of Governor Pete Wilson. Many immigrants took to the streets to protest the statewide initiative because it sought to deny undocumented immigrants access to public education, social services, and health care, and required public officials to report suspected undocumented immigrants to the Immigration and Naturalization Service. Beyond protest politics, Proposition 187 led to reactive mobilization of Latino legal permanent residents (LPRs), who became more interested in pursuing U.S. citizenship and primed eligible Latino voters to register and vote. Because it is difficult to anticipate when a political or social event or situation will lead to Latinos' reactive mobilization, the concept of reactive mobilization must remain broad so that it can incorporate future, unanticipated sources of motivation to act politically.

While reactive mobilization can become a political opportunity and catalyst for increased electoral presence, it need not lead to sustained growth when the threat is less imminent. As the threat subsides, reactive mobilization wanes; this differs from proactive mobilization, which can persist and expand even in the absence of an imminent threat. While it is clear that variation in proactive mobilization hinges on the degree of the civic infrastructure, resources, and networks, it is less obvious that variation in reactive mobilization has multiple sources. Reactive mobilization can be measured as the community response to threat. The presence of threat is the primary variation, but there is a secondary source of variation within the Latino community that has to do with heterogeneity of the Latino population and the extent to which it has been primed by experience, immigrant composition, concentration, and individuals. It is possible, for example, for legal permanent residents to react to a political threat with greater interest in both the citizenship process and voter registration in one setting of the state, but not another. The same threat could, instead, mobilize a segment of the voting-eligible population that has not previously felt compelled to register to vote. It is the combination of the primary and secondary sources of community response that determines the overall strength of reactive mobilization, and the evolution of the Latino electorate is further impacted by the convergence with proactive mobilization.

I discuss below how a state-centered approach to the evolving Latino electorate promotes the idea that this evolution cannot be understood as one particular event, but must be seen instead as the process by which this change happens. This process-oriented view highlights both the dynamism inherent in political activation (reactive mobilization), while concurrently accounting for historical contingencies (proactive mobilization, which can vary by type and longevity) that affect the geographic and temporal variation of civic and political incorporation. With this in mind, the goal of the book is to provide a novel approach to the study of Latino politics that also acknowledges relevant insights about Latinos in the three broad approaches in the extant literature: the "ethnic" model, the "pivotal vote" thesis, and the "demography is destiny" forecast.

Where Are Latinos Politically Important?

The analytical puzzle, therefore, begins with Latinos as a salient pan-ethnic group. This salience is not yet evident throughout the entire country. A group's political influence is often acknowledged only after the group noticeably changes the political calculus beyond one election cycle. Thus, where one looks to identify change that has taken place has direct consequences for identifying Latino political influence. A focus on the national level to identify such influence may miss actual influence that can better be encapsulated at the state and local levels. To better capture how Latino political behavior is shaped by and consequently shapes politics, I focus on the state level, as states are the building blocks for national party politics. Several other studies have cited instances of Latino significance on state elections, unique political behavior, and unique policy environments (Pantoja, Ramírez, and Segura 2001; Barreto, Ramírez, and Woods 2005; Preuhs 2007; Matsubayashi and Rocha 2010; Preuhs and Juenke 2011). Earlier studies of Latino influence in presidential elections, on the one hand, consistently describe Latinos as not having been influential at the national level, yet point to patterns of influence and change in select states (de la Garza and DeSipio 1992, 1996, 1999, 2005). These studies do not attempt to reconcile both accounts or to surmise when influence at the state level has indirect, yet meaningful, effects at the national level. For example, as the most populous state, California plays a critical role in setting the baseline for national strategizing for Democratic candidates (Barreto et al. 2010). What makes my state-centered approach distinctive is the focus on when Latino voters react to perceived political threat based on immigration policy and non-Latino voter preferences. This interaction between geography and political context challenges the common belief that Latino political power is simply a function of population growth or tied to their relevance for presidential election outcomes.

Given the concentration of Latinos in a few states, we can isolate the relevance of these different political contexts in the ten states where over 78 percent of Latinos live (U.S. Census 2010). These states include Arizona, California, Colorado, Florida, Illinois, Nevada, New Jersey, New Mexico, New York, and Texas. The advantage of focusing on these ten states goes beyond adequately capturing the overwhelming share of all Latinos. These states are also relevant for national politics because they account for 216, or 80 percent, of the 270 Electoral College votes necessary to win the presidency. The "demography is destiny" thesis would suggest that this bodes well for Latinos as they are the largest minority group in each of these states (U.S. Census 2011). If they are the largest minority group, it should only be a matter of time before they gain more clout in these states. However, even the "demography is destiny" thesis relies on more than population presence. The community's trajectory is also important. That is, we must also take into consideration the rate of growth in order to assess the likely direction of Latinos' future presence and influence.

Conceptually, we can divide the ten states into those with modest or substantial Latino population presence in 2010, and further delineate them into those that experienced modest or substantial percentage population growth during the period 1990–2010. This allows us to broadly classify the states into one of four typologies: Moderate, Emergent, Established, and Dynamic. Except in very competitive partisan statewide races, states with modest Latino population presence and only modest population growth are the most likely to find that Latino political influence will be "Moderate," and I therefore classify them accordingly. Conversely, "Dynamic" states are those states that have experienced significant Latino population presence *and* significant growth. This dynamism is likely to garner a lot of social and political attention. "Emergent" states are characterized by modest presence, but with substantial population growth rate; and "Established" states are characterized by substantial Latino population presence but only modest population growth.[10]

Clearly, Latinos do not enjoy the same level of population presence across the ten states. Figure 1 displays Latino population presence and growth in the ten states. The range for Latino presence in the population is between 15.8 percent in Illinois and 46.3 percent in New Mexico, with the mean percentage of the population among these states at 27. With respect to growth in the twenty-year period from 1990 to 2010, New Mexico witnessed the smallest percentage growth at only 21.1 percent. The most substantial rate of growth took place in Nevada, with 153.9 percent, and the mean rate of growth among the ten states was 70 percent. New York and Colorado both had modest presence and growth, and no states can be classified as having substantial presence and growth. Four states—Illinois, New Jersey, Florida, and Nevada—experienced moderate presence and

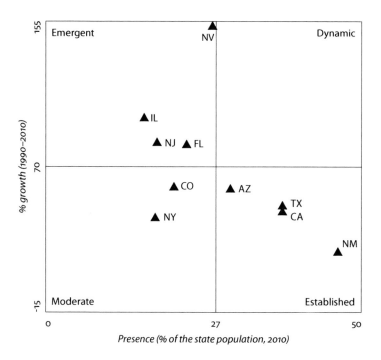

Fig. 1 Latino population presence and growth by state

substantial growth. Finally, Arizona, Texas, California and New Mexico can be classified as having substantial presence but modest growth.

The vast majority (85 percent) of Latinos in the United States who are registered to vote live in these states. While it may be true that, at some point in the future, Latinos are likely to consistently have more relative impact on state politics than other racial or ethnic minorities, this is not the case if we focus on the pool of potential and actual voters. As of 2010, Latinos are the largest minority of adult citizens, registered voters, and actual voters in only seven of the ten states. The reason for the gap between population presence and electoral presence has to do with the higher proportion of Latino nonvoters, relative to the mostly registered non-Hispanic white and black populations. If influence in politics was determined solely by population presence in the electorate, measuring influence and relevance of Latinos would be relatively straightforward. Because change in politics rarely takes place without changes in the composition of the electorate, the trajectory of presence in the electorate—or electoral presence—is also important and should be distinguished from population presence. Therefore, it is important to consider how much growth has taken place and how this has changed the calculus of non-Latino voters. How non-Latino voters behave and the nature of the two-party structure in these states are key.

At the state level, it is crucial that we understand the preferences of non-Latino voters over time. As non-Latino voter preferences become more evenly divided or competitive, Latinos may wield more influence, especially if they have *both* presence and growth in the pool of registered voters. Assuming that the non-Latino segment of the electorate is somewhat split in their voter preferences, Latinos should enjoy the greatest levels of influence in states where they also command a substantial presence in the pool of voters with substantial proportional growth (Dynamic), followed by states with substantial presence but only modest proportional growth (Established). States with modest Latino presence but substantial growth in the percentage of Latino registered voters (Emergent) are less likely to consistently witness influence in politics, but more so than in states where Latinos have modest presence and only modest growth (Moderate). One caveat that should be noted is that the focus on presence and growth is premised on pan-ethnic political identity and behavior among Latinos in each state.

Figure 2 shows Latino electoral presence and growth in the ten states. As was the case with the data on Latino population shown in figure 1, there is great variation with respect to presence and growth of Latino registered voters in the two decades under consideration. Figure 2, however, shows greater variation than figure 1 in the distribution of the states as two states are classified as "Moderate," two states are "Established," three states are "Emergent," and three states are "Dynamic." The range in the Latino presence among registered voters is between 6 percent in Illinois and 31.6 percent in New Mexico, with the mean percentage of registered voters in these states at 15 percent. With respect to growth during the twenty-year period from 1990 to 2010, New Mexico witnessed the smallest percentage growth at only 21.4 percent (which coincides with their rate of growth in the population). The most substantial rate of growth took place in Arizona, with 155 percent, and the mean rate of growth among the ten states was 88 percent. As was the case with the population typology, Colorado and New York are classified as "Moderate" because they had modest presence and modest growth of registered voters. However, the picture changes with respect to the other types. Illinois, New Jersey, and Nevada are classified as "Emergent" states because of their modest presence but substantial growth. We can classify Texas and New Mexico as "Established" due to their sub-

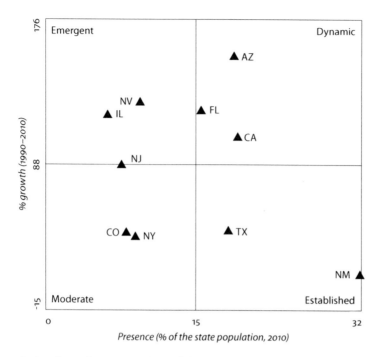

Fig. 2 Latino electoral presence and growth by state

stantial presence, but only modest growth of registered voters. Latino registered voters in the final three states—Arizona, Florida, and California—
are "Dynamic" states because they have substantial presence among those
who are registered to vote and also experienced substantial growth. The
greater variation in the classification of the states is important because it
demonstrates that population patterns, while important, do not necessarily
predestine the Latino population in a state to similar patterns among registered voters.

What Contexts Drive Latino Political Influence?

The above typologies should make clear that the path of the Latino population toward a favorable political destiny is not a smooth one. While population presence and growth are preconditions for greater political influence,
the process is not linear and uniform but nonlinear and differential. The in-
evitability of Latino influence in politics, therefore, is not as straightforward
as pundits or some scholars like Bowler and Segura (2011) have suggested.
But if demography has yet to be reflected in Latinos' political destiny, what

evidence will reveal when they have arrived politically? As indicated above, it is not enough to have occasional impact on the outcome of an election. Sustained influence can be evident in election outcomes, but it begins with translating the presence in the general population to the potential and actual voting population. Variations in turnout rate can sometimes obscure this. Therefore a more consistent indicator that this has happened is evident when the Latino share of registered voters is commensurate with their share of the population. In particular, I consider the presence of Latinos in the population and electorate through an analysis of registration parity ratios. This is a simple way to represent the relationship between population presence and electoral presence. These ratios are calculated by dividing the percentage of the Latino registered voters by the percentage of Latinos in the general population. Essentially, the *Latino registration parity ratio* illustrates how close Latinos are to attaining parity in voter registration and can identify the variation across states. While a snapshot in time, as presented by Fraga and Ramírez (2004), may tell us whether Latinos have achieved parity (1.0) in a particular state and at a particular point in time, the continuing changes in both the composition of the population and electorate ensures that Latino registration parity is a moving target and therefore requires an analysis of parity ratios over time, as well as of the forces that impact rates of voter registration. This perspective of Latino voters over time points to the relevance of proactive and reactive mobilization.

Based on the typology of electoral presence and growth, some interesting patterns emerge with respect to Latino registration parity ratios. Figure 3 displays Latino parity registration ratios between 1990 and 2010 for the ten states. The most obvious pattern observed in the data is that Latinos did not achieve parity in any of the ten states at any point in the twenty-year period. New York came closest to achieving parity in 1998 with a 0.90 parity ratio. Conversely, Illinois had the smallest parity ratio in 1996, with a mere 0.28. The former is well above the 0.56 mean parity ratio across all states during this time period, while the latter is still significantly lower. Interestingly, after almost achieving parity in 1998, New York had the largest drop in parity ratio to 0.51 in 2002 and struggled for six years to get to the 0.56 mean in 2010. There were other instances when states experienced sizable shifts in the registration parity ratio. The parity ratio has also dropped by at least 0.20 during a four-year period in New Jersey (1996–2000) and Arizona (2000–2004), and New Mexico's parity ratio improved by more than 0.20 between 1994 and 2000.

What explains the noticeable fluctuations in Latino registration parity?

Fig. 3 Latino registraton parity ratios, 1990–2010

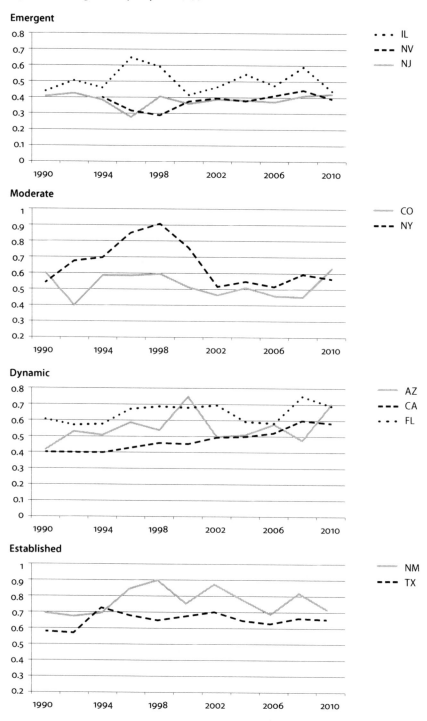

Source: Author's Calculations based on U.S. Census (1990, 2000, 2010) and Current Population Survey 1990–2000

*Parity Ratio = Percent Latino of Registered Voters / Percent Latino of State Population

Sudden population growth or loss among Latinos or non-Latinos directly impacts the stability of Latino electoral presence. Similarly, significant shifts in the segments of the Latino population who overcome the age and citizenship requirements for voter registration help structure the extent of growth. The slowest growth in the citizen voting age population (CVAP) and the slow growth of Latino registered voters during this period took place in New York at only 53 percent and 64 percent respectively. Conversely, New Mexico's CVAP grew at the fastest rate at 310 percent growth from 1990 to 2010, but had the slowest growth among the Latino registered voters in the state at 48 percent. Citizenship appears to be a bigger hurdle in New York, whereas low voter-registration rates among Latinos who recently became eligible to vote are a bigger hurdle in New Mexico. The variation in Latino registration parity ratios across states is determined by these two dynamic moving parts. Change—in this case, the growth of Latino voters—is not uniform. The variation in the growth rate can be explained by internal and external disruptions in the established pattern of growth. A state will exhibit lower parity ratios when the rate at which the percentage of Latino registered voters in the state is unable to grow at the comparable rate of growth of the percentage of Latinos in the overall population. Conversely, a state's Latino registration parity ratio will be improved as voter-registration rates increase among Latinos and they constitute a larger share of the registered-voter population relative to the Latino presence as a percentage of the state population.

Who Can't Vote?

The extant literature on political participation often begins by asking the relatively straightforward question, "Who votes"? (Wolfinger and Rosenstone 1980). Some variants include a focus on who doesn't vote (Stein, Leighley, and Owens 2005). The core of this research seeks to identify the individual-level factors and variables that shape citizens' propensity to vote, including whether they are targeted by particularistic mobilization (Rosenstone and Hansen 1993; Leighley 2001; Gerber and Green 2000). Less well understood is the experience of emerging electorates who can't vote. One notable exception to this pattern is Louis DeSipio's study of the Latino vote (1996).

In order to determine the role of new electorates, DeSipio appropriately begins with an analysis of the experience of new electorates such as women, youth, African Americans, white ethnics, and Latinos in the twentieth century as they became socially and politically relevant in the United

States. In particular, he considers whether these electorates were distinct and the consequences of the expansion of the electorate on party politics. DeSipio disaggregates the Latino nonvoting population into those who are registered but did not vote ("reticents"), citizens who have not registered to vote ("reluctants"), and noncitizens ("recruits"). By identifying the potential electorate, DeSipio lays the groundwork for understanding the fundamental shift among the Latino electorate during the 1990s and since 2000, including strategies for incorporating non-U.S. citizens, or those defined as the "excluded."

DeSipio's (1996) analyses of the attitudes and behavior of the Latino voters and nonvoters provide an important initial portrait of the Latino electorate in the United States. This baseline understanding is drawn from the 1988 Current Population Survey, the 1989 Latino National Political Survey (LNPS), and the 1988 National Latino Immigrant Survey (NLIS). The current Latino electorate, however, is not George H. W. Bush's Latino electorate from 1988 and 1989. More than 60 percent of today's Latino registered voters were not part of the Latino electorate in 1990. This substantial shift in the composition of the Latino electorate requires that we update our theoretical understanding of Latino voting behavior, especially of those Latinos who became part of the electorate since 1990, and that we reassess the potential significance of Latinos who could become voters, but who have not yet been mobilized.

There are two segments of the Latino population who can't vote that deserve special mention. In both instances, agency within the Latino community cannot directly expedite the mechanisms by which they can inch closer to becoming registered voters. The first segment consists of the unauthorized Latino immigrant population, but it is difficult to accurately determine the effect of this population because the data are largely based on estimates. What is known is that about 8.3 million, or 77 percent, of all unauthorized immigrants were born in Latin America (Hoefer, Baker, and Rytina 2012). Given that almost 69 percent of the estimated 10.8 million unauthorized immigrants live in the ten states under consideration,[11] it is reasonable to conjecture that the bulk of unauthorized Latino immigrants live in these states. If comprehensive immigration reform regularizes the status of many of these immigrants, the pool of potential Latino legal residents, citizens, and voters could prove significant. Thus, while there is a sense of agency involved in helping to advocate for comprehensive immigration reform, it is far removed from direct effects of mobilization from within the Latino community.

Another segment of the population that receives little attention, the "emerging electorate," consists of U.S.-born children of Latinos who are not yet of voting age. In the coming years, this will be the biggest growth segment of the Latino electorate. Consistent with the general distribution of the Latino population, an estimated 76 percent of the 15.8 million native-born who are younger than eighteen years live in the ten states. Given the size of this population, this is where most of the growth will take place in the next seventeen years. The potential impact of this population nationally is even more dramatic. According to the National Council of La Raza, between 2011 and 2028, an estimated 15.8 million Latino citizens will turn eighteen and will be eligible to register to vote (NCLR 2012).

There is reason to believe that the political context will continue to change well before all of the above-mentioned native-born children turn eighteen. The most likely engines of immediate growth come from the three categories of Latino nonvoters identified by DeSipio (1996): the "recruits," the "reticents," and the "reluctants." The effect on Latino registration parity will be felt more in some states than others. My initial focus is on the harder case of those who can't vote, and I work my way to those who don't vote. With respect to "recruits," 83.5 percent of the 6.6 million Latino legal permanent residents (LPRs) who have not naturalized also live in these states.[12] They are not equally distributed across the ten states. California alone accounts for just over one-third of these Latino LPRs who have yet to naturalize. If a greater percentage of these LPRs pursue citizenship, they are likely to have significant effects on the Latino registration parity ratios across the states.

With respect to "reluctants," only about half of all eligible Latinos are registered to vote. When we broaden our focus of this pool of potential voters to consider geographic distribution, we find that 80 percent of the U.S. Latino citizen voting-age population (CVAP) that is not registered to vote lives in the selected ten states (Current Population Survey 2010).[13] The distribution and impact of the "reticent" Latino voters is harder to pinpoint over time and place. Variation in turnout rates is sometimes a result of election and/or candidate-specific effects. In order to more fully identify the overall influence that Latinos can have on politics, it is increasingly evident that understanding "who doesn't vote" is as important as understanding which Latinos do vote. Beyond the estimated 12 million Latinos who did vote in 2012, and the 7 million Latino unauthorized immigrants who may not gain residency or citizenship, I estimate that the combined pool of distant, potential, proximate, and eligible voters in the next eighteen years will be more than 40 million Latinos. This would represent the single-largest potential influx of new voters since women's suffrage. As they become engaged in politics, the established patterns indicate that they likely will uniquely impact politics in the selected states. As I discuss throughout the book, this relationship between the potential and promise of a Latino vote is not a static, but a dynamic one. The next step is to identify variation in the scope and nature of the change that has already taken place in these states as a result of the Latino community.

When and How Change Happens

Latinos are clearly a growing force in American public life. From 1991 to 2008, more than a third of all new U.S. citizens—nearly 3.8 million—were Latinos. Concurrently, many U.S.-born Latinos became eligible to vote, as the number of Latinos between the ages of eighteen and twenty-four almost doubled, growing from 1.8 million in 1991 to 3.2 million in 2006. These shifts raise a host of critical questions about how Latinos and other groups are changing the political landscape in the United States.

Pundits and scholars tend to answer these questions by pointing to the sheer population growth among Latinos. This is not surprising. Not only are Latinos the largest ethnic minority group in the nation today, the group is expected to account for most of the nation's population growth over the next forty years and comprise one out of every three people in the United States by 2050 (Passel and Cohn 2008). As stated earlier, it is often assumed that demographic growth will automatically translate to greater influence in election outcomes as well as greater descriptive and substantive representation. However, this often leads to facile conclusions regarding political influence that focus on whether or not Latinos provided the margin necessary to win a particular election at the mass level, or whether increasing descriptive representation necessarily results in greater substantive representation. A preoccupation with whether Latinos constitute the "pivotal vote" in a specific election or whether there is distinctive legislative behavior of Latino elected officials neglects the many and various ways that Latinos have reshaped state political competition and national campaign strategies. It fails to account for how proactive mobilization and reactive mobilization have been determinative of the growth and evolution of Latino state electorates.

Identifying nonvoters and the pool of potential voters is a crucial first step toward detecting the factors that enhance or depress Latino registration parity. Several scholars have raised concerns about the dampening effect of Latino immigrants on the overall registration and turnout rate of Latinos at the polls (Highton and Burris 2002; Tam Cho 1999; de la Garza, Falcon, and Garcia 1996; DeSipio 1996; de la Garza and DeSipio 1992). More recently, there is evidence that rather than depressing turnout, immigrants vote at higher rates once they are registered to vote (Logan, Darra, and Sookhee 2012; Barreto, Ramírez, and Woods 2005; Pantoja, Ramírez, and Segura 2001). The noticeable change in the behavior of the Latino electorate necessitates a revised assessment of the effect of nativity on Latino registration and turnout. I draw on earlier contributions among Latino politics scholars but extend my examination to the next analytical dimension, which focuses on *when* meaningful change happens and *how* that change in the pool of eligible and actual Latino voters occurs. To identify when this change happens, I begin by exploring the nature of the growth in Latino naturalization and registration rates during the twenty-year period from 1990 to 2010.

Taking into consideration the moving parts of where Latinos are significant in politics, what state contexts present opportunities for political power, and who can and cannot vote lays the groundwork for a systematic explanation of the future of Latino politics. Answers to the questions of when and how change happens as a function of population growth, for example, are not only more difficult to craft, but also more useful for predicting the contours of Latino politics in U.S. democracy. The catalysts for change, or mobilizing opportunities, help explain the "how." I provide a framework for understanding how the state political context impacts the electoral behavior of citizen and noncitizen Latinos. I present a model of "mobilizing opportunities" (consisting of proactive and reactive mobilization) that draws on literature related to political participation, state politics, social movements, and racial and ethnic politics. This approach is unique because it highlights the dynamic interaction between endogenous factors, including Latino demographic characteristics, Spanish-language media, and organizational capacity and exogenous factors such as perceived political threat.

To understand the utility of this approach, we can begin by considering three state examples: Texas, California, and New Mexico. These three states in the continental United States already have majority-minority populations but exhibit three diverging experiences among Latinos with respect to influence in state politics. Despite the fact that Texas, California, and New Mexico have *similar* presence of Latinos as a percentage of the population, they have very *different* levels of Latino electoral power. I focus on Texas in this section, and the concluding chapter ends with my outlook of the role of Latinos in Texas politics. The Latino population in Texas grew from 25.5 percent of the state population in 1990 to 37.6 percent of the state population in 2010. During this same time period, there was comparable rate of growth in the percentage of registered voters in the state who were Latino, going from 14.8 percent of all registered voters to an estimated 24.1 percent. Despite growth in both the Latino share of the state population and the electorate, the number of Latinos in the legislature was 25 in 1990, peaked at 36 in 1996, but returned to 25 in 2008.[14] The relative influence of Latinos in Texas state politics has remained stagnant because demographic growth has not yet translated into sustained growth of descriptive representatives.[15]

California also witnessed growth in the presence of Latinos in the electoral arena. The confluence of factors at the center of party politics such as increasing naturalization rates by Latino immigrants, favorable redistricting outcomes, and mobilization of Latinos in reaction to race-targeting state propositions resulted in greater growth in the electorate than would be expected by mere population change. Not only do Latinos in California represent an increasing share of the governing coalition that has pursued policies beneficial to Latinos in education and healthcare, but more importantly, Latinos are largely credited with putting the state out of reach for Republican presidential candidates and any other statewide candidates. Chapter 4 delves further into how this took place in California during the 1990s. The case of Latinos in New Mexico is unique in that they have not experienced the same level of population growth attributed to immigration and because they have long represented the largest share of the nonwhite population and electorate. As such, they have enjoyed periods where Latinos have been elected as U.S. senators, but more importantly, the two most recent governors of New Mexico are both of Latino descent. The level of integration within the state's political elite is unparalleled. While Hispanos in New Mexico have experienced significant gains in representation, the slower rate of growth and the lower rates of voter registration of eligible Latino voters have stunted the potential to institutionalize long-term incorporation into New Mexico's party politics.[16] In the concluding chapter, I delve further into why this is the case and provide an outlook for the future of New Mexico party politics.

Earlier works have considered whether state context matters for Latino incorporation vis-à-vis policy outcomes and focused on the "political culture" of the states as conceptualized by Elazar (1984) and on the patterns of "social diversity" across states (Hero 1992, 1998). Others have focused on how increased Latino presence in state legislatures matters for policy outcomes (Preuhs 2007; Preuhs and Juenke 2011; Juenke and Preuhs 2012). These perspectives focus largely on snapshots in time, without considering the longitudinal nature of influence or the possibility that two similarly situated states with respect to social diversity and party competition can have distinct outcomes. I argue that a process-oriented perspective is necessary to understand the dynamic interactions and symbiotic relationship between state political context and the pace by which a state's electorate and representative institutions become more diverse.

The future role of Latinos in American politics cannot be understood simply by their demographic presence nationally or vis-à-vis national party politics. Demographic presence is a key factor to consider, but a state-centered approach that takes context seriously gives a greater sense of the variation in scope and size of the Latino presence, but more importantly the extent to which the influx of Latinos into state politics is gradual and expected or sudden and unexpected. Changes to the political status quo across states, therefore, prompts Latinos to become politically engaged at higher levels than expected, or reflect the efforts by Latinos to become politically relevant in ways that forces the political system to react to their increased role. It is the case that changes in the political behavior of both current Latino and non-Latino voters have the potential to shape the future of party politics across states.[17]

To make sense of how emerging and evolving electorates matter, one must adopt an approach that seriously considers other catalysts of growth, particularly those related to political context. It is therefore important to understand when and how Latinos are activated as political participants, citizens, and voters, as well as the state partisan context where they find themselves embedded. The relationship between Latino presence and state political context has not been fully explored. Rodney Hero indirectly addresses Latino presence in states by considering how social diversity can impact policy making at the national and substate level in his award-winning book *Faces of Inequality: Social Diversity in American Politics* (1998). Although the book begins to address the impact that the presence of Latinos and other minority populations may have on state policies, it does not account for structural mechanisms such as the partisan composition of state legislative and executive offices, or minority community agency in the outcomes because it does not allow for variation in electoral presence and outcomes that are driven by organizational mobilization.

I make the case that reactive mobilization is evident when Latinos respond to political threat by engaging the multiple access points in the political system, from protest politics to electoral politics. I argue that those who primarily rely on the notion that demography is destiny ultimately neglect the interaction of proactive and reactive mobilization as evident in the four important antecedents to Latino electoral presence in politics: (1) mass media and language; (2) naturalization patterns; (3) threat of Latino voter activation; and (4) organizational mobilization.

It should be noted that all four of these antecedents are shaped by and help shape state two-party politics. The core argument makes the case that the extent to which demographic change will translate into Latino political influence is conditioned by the presence of these four catalysts and their unique interaction as moving parts. For Latinos, there are three notable instances of activation into electoral politics. These include direct participation and/or support of protest activity (1) in the 1960s in the Southwest, (2) during the 1990s in California, and (3) throughout the United States in 2006 (Barreto et al. 2009). The political science literature often focuses on the central role of grassroots organizations to coordinate protest activity, but largely overlooks the role of alternative media. The 2006 immigrant protest marches are unique in that Spanish-language media proved to be the key to widespread efforts to mobilize Latinos. Rather than a hurdle to overcome, Spanish-language skills became essential to the success of the demonstrations. This should not discount the relevance of Latino organizational capacity, but without Spanish-language media as a resource, it is highly unlikely that the marches would have been as widespread or as large.

Latinos as residents, citizens, and voters can draw upon endogenous resources (proactive mobilization) that they can mobilize to create opportunities to enhance their relevance as political actors, but they can also encounter opportunities to mobilize (reactive mobilization) in response to exogenous disruptions in the behavior of the existing non-Latino electorate. In both circumstances, these are mobilizing opportunities, one in response to external stimuli and the other created from within. There are no existing analytic frameworks that simultaneously capture this dynamic interaction between emerging electorates and political context. *Mobilizing Opportunities* fills this critical gap by articulating a theory specifying the interaction of Latino demographic presence and growth, the role of Spanish-language media, group-based organizational capacity, and the perception of political threat in mobilizing opportunities for political influence among Latinos in the United States.

Structure of the Book

The remainder of the book consists of five chapters. Chapter 2 discusses the role of Spanish-language radio in mobilizing Latino immigrants and their supporters to take part in the 2006 immigrant protests against House Resolution (HR) 4437. Spanish-language media, particularly radio, emerged as important and novel resources in the political mobilization of immigrants and Latino youth, the largest growth segments of the Latino electorate. I use data about the location and established market share to highlight its impact on political activity. Beyond the sheer numbers, I discuss the evolution of Spanish-language radio and assert that it should not have been surprising that this relatively new media was a willing and active participant in the weeks and months leading up to the 2006 immigrant protest marches and embraced this role in the months that followed. The analysis provides compelling evidence to counter the claim in the existing participation literature that consuming non-English-language media diminishes political activity. I demonstrate that the direct and indirect activation into politics through protest, along with Spanish-language media usage, collectively have downstream effects on the intent to naturalize, the acquisition of citizenship, and higher electoral participation among Latinos. At the same time, by tracing the corporate and pan-ethnic evolution of Spanish-language radio beyond 2006, I explore the limits of its mobilizing capacity.

Chapter 3 takes a closer look at the relationship between perceived political threat and defensive naturalization as evidence of reactive mobilization. Perceived anti-Latino/anti-immigrant context, it is argued, was the catalyst for the belief among immigrants that they should respond with action. However, anger without direction yields very little. The novel interactions between the proactive mobilization of Latino grassroots organizations and Spanish-language media helped channel the anger into outcomes by framing the necessary reaction as increased attention to citizenship and voting. The analysis investigates whether and the extent to which the decision by Latino immigrants to initiate the naturalization process can be linked to the 2006 immigrant protest marches. I provide evidence to support the hypothesis that the policies embodied in HR 4437 promoted a sense of political threat among Latinos and spurred naturalization. Chapter 3 documents how unprecedented efforts by Latino organizations and Spanish-language media to seize the opportunity to increase the pool of voting-eligible Latinos had noticeable effects on naturalization rates of Latino immigrants. It presents a clear example that reactive mobilization can enhance levels of civic engagement when proactive mobilization is already in place. This chapter makes use of the 2006 Latino National Survey, the 2009 Ya Es Hora *Ciudadania*/Naturalization Survey, and published and unpublished data from United States Citizen and Immigration Services (USCIS). If reactive mobilization had an effect on Latino immigrants, the expectation is that defensive naturalization is evident when more Latino immigrants seek citizenship in response to increased anti-immigrant sentiment (a form of political threat). The analysis supports this, but also highlights the crucial role of proactive mobilization by Latino organizations and Spanish-language media in helping interested immigrants through the laborious and increasingly complex citizenship application process.

It is one thing to speculate what the combined effects of proactive and reactive mobilization could look like throughout the United States, but it is also necessary to present evidence of the likely outcome. Chapter 4, therefore, highlights the importance of temporal effects of reactive mobilization in state-specific contexts and subsequent effects on actual voter participation over time. With this in mind, I turn to California as a case study. Overcoming the citizenship hurdle will not necessarily translate an increased pool of eligible voters into presence and influence at the polls, but this can and does happen when the political context becomes a catalyst for participation in politics. The data come from the 1996 Tomás Rivera Policy Institute Survey of Latinos in California, with appended validated voter turnout in 1996, 1998, and 2000. The influx of new Latino voters (both native-born and foreign-born) can be credited with increased turnout among Latino voters in elections when race-targeting initiatives are on the ballot. What is unique about California is that the behavior of the Republican Party during the 1990s led to more sustained participation among new voters! There were also downstream effects well beyond the political threat. The downstream effects were twofold. First, the perception that Latinos don't vote had less traction among partisan campaigns. The second was the realization that there was a shared sense of political identity among those Latinos who were activated into politics and mobilized to vote. The significance of this chapter to our understanding of the political relevance of Latinos nationally depends on the extent to which we believe that "as go California Latinos, so go Latinos nationally." Only time will tell if the effects of the immigrant protest marches in 2006 will resemble those of the 1990s experience in California.[18]

Given that the mobilizing effects of external catalysts are not uniform across all Latinos, chapter 5 examines how Latino organizations have developed mobilization strategies and taken the opportunity to bring the large segment of low-propensity Latino voters into electoral politics. These are populations of voters and potential voters that are largely ignored by political parties and campaigns.[19] From 2000 to 2012, nonpartisan Latino organizations conducted "get out the vote" (GOTV) campaigns among these neglected Latino voters. These efforts have evolved into sophisticated, coordinated multicity and multistate campaigns to maximize Latino mobilization efforts. As was the case in the mobilization of Latinos into protest politics and motivating them to pursue citizenship, Spanish-language use matters in these GOTV efforts. Not only was Spanish used to more effectively convey mobilization scripts or as a sign of solidarity, but it was used more instrumentally to target Latino voters through a combination of Spanish surname lists and geography.[20] I use data from a quasi-experiment in 2000 and four subsequent randomized field experiments to test the hypothesis that GOTV mobilization efforts can activate low-propensity voters to turn out on election day. Interestingly, the same efforts have yielded uneven effects across place and time, but have nevertheless transformed existing narratives and perspectives about the viability of mobilization efforts among Latino voters. That is, it is not just at the mass level that Latino voters have reacted to and have been mobilized to vote by a political threat; it is equally important to understand the day-to-day decisions of organizations to proactively seek to reduce barriers to participation.

The book's concluding chapter takes stock of the empirical evidence analyzed on Spanish-language media, political threat and defensive naturalization, ballot initiatives, and state context, as well as GOTV efforts and the effects of these mobilization efforts on Latino political activation and participation. I discuss the significance of identifying mobilizing opportunities among emerging electorates and consider the implications for the future of an increasingly diverse American electorate and its relationship to the extant two-party system. In particular, the final chapter emphasizes that while African American interests have been marginalized and Asian American interests ignored by the history of two-party competition, the new demographic reality and voter preferences of blacks, Asians, and Latinos have opened up the possibility of breaking from the status quo. As the largest racial/ethnic minority group, Latinos are likely to help set the stage for the next phase of American party politics. I conclude with an outlook of what the future may hold in selected states based on existing evidence of proactive and reactive mobilization, while still acknowledging that the next twenty years will likely give rise to even greater change than the twenty-year period after 1990.

The media's focal shift during the 2008 and 2012 presidential campaign from population size to electoral presence and preferences is notable in that it also represents a concurrent shift from earlier ethnicity-based accounts and affords a future-oriented consideration of political salience. Latinos are at the heart of recent scholarly analyses about significant changes in the electorate, shifting partisan preferences, and variation in levels of voter turnout. If we are to understand how the Latino vote, as a new electorate, is redefining American democracy, we must identify the conditions that determine the processes by which selected segments of the population are activated into politics and that subsequently mobilize some to vote and not others. We need to understand when those favorable opportunities to mobilize exist, when Latinos have seized upon them, and when they represent missed opportunities.

2

MOBILIZATION EN ESPAÑOL

Spanish-Language Radio and the Reaction to HR 4437

The U.S. Congress faced several controversial issues at the end of its first session in 2005. Among these, U.S. House and Senate Republican leaders tried to salvage legislative priorities such as the renewal of the USA Patriot Act, efforts to allow oil drilling in the Arctic National Wildlife Refuge, formulation of a clear policy on the use of torture, and the passage of a budget agreement. There were also questions about whether Republicans in the U.S. House would permanently replace Tom DeLay, the former House Majority leader, after he was indicted by a Texas grand jury in a finance probe. Given this political context, the media paid very little attention when a controversial immigration measure was approved by the House Judiciary Committee in early December.

On December 16, 2005, three days before the close of the winter session, the "Border Protection, Anti-terrorism, and Illegal Immigration Control Act of 2005," or HR 4437,[1] was passed by the U.S. House of Representatives by a vote of 239 to 182. The mainstream media devoted very little attention to the passage of this punitive immigration bill, which called for enhanced physical barriers at the U.S.-Mexico border and harsher scrutiny of suspected "undocumented aliens," and made it a felony for undocumented immigrants to be in the United States (Félix, González, and Ramírez 2008; Barreto et al. 2009). In the days after this bill cleared the lower house of Congress, there were protests by immigrant rights advocates, but these were very limited in scope and size. For example, on December 28, a small group of about two dozen Latino community activists gathered in front of

Table 1   Key moments in immigration-related legislation and mobilization, 2005–2006

December 16, 2005	Border Protection, Anti-terrorism, and Illegal Immigration Control Act of 2005 ("Sensenbrenner Bill") passed by U.S. House of Representatives
December 28, 2005	Small group of protesters gather in Chicago to protest Sensenbrenner Bill
February 14–March 24, 2006	Protests of 10,000–100,000 in Chicago, Milwaukee, Phoenix, and other cities
March 25–May 1, 2006	Protest marches of 500,000–1 million in Los Angeles and other cities

the office of U.S. Rep. Daniel Lipinski (D-Ill.) on the Southwest Side of Chicago to protest his vote in favor of HR 4437 (Wang 2005).

The size of demonstrations protesting HR 4437 would grow rapidly. As early as February 2006, thousands of protesters gathered in many of the largest cities in the United States. On February 14, more than one thousand people gathered at Independence Mall in Philadelphia (Bahadur 2006). This was followed by anti-HR 4437 protest gatherings of 100,000 in Chicago, 10,000–15,000 in Milwaukee, and 20,000 in Phoenix on March 10, 23, and 24 respectively (Johnson and Spice 2006; Gonzalez and Wingett 2006). The most dramatic show of resistance to the legislation occurred on March 25 in Los Angeles. On that date, an unprecedented 500,000 to 1 million people took to the streets of downtown Los Angeles to peacefully protest the HR 4437, or Sensenbrenner Bill, and surprised many by the coordination of the protest participants who wore white shirts and waved American flags (Watanabe and Becerra 2006).

Analysts speculated that coordinated efforts between immigrant rights groups and Spanish-language disc jockeys drove the massive turnout between March 25 and May 1, 2006.[2] The role of Spanish-language media was made clear in the different responses to the protests by the mainstream media and English-dominant populations compared to the Spanish-language media and their audiences. Most English-speaking residents in Southern California and mainstream English-language media outlets were largely, if not completely, caught by surprise during the protests in Los Angeles on March 25. Editorialists with the *Christian Science Monitor* underscored this sentiment in their commentary:

> The turnout surprised everyone. More than 500,000 Latino protesters in Los Angeles last month. Nearly as many in Dallas Sunday. On Monday, hundreds

of thousands nationwide. It's big, it's unprecedented—and no one knows what it portends.

Quite unexpectedly, a population living in the shadows of American society has emerged into full view and found its voice. Illegal immigrants and their supporters are on the march, galvanized by a House immigration bill heavy on enforcement and offering no path to citizenship. (*Christian Science Monitor,* "The Monitor's View," April 13, 2006)

Conversely, Spanish speakers largely expected the initial demonstration because the Spanish-language disc jockeys had been promoting the protests for weeks before the marches to their listening audience. In the days leading up to March 25, 2006, Luis Garibay, the producer of the radio show *Piolín por la mañana,* anticipated the huge turnout: "It's incredible, the people's response. Everywhere we go, they are talking about it, even at Disneyland. . . . We have been getting e-mails, telephone calls, faxes—everything."[3] Initial media reports after the protests largely focused on the unprecedented collaboration that took place among disc jockeys from competing radio stations to mobilize their listening audience to participate in the March 25 protest in Los Angeles (Hernandez 2006).

This demonstration attracted nationwide media attention and also served to further motivate organizers and other DJs across the country in what would prove to be the largest coordinated effort for a one-day protest throughout the country on May 1, 2006. In total, it is estimated that from 3 to 5 million immigrants took to the streets in several cities across the United States to peacefully protest anti-immigrant congressional legislation between February and May 1, 2006 (Bada, Fox, and Selee 2006). Moreover, the unprecedented incipient social movement reverberated beyond the territorial confines of the United States.[4]

A focus on demographic change alone fails to adequately explain the Latino political participation in the 2006 immigrant rights marches. To understand Latino political mobilization in this case, we must attend to institutional capacity and history. First, we must reconsider the Spanish-language media and its capacity to create opportunities for political mobilization. Pundits and mainstream media have reported that Spanish-language radio was the primary source of information about protest march against HR 4437 in downtown Los Angeles and subsequent marches throughout the United States. On March 29, 2006, an Associated Press story underscored the potential power of Spanish-language radio as a political institution:

Many of the 500,000 people who crammed downtown Los Angeles on Saturday to protest legislation that would make criminals out of illegal immigrants learned where, when and even how to demonstrate from the Spanish-language media. For English-speaking America, the mass protests in Los Angeles and other U.S. cities over the past few days have been surprising for their size and seeming spontaneity. But they were organized, promoted or publicized for weeks by Spanish-language radio hosts and TV anchors as a demonstration of Hispanic pride and power.

Yet the role of Spanish-language media in the mass mobilization is also subject to question. The assumption that it played a large role in direct mobilization is countered by the fact that Spanish-language media was not widely available in many states where the marches took place. Further, it is possible that protesters would have gathered with or without the encouragement of Spanish-language media personalities. If speculations about the role of Spanish-language media are correct, however, conventional wisdom that non-English-language use inhibits political participation must be revised.[5]

The unique potential for Spanish-language media in creating mobilizing opportunities is at the heart of this chapter. I investigate that institutional role, and consider it in light of a long history of political mobilization via radio. That is, I examine how the role of Spanish-language media in political mobilization has varied over time. I also examine the conditions, having to do with demographic targets and market forces, that shape its potential—and limitations—as a resource for political mobilization.

Not Lost in Translation

It would have been hard to predict in December 2005 or even January 2006 that the Sensenbrenner Bill would combine with inflammatory rhetoric from political elites, media pundits, and the general public to create a hostile national political environment reminiscent of mid–1990s in California (Ramírez 2007; Bowler, Nicholson, and Segura 2006; Pantoja, Ramírez, and Segura 2001). Clearly, a hostile political context can become an opportunity for individuals to mobilize, which is illustrative of reactive mobilization. What is unique about the 2006 immigration protest marches is the process by which new and existing Latino civic leaders and Spanish-language media unexpectedly converged on this issue as a mobilizing opportunity to motivate Latino immigrants and their supporters to take part in protest politics with the intent of enhancing the civic and political status of Latinos in an increasingly diverse American democracy.

Why did so many people in Southern California (and elsewhere throughout the United States) participate in a protest, when very few people ever participate in this form of political participation? One of the most widely accepted explanations for all forms of political participation is that being recruited to participate has a predictably positive impact on political participation (Rosenstone and Hansen 1993; Verba, Schlozman, and Brady 1995). This is especially true when the appeals are more personal (Green and Gerber 2001; Ramírez 2005; Michelson 2005). Less well-known, but no less accepted, is the view that English-language ability helps determine levels of participation. The rationale for why non-English-language use inhibits participation is concisely articulated by Uhlaner, Cain, and Kiewiet: "Not speaking English as a primary language inhibits the acquisition of information and increases the difficulty of certain activities" (1989:203). Similarly, David Leal contends that "non-citizens often have difficulty with the English language, which would make non-electoral political activities much more challenging" (Leal 2002:356). This view is reiterated by other studies of political behavior (MacManus and Cassell 1982; Calvo and Rosenstone 1989; Lien 1994; Verba, Schlozman, and Brady 1995).

Taken together, we should expect higher levels of political participation among those who are mobilized through more direct means and who are English-dominant. It is therefore not surprising that appeals to participate resulted in participation in the protest marches. What is surprising is that the appeals largely came from mass media (as opposed to personal contact) and that the language of mobilization and participation in the protests was primarily Spanish rather than English.

Despite the strong assumption that Spanish-language media played a key role in the mobilization of Latinos to participate in the protest marches, there is no consensus as to whether Spanish-language radio was a tool utilized by others or a purposive player in the event planning, the coalescing of diverse communities, and the broad mobilization of protest participants.[6] The diverging views about the role of Spanish-language radio are clearly evident in the headlines of the leading California-based newspapers. On March 28, a headline on the front page of the *Los Angeles Times* read, "The Immigration Debate; How DJs Put 500,000 Marchers in Motion." Almost as if in reaction to the story in the *L.A. Times,* the print edition of the *San Francisco Chronicle* on the following day included a headline that read "Spanish-Language Radio Spread Word of L.A. Protest; Others Laid the Groundwork, but DJs Told the Masses." There is some merit in clarifying whether Spanish-language radio was at the forefront of the immigrant response to HR 4437 or was merely an instrument used by existing organizations.

The confusion about the role of Spanish-language radio did not end after the March 25 protests in Los Angeles, but continued, with many protest marches taking place throughout April and on May 1, 2006. Additionally, reports in 2007 highlighted the significant drop-off in the levels of participation in the one-year anniversary of the May 1 protests and led some to question the established or potential influence of Spanish-language radio and to point to a seeming failure of disc jockeys to unite and mobilize their listening audience (Gorman and Abdollah 2007; Hernandez 2007). Without substantial archived recordings of all of the major radio stations and presence at protest planning meetings before the events across various localities, it is difficult to accurately appraise the primary effects of Spanish-language radio or its DJs. A truly representative sample of interviews of participants and organizers is unlikely, and there is potential for selective memory of the period leading up to the protests in 2006 and subsequent years. Given the methodological challenges of such a post-hoc analysis, this chapter pursues two equally or more important overarching lines of inquiry. First, irrespective of its precise role in the 2006 protests or beyond,[7] what is unique about Spanish-language radio that allowed it to be become a powerful resource for promoting political participation among Latinos? Second, given this history of involvement leading up to 2006, how does Spanish-language radio enable or constrain the social and political incorporation by Latinos in the United States?

In order to answer these questions, I begin with the controversial hypothesis of Johnson, Stein, and Wrinkle that "choosing to speak a language other than English—in this case, Spanish—may represent an individual's access to social and community resources that enable, rather than impede, political participation" (2003:413). I then specifically focus on systematic questions about whether one could have predicted, a priori, that immigrants and other Spanish-speaking supporters would participate in such large numbers and that Spanish-language radio would be at the center of the mobilization efforts for the immigrant rights demonstrations. Rather than dismiss the participation by hundreds of thousands of people engaging in protest politics as aberrant and unexpected, this chapter focuses on the distinctive nature of Spanish-language radio and its potential for mobilizing political opportunities. I make the case that a more discriminating account of the role of Spanish-language radio in the immigration protests reveals an established capacity to mobilize opportunities among Latinos by appealing to and activating a common ethnic identity in response to external shocks or urgent needs of the community, including aiding those affected by natural disasters, the immigration protests, and naturalization and voter-registration drives.[8] This alternative analysis of Spanish-language radio requires the consideration of two important factors. The first is the evolution of Spanish-language radio and its relation to other mediums. The second has to do with confluence of geographic, demographic, and market forces that shaped the circumstances of mobilization of protest participants, information diffusion, and message framing.

I make the link between Spanish-language radio and Latino political participation by drawing on the media effects literature in political science, sociology, and communications. Although these disciplines have not explicitly tackled the question about the relationship between media, language, and political participation, there are enough insights to formulate a hypothesis that Spanish-language radio is a key mobilizing agent in Latino civic engagement and political activity. To further substantiate this hypothesis, I examine the changes that have taken place in Spanish-language radio and the related response by the Spanish listening audience. I challenge the conventional wisdom that non-English-language use inhibits political participation. At the same time, I suggest the specific limitation of Spanish-language media as a resource for future political mobilization.

Media and Political Behavior

There are two distinct branches in the political behavior literature that focus on mass media effects. First, it is widely accepted that the mass media can affect political attitudes through priming, framing, and agenda setting (Iyengar and Kinder 1987; Iyengar 1991; Zaller 1992, 1996; Mutz and Soss 1997; Peter 2004). There is less agreement about the ways in which mass media impacts political participation. "From one perspective, media use diminishes involvement and contributes to political cynicism and declining turnout; from another, media use contributes to political involvement, trust, efficacy, and mobilization" (Aarts and Semetko 2003:760). More recent work suggests that media has the power to mobilize or depress participation, depending on media type, levels of exposure, and content (Prior 2007; Aarts and Semetko 2003; Newton 1999). This is consistent with social movement research that places radio at the center of participation in the southern textile worker insurgency of the late 1920 and early 1930s, as well as the civil rights movement of the 1960s (Roscigno and Danaher 2001; Ward 2004).

Even with these supplemented views, there are two relative omissions in this literature. First, the effect of media on political attitudes and behavior is overwhelmingly seen through the lens of mainstream mass media rather than alternative media (that is, media outside of mainstream corporate control). Second, non-English-language mass media is a pronounced omission in the extant literature and has been almost entirely overlooked by political scientists or sociologists. These omissions are partly attributable to the fact that alternative media and non-English-language media affect only a subset of the population who either by choice or by necessity opt for something other than mainstream mass media. However, both forms of communication are growing in usage, as is evident in the rise of noncorporate online newsletters, newspapers, and Internet blogs, as well as the increasing popularity and demand of Spanish-language media in the biggest media markets in the United States. Thus, emerging studies of media and political behavior must incorporate these growing forms of communication if they are to remain relevant.

Can insights by communication scholars about alternative media inform the mobilization hypothesis and be extended to Spanish-language media? There is evidence that alternative media, mainly in the form of newsletters and newspapers, helped to mobilize supporters during the black and Chicano civil rights movements by providing relevant information and serving as facilitators of communication for civil rights leaders and organizations (Garland 1982; Rojas 1975). It is even the case that mainstream radio stations were effectively used by labor during the southern textile strike campaigns of 1929 to 1934, when more than four hundred thousand workers throughout the South walked off their jobs. Roscigno and Danaher make the connection between radio and strike activity through a variety of sources to "show that the geographic proximity of radio stations to the 'textile belt' and the messages aired shaped workers' sense of collective experience and political opportunity: Walk-outs and strike spillover across mill towns resulted" (2001:21). Radio was also used by African Americans during the 1960s civil rights movement to educate and inform both white and black radio listeners (Ward 2004).

In the context of the 2006 debate over immigrant rights, Spanish-language media was the necessary alternative to mainstream English-language media for diffusion of information. I argue that the immigration protests of

2006 were successful because Spanish-language radio transmitted information about when and where they were to take place.[9] Advocacy organizations helped with logistical support and provided some of the background information about HR 4437 as the impetus for action. However, Spanish radio stations were not simply tools for information diffusion where national leaders and organizations could activate a captive audience. Unlike in the civil rights era, the more recent contestation over immigrant civil rights has not been led by national organizational or political leaders who command mass recognition like Martin Luther King Jr. or, more recently, Bill Clinton and Jesse Jackson. Without a national leader or even a national organization to frame a unified message or response, something else had to situate the issue and the unified response by millions of people throughout the United States. Through their syndicated morning shows, disc jockeys Eduardo "Piolin" Sotelo and Renán Almendárez Coello "El Cucuy" were instrumental in activating a collective Latino identity to become engaged by directly participating in the March and May immigrant protest marches or supporting them in some other way.[10] The use of Spanish in this medium presents one significant alternative to the mainstream mass media, and one very important cultural process that induced "individual participation in collective action to ensure social solidarity, even in the face of harsh countermobilization" (Roscigno and Danaher 2001:24).

Chicago-based DJ Rafael Pulido "El Pistolero" asserted this commitment to the Latino community and his discussions with DJs in Los Angeles and San Francisco in the weeks leading up to the May 1 protest marches and his belief that protest politics would be at the heart of any real change:

> I believe if there's not a clear and fair legalization for the 14 million illegal immigrants, I think that we will continue to push and to support groups or to do it ourselves, to take initiative to send the message to the people as of the importance of coming together. . . . If it's necessary, I've spoken to my colleagues in L.A., I've spoken to the people in the Bay Area, I've spoken to the people in Houston and they're all for it. They're willing to use their airtime at all cost. . . . I believe it's all about strategy and we all need to see which way the Senate is moving, the government is moving, how serious are they taking this. (March 28, 2006, NPR interview)

El Pistolero's comments do suggest that, from the DJs' point of view, Spanish-language radio and the personalities associated with it sought to challenge the status quo. Their involvement in encouraging their listeners to gather and protest is more in line with Hamilton's assertion that ethnic mass media "often view their role more or less explicitly as one of educating and mobilizing the 'masses' in the service of the cause or movement" (2000:359). It makes sense, then, that some mainstream media accounts portrayed Spanish-language radio disc jockeys as leaders in the immigration protests. The reality was that they served to support the efforts of grassroots organization and framing the response to a perceived threat while also engaging in direct mobilization by emphasizing collective identity, solidarity, and political opportunities (Zepeda-Millán 2011). In particular, the disc jockeys helped educate and mobilize the masses while organizational and other community leaders provided the requisite leadership and institutional capacity to carry out a mass-scale protest.[11] National survey data from the summer of 2006 reveal that media and this sense of solidarity were crucial not only for participation in the protest marches, but for support for them among those who could not attend (Barreto et al. 2009).

Radio and Mobilization: A History of (Re)action

The role that Spanish-language radio disc jockeys played during the fight against HR 4437 was characterized by mainstream media as new or unique. However, Ward makes the case that radio was also essential for mobilizing support for the civil rights movement: "By helping to publicize the goals and methods of the early movement beyond Dixie, radio contributed to a national process of legitimization that by 1965 had persuaded even some southern stations to allow pro–civil rights programming" (Ward 2004:124). Moreover, the African American community in urban centers has a history of utilizing black radio for the community mobilization and ensuring a strong link between black radio and community in the 1960s (Johnson 2004; Squires 2000; Barlow 1998). There is, for instance, one account about Jack Gibson, a leading black disc jockey, who shared the microphone with Martin Luther King Jr. to rally listeners to attend meetings and become involved in the civil rights movement (Barlow 1998). Black radio disseminated information about and encouraged a host of civic activities, ranging from attending meetings to taking part in voter-registration drives. Again, it should be noted that disc jockeys in black radio stations facilitated the diffusion of information, but it was largely national leaders such as Martin Luther King Jr. who provided the rationale for the call to action.

Political mobilization via radio would not have been possible if disc jockeys on black radio had been unable to create an intimate relationship with the audience. Despite its commercialization, black radio maintained a level of connection with the community through identity that is not readily available for other mass media.[12] Squires (2000) argues that black radio offers an example of how "commercial media can play a positive role in forming and sustaining serious discourse within a subaltern public sphere, especially through a small market or niche format" (84).

Providing a more proximate example to the contemporary case of immigrant rights in Los Angeles, Johnson (2004) delineates the role of black radio, especially in times of crisis. Her account of KJLH, a black-owned radio station in Los Angeles, suggests that the station played a pivotal civic activist role in the aftermath of civil unrest that followed the May 1992 "not guilty" verdict of the police officer charged with the Rodney King beating.

> Through its service to the community, KJLH-FM countered some of the negative images strewn across television. More important, the radio station became the focal point for discussion and implementation of nonviolent solutions to the social ills of southern Los Angeles and to the larger African American community across the nation. KJLH-FM's social and political identity, subsequently, was not merely established via on-air dialogue but also through the civic participation it inspired from its staff and community. The station's political activism appears as an important component of its larger community role both before and after the 1992 events. KJLH-FM listeners' interest and willingness to participate in rallies and voter registration drives became unifying forces within the Black community during 1992. KJLH-FM fostered a shared identity among its listeners as they called to voice their outrage with the Rodney King verdict. (Johnson 2004:354)

Johnson and others make it clear, however, that 1992 was not the origin of this phenomenon. Rather, there is a history of such involvement in the preceding decades, including during the civil rights movement. These include community service efforts to raise money during the 1950s and 1960s, as a unifying force immediately after the assassination of Martin Luther King Jr., and through participation in voter-registration campaigns that led to the election of black mayors for the first time in several cities, including Harold Washington in Chicago in 1983 and Willie W. Herenton in Memphis in 1991. Even as recently as October 27, 2000, there was an on-air one-hour conference call by Bill Clinton and Jesse Jackson to forty National Association of Black-Owned Broadcasters (NABOB) to ask the listening audience to mobilize the black vote on election day. Others have noted that ethnic media have historically served a similar role for immigrants and ethnic communities. "For immigrant communities, these media . . . are often used as a means of mobilizing support or opposition. They also serve as a focal point for the development of a local consensus, and a means of expression of the community's demands upon the wider host community" (Gandy 2000:3). The role that Spanish-language radio played in reaction to the HR 4437 and anti-immigrant rhetoric is strikingly similar to the role that black radio has played. It is also similar to that of ethnic media among other immigrant communities including Italian, German, and French (Gandy 2000).

By the fall of 2006, the mass mobilization that characterized the immigrant rights movement across the United States seemed to have faded. Fewer than five thousand demonstrators gathered at a Labor Day weekend rally in Washington, D.C. (Brulliard 2006). Many fewer attended a rally for immigrant rights that weekend in Los Angeles (Prengaman 2006). Tempting as it may be to view the decline in the number of protest participants and the diminished role of Spanish-language radio after the spring of 2006 as "return to normalcy,"[13] I argue that the swell of participation by both the protest participants and disc jockeys and the noticeable drop in their participation can be better explained by paying closer attention to the growth and evolution of Spanish-language radio before and after the 2006 marches. An overview of the contemporary development of national Spanish-language radio reveals various indicators of the potential role of this communication resource in the mobilization of immigrants, albeit ones that have gone largely unnoticed by political scientists and sociologists.

Spanish-Language Radio, Identity, and Market-Share Politics over Time

As noted earlier, communications scholars have made it clear that the community involvement by black radio in 1992 was rooted in a history of involvement since the 1960s. Similarly, an examination of the growth and evolution of Spanish-language radio yields a similar conclusion that its contemporary role in community affairs is rooted in a history of involvement. Without this historical perspective, any attempts to gauge the relevance of Spanish-language radio for the immigration protest marches will miss a crucial factor that explains the groundswell of opposition to HR 4437 across the United States. A closer review of the history of Spanish-language radio inevitably will begin with a recognition that it has grown dramatically over time and has been seen as a means to tap into the growing Latino population in the United States. In 1980 there were only 67 Spanish-language radio stations in the United States (Castañeda Paredes 2003). As figure 4 demonstrates, the number has grown dramatically to 533 in 1998, 835 in 2006, and more than 1,000 in 2008.

This growth can be attributed to the existing practice of audience segmentation. According to Oscar H. Gandy (2000), "audience segmentation . . . is both the product and the source of strategic information about individuals who share an identifiable status based on any number of attributes . . . or claimed membership in groups defined by race or ethnicity" (44). There are various ways of segmenting demographic minorities, but one of the most direct ways to segment ethnic audiences is through language. In the case of Latinos, even as they assimilate in the second and third generation and their use of Spanish-language media decreases, they still listen to Spanish-language radio, especially "Mexican Regional" and "Spanish Contemporary," the top two Spanish-language formats. A *Hispanic Radio Today 2011* report makes reference to a decline among younger audiences, based on Arbitron data, but emphasizes that "significant percentages of English dominant listeners come from teens and young adults, a reflection of this audience segment's desire to retain their cultural connectivity" (6). Moreover, the inflow of Latino immigrants has ensured the maintenance and growth of a sizable segment of a linguistically defined audience. The rapid growth of the Latino population, consistently high ratings,[14] and Latinos' increasing spending power have not gone unnoticed by advertisers, as they realize that what was true in the 1970s is even more relevant today: "Every morning millions of persons across the United States wake up and turn to their radio for music, news and traffic reports. During the day they listen to radio as they drive to work, go about their daily tasks, and make their way home. For them radio is a 'constant companion,' the communication medium that follows them wherever they go" (Gutiérrez and Schement 1979:3).

In an age when the traditional English-language radio format has lost many of its audience to iPods and satellite radio, the characterization of Latinos from the late 1970s holds true today because Latinos listen to radio more than any other media and they listen more than non-Latinos. According to the 2007 Arbitron report *Hispanic Radio Today*, "while TSL [time spent listening] for radio in general has struggled, not so in the Hispanic world" (Arbitron 2007:9). While white-collar workers are often able to stay connected to the news during business hours through the Internet, many Latino immigrants who work in the service sector are able to listen to radio while they work and effectively "stay connected" throughout the day

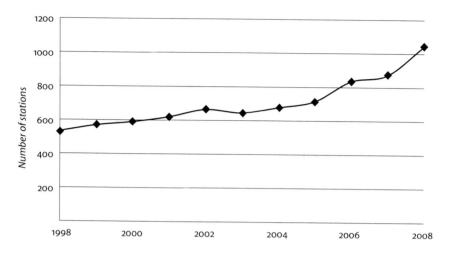

Fig. 4 Spanish-language radio stations, 1998–2008

to the Spanish-language news and entertainment. Latinos listen to radio more than non-Latinos as evidenced by "radio's reach among both English-dominant and Spanish-dominant listeners continues to land between 94% and 96%—a constant since *Hispanic Radio Today*'s first study back in the 1990s" (Arbitron 2010).

In order to determine whether a communication resource can be used to mobilize Latino immigrants for a particular cause, it is important to recognize the nature of the radio industry and the forces that pushed Spanish-language into a prominent social, economic, and intermittent political role. In addition to considering the evolution of Spanish-language radio, it is also important to factor in the public nature and content provided by these radio stations. It is not simply that the on-air programs and advertisements are in Spanish, but the content often uses identity to appeal to and connect with a "sub-ethnic" audience, thereby enhancing the goal of marketing practices to direct advertising to clearly defined consumer groups. For example, "advertising campaigns on Spanish-language radio can be developed with the sub-ethnic in mind, such as Mexicans in Los Angeles or Cubans in Miami, each of whom has a unique set of Spanish words and cultural customs" (Castañeda Paredes 2003:7). Interestingly, the sub-ethnic marketing, it is argued, happens less in the Spanish-language television format. Arlene Davila (2000) argues that rather than emphasizing or targeting specific Latino sub-ethnics, Spanish-language television and marketing industries attempt to forge a transnational diasporic culture of Latinidad that deemphasizes cultural distinctiveness across national origin groups. More recently, Cristina Mora similarly makes the case that the evolution of "Hispanic programing" on Spanish-language television networks catered to a national pan-ethnic audience and helped to institutionalize Latino pan-ethnicity (2009).

Sub-ethnic marketing strategy and the creation of Spanish-language radio stations to reach Latinos is currently the accepted norm,[15] but that was not the case twenty years ago, when this segment of the population was largely neglected by mass media. A series of events and recognition of the changing demographics transformed this. Among all the major radio markets, the change began in Los Angeles in 1992, when a new Spanish-language radio station sought to capitalize on the presence of millions of Latino immigrants in Los Angeles. While there was one FM station at the time, KLVE, the programming could be characterized as Spanish contemporary music. The new radio station, KLAX, or "La X," chose two relatively new DJs who were former immigrant farmworkers to head its morning show. More surprising was that it opted for an untested music format on FM in Los Angeles consisting of Mexican Regional and Banda music. At that point, banda music[16] enjoyed no more acceptance in California than did the immigrants themselves.

By 1992, in a surprisingly short amount of time, KLAX had captured the largest percentage of the radio market. While the accuracy of the Arbitron[17] ratings was originally questioned by other stations, its continued success made it clear that KLAX's programmers had discovered a large and un-tapped pool of listeners consisting of recent Mexican immigrants, children of immigrants, and blue-collar Latinos who maintained Spanish competence. The combination of ethnic pride in the music, the down-to-earth style of KLAX's disc jockeys, and the concentration of the Latino population set the stage for the continued transformation of the second-largest media market in the country, as well as the influx of other Spanish-language radio stations throughout the country.

The levels of success surprised everyone, including the DJs, Juan Carlos Hidalgo and Jesus Garcia "El Peladillo," who were largely responsible for the dominant position of "La X" and the positive response by their listeners. As these two radio personalities boosted ratings for KLAX through their focus on family values, they simultaneously built a relationship predicated on trust and reciprocity with their listeners, tending to the needs of their listeners and of the Latino community more broadly. By constructing and attracting a dedicated audience, they were able to create a media environment whose commercial goals and community goals overlapped (Squires 2000).

These disc jockeys also heavily criticized politicians whom they perceived as immigrant bashers. For example, they thought then-governor Pete Wilson blamed California's problems on illegal immigrants, and they took every opportunity to air those sentiments (Ginsberg 1994). They used the power of the airwaves to berate Wilson for using immigrants as scapegoats for California's struggling economy and for creating the perception that immigration was out of control and that most Latinos were in the United States illegally.

In her analysis of the role of the interaction between radio, music, and politics in California during the 1990s, the ethnomusicologist Helen Simonett asserts that "not only did recent immigrants feel unwelcome in California, but longtime Latino residents and Mexican Americans of several generations were also faced with growing resentment, open hostility, and hardly disguised racism" (2000:2). Rather than sit on the sidelines or merely talk about empowerment, Juan Carlos Hidalgo and "El Peladillo" also set a precedent for direct involvement in real-world politics during the 1994 protest against a 1994 ballot measure widely seen as anti-immigrant, Proposition 187. "El Peladillo" recalls that at that time he was unaware of the influence that came with his position as a popular DJ. His participation in the pro-immigrant marches in 1994 transformed him and further connected him to his audience. "El Peladillo gradually but increasingly identified with his audience and became 'raza,' seeking to help those who hear his show. . . . 'The first march that we took part in was in 1994 against Pete Wilson, that is how we came to identify as a united people'" (Radionotas 2006).

While the popularity of their morning show was evident in their Arbitron ratings, the consonance of their message with the audience was more directly evident when Governor Wilson visited Los Angeles to give a speech at the opening of the new 105 "Century Freeway." The disc jockeys asked any listeners who might be cruising nearby on the San Diego (405) Freeway to honk in a sign of unity and protest to drown out Wilson's speech. In a pattern that would be replicated in 2006, it appears that part of the reason why a Spanish-language station topped Arbitron's ratings has to do with its willingness to take on social and political issues that are important to its audience. However, after a reduction in the civic activist role of the radio station, the top spot was then achieved by another Spanish-language station with less of a civic activist role. KLAX, which held top spot from 1992 to 1994, ceded its first-place rank to KLVE in 1995.

The emergence of other Spanish-language stations in all of the top radio markets is important not just because they played similar Mexican Regional music formats in places like Chicago, Houston, and Dallas, but because of the connection between the local morning DJs and the listening audience. It was throughout the mid- to late 1990s that multiple Spanish-language stations emerged and were consistently among the top radio stations in many of the largest media markets in the United States. According to Felix Gutierrez (2006), there was a transformation of Spanish radio during this time period from a medium of chance to a medium of choice. "You listened to the radio station because you preferred Spanish or you only spoke Spanish, and you only had one or two choices. Now it's a medium that's replicated English-language media. . . . So whatever flavor you want in Spanish, you can get it." To highlight the many "flavors" of Spanish-language radio, in 2001, Arbitron reported six distinct Spanish-language radio formats. By 2011, they have reported on twelve different formats that have flourished in regions and states.[18]

Strength from Within: Identity and New Mobilizing Opportunities

It is useful to compare Spanish-language radio to black radio for a better understanding of the opportunities as a potential resource for mobilization. Both black radio and Spanish-language radio have demonstrated a commitment to attending to the community and have built this capacity over time. Just as black radio mobilized around exogenous shocks or crises that require community involvement, so too has Spanish-language radio been effective in developing this close connection with its audience. While this intermittent civic role may appear to be reactionary and haphazard, that characterization does not fully encapsulate the opportunities and challenges faced by Spanish-language radio. This is because one must understand the role of exogenous and endogenous factors in the decision among radio stations to engage in civic activism. Exogenous forces include natural disasters and political threat that require engaging personalities that can motivate and mobilize the community for a specific outcome. There are instances when Spanish-language radio has been used outside of the political realm as a communication resource to diffuse information and others when it has independently sought to mobilize the community. For example, when communities in the United States and Latin America have experienced natural disasters, Spanish-language radio has a track record of addressing the pressing needs by raising funds to help the victims, even when there is no other grassroots organizational activity for this purpose.

There is an established history of DJs on Spanish-language radio helping to raise funds for disaster relief. For example, while at KSCA and KLAX, Renán Almendárez Coello "El Cucuy" devoted on-air programming and formed the "El Cucuy" Foundation to mobilize his audience to help with financial and other contributions in reaction to natural disasters. He helped raised hundreds of thousands of dollars for aid to victims as well as for other notable public projects. There is indeed a history of mobilizing around a cause, and his appeals were very much infused with calls for Latinos to step up and help. These include efforts to help victims of major hurricanes in Honduras, Mexico, and New Orleans in 1998, 2002, and 2005 respectively, as well as the victims of major earthquakes in Latin America.

Another similarity between Spanish-language radio and black radio is that their social and political identity is inherently tied into the identity of the listening audience. Yet, there is one notable difference between black radio and Spanish-language radio with respect to the role of identity. Barlow's (1998) account of black radio suggests that it is important to look at the construction of racial identity through voice. He explores the history of white DJs "passing" for black over the air and vice versa, a phenomenon dubbed "racial ventriloquy" (Watkins 1994; Barlow 1998). The reason why this is an important difference is that while both rely on and encourage identity formation, there is much less ambiguity about whether the Spanish-language DJs are Latino than about whether a DJ on black radio is black. In other words, by its very nature, the language of transmission ensures some common identity with the mother tongue as a possible unifying mechanism.

However, while both black radio and Spanish-language radio rely on the strong identity connection with the audience to effectively transmit their message, their target audience and the overarching goal were very distinct. Black-oriented radio can be characterized as primarily having an information-diffusion and proselytizing function. "Although television and the print media were vitally important in promoting northern white and federal support for the attack on Jim Crow, movement workers also appreciated the unique potential of radio to help fashion favorable national attitudes toward the southern struggle" (Ward 2004:116). The linguistic isolation of Spanish-language radio precludes any possible effort to build alliances and fashion favorable attitudes toward the immigrant struggle. This may seem likely to hinder Spanish-language radio's ability to mobilize listeners to become active in a cause, but Spanish-language radio is also less likely than black-oriented radio to be scrutinized by those outside the target audience. This was evident during the civil rights movement in the South. "Since many white southerners had originally become hooked on African American music by secretly listening to black-oriented shows . . . this racially transgressive capability alone justified closer examination of what was being said, as well as what was being played, on southern radio" (Ward 2004). It is not surprising that "black-oriented" radio was wary of taking an explicitly activist tone and making direct calls to action as Spanish-language radio did during the protest marches of 2006. Thus, unlike the case in the 1960s when there was fear of immediate backlash and outside guests were the driving force in crafting the message, DJs such as "Piolin," "El Cucuy," "El Mandril," "El Pistolero," and Humberto Luna, in their respective geographic radio markets, were able to use the linguistic isolation to directly mobilize people to protest and were themselves instrumental in formulating the symbols and message.

Another significant difference between black radio and Spanish-language radio has to do with the endogenous forces affecting the very nature of Spanish-language radio. The sheer size and concentration of the Latino population has allowed Spanish-language radio to achieve significant audience share in the largest media market in the United States. In 2012, Latinos comprised 20 to 43 percent of the audience in the top six radio media markets.[19] In each of these media markets, at least one Spanish-language radio is in the top ten rated stations,[20] and Spanish-language morning radio shows have, at different points in time, garnered the top spot, beating out nationally syndicated English-language shows like Howard Stern and Ryan Seacrest. This level of success, in turn, has created an extremely competitive market for Spanish-language radio audience. The diffuse nature of the Spanish-language radio market requires extreme coordination and willingness to overlook their competition in responding to community needs such as the immigration protests in 2006. While this does not prevent any one station from taking on a civic activist role, it simply makes a unified response to exogenous shocks less likely, though still possible.

Spanish-language radio has evolved and grown so much that there are limits to the extent that it can be compared to black radio. Unprecedented levels of commercial success put Spanish-language radio in uncharted territory. This success can be directly attributable to the ease with which

Spanish-language radio segments a linguistically identifiable target audience. The challenge, however, is that despite its impressive combined market share, there is very little chance that Spanish-language radio and its listening audience will be fully integrated within society. This is because the language barrier inherently prevents most non-Latinos from becoming regular audience members.[21]

On a more localized level, there are similarities between black radio's civic activism in Los Angeles early in the 1990s and contemporary successes of Los Angeles–based Spanish-language radio to help disseminate information, relate the community's views on immigration, and strategically use its political power to mobilize its audience into protest politics. The immigrant rights protests of 2006 were a cumulative response to a national anti-immigrant political environment and coordinated by a partnership between civic and community organizations and the Spanish-language media. Just because there is a capacity to mobilize does not mean that the radio stations are always in mobilization mode, however. To a degree, strategy and selectivity have been employed. More importantly, one must factor in the unmistakable reality that at its core, Spanish-language media is corporate mass media and that therefore this capacity is constrained to a greater degree than locally owned black radio.

The short-sighted critiques leveled at the disc jockeys in Chicago and Los Angeles Spanish-language radio for their diminished role in the May 1 protest marches after 2007 and 2008 fails to consider the unprecedented nature of what Spanish-language radio was able to do in 2006. Spanish-language radio has shown that it can introduce innovation. When there are opportunities for innovation, radio has the power to engage and reach a broader spectrum of people than existing grassroots organizations or even network television. The first innovation was the ability of disc jockeys from competing stations to come together to jointly mobilize the Latino community to participate and to help frame the response to the political threat with a sea of white shirts and American flags. Spanish-language radio did what would have likely taken months of negotiation for grassroots organizations with different goals and constituents.

Challenges and Uncharted Waters for Spanish-Language Radio

It is one thing to examine the effects of alternative media, including non-English media, which take the form of newsletters or community newspapers that help disseminate information and mobilize the audience at a localized level. It is wholly another proposition to consider what happens when the medium is growing rapidly and must inherently address the mass public, such as radio or television. This is the case in many media markets, such as in Los Angeles, New York, Chicago, and Dallas, where Spanish-language radio and television have witnessed impressive growth in market share. Mass media opens up opportunities for mass mobilization, but also gives rise to challenges. As Spanish-language television and radio have become key players in the national corporate media, organizations and social movements have to figure out how to deal with the tradeoff between political effectiveness that could result from mass-produced and disseminated media and the increased costs associated with such mass-scale production and distribution.

This is a valid concern with mass media. In order to sustain the expanded capacity, Spanish-language media must seek capital, often through commercialization to secure financial support, which then has the potential to deviate from grassroots origins or desire to represent the community (Mora 2011). As Hamilton (2000) notes, alternative media are faced with a dilemma where "on one hand, they seek to become influential and powerful to help bring about changes to the current commercial media system and the society that supports it; yet, efforts to do so mean adopting the same large-scale, capital intensive, technologized means typical of mainstream media, which limits popular participation" (358). Mass Spanish-language radio works within the same mass-culture context as mainstream mass media and therefore faces the dilemma of seeking to increase distribution while maintaining a sense of commitment to the community.

Owen and Wildman's (1992) insights about the nature of the television industry are instructive for those interested in the opportunities and challenges presented by Spanish-language radio. Their critique of television analysts is particularly useful if applied to the radio industry:

> The first and most serious mistake that an analyst of the television industry can make is to assume that advertising-supported television broadcasters are in the business to broadcast programs. They are not. Broadcasters are in the business of producing audiences. These audiences, or means of access to them, are sold to advertisers. The product of a television station is measured in dimensions of people and time. The price of the product is quoted in dollars per thousand viewers per unit of commercial time. (Owen and Wildman 1992:3)

With the caveat in mind that Spanish-language radio is first and foremost a money-generating business, one can explain the fact that the disc jockeys were allowed to devote airtime to rallying listeners around a political cause by noting that such programming boosted ratings. In Chicago, for instance, after a gradual climb to the third-highest-rated morning show, Rafael Pulido "El Pistolero" captured the top spot in the spring and summer of 2006, at the very time he was encouraging his listeners to take part in the immigrant rights protests. Similarly, according to the summer 2006 Arbitron ratings, five of the top ten radio stations in the Los Angeles media market were Spanish-language stations. However, after the mass marches, they likely felt pressure to return to their traditional format or face a potential loss of the core audience that tunes in for entertainment and general news and information. Even Spanish-language radio is bound by tradition and social and economic constraints.

Recall that the Spanish-language DJ Piolin was one of the most influential in calling for mass protests in 2006. By January 2007, Univision expanded the syndication of *Piolin por la mañana* in several of the top media markets, including Chicago and New York, making this the most syndicated morning show in the history of Spanish-language radio. The syndication of *Piolin por la mañana* has expanded to fifty markets covering twenty-four states. This is a significant increase from the fifteen markets covering seven states in 2006. Liberman Broadcasting, Spanish Broadcasting System, and Entravision Communications Corp—Univision Radio's primary competitors—are also shifting to more syndication of their morning shows. Interestingly, the reduced coordination across cities and formats results in a less intimate relationship between morning DJs and the local audience. It was this relationship that helped generate the interest among the listening audience to take part in the protest marches.

As both syndication and the competition for audience share among Spanish-language radio stations increase, so too does the pressure for "commodification" of a pan-Latino identity expressly for commercial purposes, not for social and political ends. The elimination of national ownership caps of radio stations (Telecommunications Act of 1996) has led to industry-wide consolidation and mergers such Univision's acquisition of the Hispanic Broadcasting Corporation in 2002. This corporatization of Spanish-language media has changed the dynamics of what Spanish-language radio is willing to do with respect to political activism and may limit to the extent to which Spanish-language radio can be used as a means to mobilize. In short, corporatization and corporate mergers encourage media to adopt risk-free programming to avoid loss to competition or alienating potential listeners. Political messages may be effective in gaining listeners' attention, but they may also prove to be controversial. Corporate leaders are unlikely to rely on controversial political messages to attract a stable listening audience.

As successful as Spanish-language radio has been before, during, and after the protest marches, it is important to have a balanced view of some of the challenges and limitations of this media for political mobilization. In addition to some of the inherent limitations that the mass broadcast media format imposes on Spanish-language radio, these stations increasingly behave more like mainstream radio. At the end of the day, the primary goal continues to be to make money. It is likely that the very connection between the DJs and the protesters becomes a means to compete for greater market shares, which, once achieved, may diminish the likelihood of future mobilization efforts. Attaining greater market share may often mean relying on a pan-ethnic format without political content to attract as many listeners as possible.

There is evidence of this as the only DJ who has maintained a consistent presence on Spanish-language radio has been "Piolin." Most of the DJs who played a significant role in planning the marches have had a diminishing and inconsistent presence. In late 2006, Ricardo Sanchez "El Mandril" left KSCA and joined KLAX, but in the afternoons. The expansion of *Piolin por la mañana* in January 2007 meant that Rafael "El Pistolero," one of Chicago's local DJs who had mobilized the Latino community to participate in the protests of 2005, March 2006, and May 1, 2006, had to be shifted to an afternoon time slot. In mid-September 2008, Almendárez Coello "El Cucuy" left KLAX to pursue his own radio network. Around the same time, Marcela Luevanos, a fixture on *Piolin por la mañana* and one of the few female personalities on Spanish-language radio, was dismissed from Univision. In 2009, several other major changes took place. Rocio Sandoval "La Peligrosa," whose afternoon slot had continued the discussions about the protest marches in 2006, was replaced on KSCA. "El Pistolero" was fired from Univision Radio in 2009. Similarly, Humberto Luna left his long-running morning show in Los Angeles on KHJ-AM, to join Clear Channel's La Preciosa network, which is syndicated in several cities, but not Los Angeles. This volatility among the DJs is also evident in the volatility in ratings for individual radio stations in many of the top Spanish-language radio markets.

Furthermore, as Spanish-language radio seeks to expand its audience nationally, it will attempt to mobilize a pan-ethnic identity, rather than an ethnic-specific one. That move may well inhibit political content as well, as corporate strategists know well that support for immigrant rights, particularly the rights of those without documents, varies across national-origin groups. Though some may believe that political strength is tied to numbers, the case of pan-ethnic-targeted radio may challenge that assumption. The quest for a larger, pan-ethnic audience may well lead Spanish-language radio to deemphasize politics to avoid the appearance of taking up an issue perceived to affect some Latino groups more than others.

The competition between and among radio stations presents a challenge for the future of political activism in Los Angeles and beyond. Even with this challenge, it is also important to remember that scholarly understanding about the capability of Spanish-language radio to mobilize its listening audience has neglected its long history and its unique potential. Thus, this chapter closes where it began: with a critical view of the extant political science and sociology literatures for their inability to adequately update the mobilization and participation theories to help explain the mobilization and participation of immigrants in 2006.[22] These literatures fail to offer an explanation for the activation of immigrants and/or their sympathizers and, especially, the fact that non-English-language use and non-English-language radio enabled rather than inhibited participation. Evidently, most of the prominent scholars were off the mark with respect to the effects of language.

To be fair, the assertions about the role of language in participation were made before Spanish-language stations reached their current levels of success. Verba, Schlozman, and Brady (1993) do indicate that protests were perhaps the exception to the rule that non-English-language use inhibits participation. However, even in the most civic-oriented activities like naturalization and voter registration, Spanish-language radio has prompted and encouraged greater participation through the activation of identities and naturalization and voter-registration drives. It is also discouraging that even recent studies about the effect of mass media on political behavior continue to largely overlook the Spanish-language media. It is important that the subsequent research begins to incorporate these social, economic, and political changes that are under way as a result of the growing immigrant population and its established presence in the largest media markets in the country.

3

DEFENSIVE NATURALIZATION AND THE OPPORTUNITY TO MOBILIZE

In the last chapter, I explored the reactive mobilization of Latinos into protest politics as a result of an exogenous political shock, but I suggest that existing studies of minority politics have largely been looking in the wrong place for additional catalysts of political mobilization. By neglecting the proactive mobilization that took place as a result of the convergence of Spanish-language media and Latino organizations, the existing literature misses a piece of the puzzle key to understanding the evolving role of Latinos in American politics. The activation of Latinos into protest politics, according to the established work on social movements and political participation, should have consequences on the nature of Latinos' engagement in American democracy. However, Browning, Marshall, and Tabb (1984) make a compelling case that if we are to adequately consider the struggle for equality in politics for blacks and Latinos, we must look to their levels of political incorporation in the electoral arena because "protest is not enough." While noncitizenship does not prevent Latino immigrants from participating in protest politics, it is the primary barrier to the electoral participation of many Latino immigrants. In order to fully consider the evolving Latino electorate, we must begin with an understanding of when there is a change in existing rates of naturalization among Latino immigrants and the catalyst(s) for that change. I draw on multiple sources of administrative naturalization statistics, aggregated at multiple levels of geography, as well as one nationally representative survey of Latinos and a regional survey of Latino immigrants who began the process of naturalization. I explore the convergence of exogenous and endogenous factors that helped transform noncitizenship, one of the most pressing barriers to Latino electoral presence, into a mobilizing opportunity. The purpose of this chapter is to demonstrate the instrumental role of political context for understanding the motivation to pursue U.S. citizenship. I also emphasize the crucial role of endogenous resources within the Latino community in navigating the increasingly complex and bureaucratic process of naturalization.

Between March and May 2006, thousands of marches were staged across America to protest the passage of the Sensenbrenner Bill (HR 4437),[1] regarded as one of the most punitive anti-immigrant pieces of legislation in the last seventy years. HR 4437 included provisions that would criminalize the presence of undocumented persons in the United States, construct additional fencing along the U.S.-Mexican border, and impose criminal penalties upon anyone who knowingly assisted any individual with an unauthorized immigration status. It is estimated that there were more than 5 million participants in these pro-immigrant marches, making it one of the largest and most widespread civil rights actions in U.S. history (Lazos 2007).

Clearly, the scope and size of the pro-immigrant demonstrations make them distinctive. Beyond the levels of participation, however, a unique prevalent characteristic of the marches was the pronounced use of a common slogan, "We Are America," that would continue well after the demonstrations. While there were non-Latinos at the immigration marches, the word "we" in this message implicitly references Latino immigrants and highlights the integral nature of Latinos in the United States. The first message was further reinforced by the symbolic use of American flags.

A second equally important slogan was prevalent during the demonstrations. The slogan, "Today we march, tomorrow we vote," was powerful because of the message and because, more than other messages, it appeared in both Spanish and English.[2] It sent a message to elected officials that while many could not vote now, they would in the near future. In Spanish, it was not only a slogan, but a call to action among Spanish-speaking Latinos for a united social movement. The intent was to spur voter-registration activities among those already eligible, but the slogan also evoked renewed energy among legal immigrants to pursue citizenship. Did Latinos heed this call to action or at least perceive that a unified social movement was possible? According to the first major nationally representative public opinion poll of Latinos in the United States following the pro-immigration marches, 63 percent of Latinos agreed with the statement that "the immigrant marches were the beginning of a new Hispanic/Latino social movement that will go on for a long time" (Suro and Escobar 2006:1). If the pro-immigrant demonstrations are indeed the beginning of a new social movement, what are the likely political effects? Will Latino legal permanent residents seek U.S. citizenship at higher rates than has been historically the case? Irrespective of whether there is a noticeable change in the rates of naturalization, what was the effect of the immigration marches on the predictors of who indicates that they are interested in becoming U.S. citizens? This chapter focuses on the latter question. Specifically it seeks to shed light on whether the contentious political context nationally that activated Latino immigrants to "come out of the shadows" can be linked to the underlying decision of Latinos to seek full political membership in the United States.

Great Expectations: Patterns of Naturalization among Latino Immigrants

The rhetoric and slogans of an energized Latino immigrant community during the immigrant protest demonstrations are both optimistic and aspire to seize on the reactive mobilization of the Latino community in protest politics to change historic patterns of naturalization among Latino immigrants. This great expectation of growth runs counter to most of the scholarly work about Latino immigrants and political incorporation. Studies interested in the differential rates of naturalization of all immigrants have concluded that immigrants from Latin America, relative to other regions or countries, have lower rates of naturalization and that there is a longer time lapse between when Latino immigrants are eligible to apply for citizenship and when they actually naturalize. Personal characteristics, such as limited English-language skills, lower levels of formal education, lower income, and lower homeownership rates explain, in part, why Latinos pursue citizenship at lower rates given that these characteristics discourage naturalization (Portes and Mozo 1985; Jasso and Rosenzweig 1990; DeSipio 2001). Latino immigrants have also been said to exhibit behavioral and attitudinal predictors of lower naturalization because they are more likely to interact with other immigrant noncitizens or subscribe to the "myth of return" to their birth nation, making them less likely to naturalize (Portes and Curtis 1987; Jones-Correa 1998). Additionally, some have focused on the bureaucratic roadblocks and barriers to naturalization in the current citizenship process (Félix 2008). Taken together, the characteristics, behaviors, and attitudes of Latino immigrants do not bode well for changes in the sluggish rate of naturalization (Barreto, Ramírez, and Woods 2005).

Is there a reason to expect that Latino political leaders' great expectation of change among Latino immigrants could be realized? It is important to counterbalance two realities when it comes to Latino immigrant naturalization and the question of whether the gap between the rhetoric and reality can be overcome. First, many of the conclusions in the comparative studies of naturalization draw on data that do not capture the changing pool of Latino immigrants. Second, given the significant increase in the number of Latino legal permanent residents (LPRs) since the late 1980s, there is potential for growth of the number of Latino naturalized citizens. If we consider all immigrants who became LPRs between 1985 and 2010, Latino immigrants comprise 39.14 percent of immigrants eligible for citizenship (CSII, USC 2011). However, among these LPRs, non-Latino immigrants make up 67 percent of those immigrants who had naturalized by 2011, which means that Latino immigrants constitute just over 33 percent of naturalized citizens during this time period. Clearly, in the aggregate, Latino immigrants do not pursue citizenship at the same rate as non-Latinos, but the compositional differences between LPRs and naturalized immigrants are not dramatic. The lower rates of naturalization are impacted by the fact that Mexican immigrants, who have among the lowest shares of naturalization at 32 percent, comprise the overwhelming share of Latino LPRs and these immigrants. Two other countries, Canada and the United Kingdom, have lower rates of naturalization at 26 percent and 30 percent, respectively, but are a much smaller share of all LPRs relative to Mexico or other Latin American countries. This pattern of lower rates of naturalization is evident geographically if we consider the demographic composition and naturalization rates of metro areas throughout the United States.

As figure 5 indicates, metro areas with higher concentration of Latino LPRs have lower rates of naturalization as of 2011. The geographic patterns reinforce the notion that many citizen-eligible Latino immigrants do not pursue U.S. citizenship. While the disparity between the aggregate composition of Latino LPRs (39 percent) and Latino naturalized citizens (33 percent) does not immediately raise a red flag, aggregate statistics mask important patterns over time. It is possible that there are some compositional effects, in addition to the effects of political context.

The pattern over time uncovers what is missed by aggregating all LPRs during this period. Figure 6 makes clear that in many instances, the number of naturalizations fluctuates over time and that the rate of naturalization among Latino immigrants is not always consistent with their share of LPRs. The percentage of those Latino LPRs who become naturalized citizens is

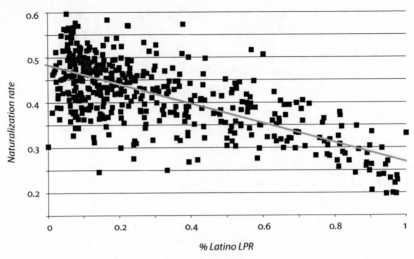

Fig. 5   Naturalization rate by metro area percent Latino, 1985–2005 LPR cohort

less than 32 percent in eleven of the twenty-one years observed. There are two noteworthy take-home points. First, the number of immigrants obtaining citizenship is not static over time. Second, there are instances when there are sudden spikes in the number of immigrants who become part of the citizen voting-eligible population. In two periods, 1995–2000 and 2007–2009, the percentage of all naturalized citizens who are Latino is greater than the 32 percent that they constitute of all LPRs who are eligible for citizenship. Clearly, the great expectations among Latino elites that the established patterns of naturalization could be disrupted were well-founded. It is important, therefore, that we understand how and when change happens. Before turning to the changes in 2007–9, I briefly turn to the prior disruption in naturalization patterns (1995 to 2000) and the explanations for the prior change.

There are four possible explanations given for why the greatest increase of naturalizations among Latino immigrants took place after 1992. First, starting in 1993, the large cohort of immigrants who were granted legal permanent residency under the Immigration Reform and Control Act of 1986 (IRCA) became eligible for naturalization.[3] Although this significantly expanded the pool of potential Latino citizens, it does not explain why Latinos would behave differently than they had in the past, where the time lag between legal residency and naturalization has been particularly high (DeSipio 2001).[4] Analysis of the naturalization rates through 2001 by Nancy Rytina from the Statistics Division of the U.S. Immigration and Naturaliza-

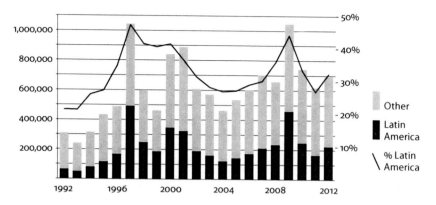

Fig. 6 Naturalizations by immigrant's region of origin, 1991–2011

tion Service[5] concluded that the simple influx of IRCA LPRs did not lead to higher rates of naturalizations. "The impact of IRCA was much more concentrated with respect to legal immigration than naturalization. IRCA LPRs represented more than 40% of all immigrants in fiscal years 1989–1991 but never accounted for more than 23% of naturalizations in any one year" (Rytina 2002:3).

A second explanation for the increased rates of naturalization during the mid–1990s is a simple cost-benefit analysis by immigrants. Specifically, Latinos and other immigrants are believed to have made the decision to pay the one-time fee of ninety-five dollars for the application to naturalize as opposed to the mandatory seventy-five-dollar fee to renew the Alien Service Receipt Card, which a 1996 Immigration and Naturalization rule states must be updated every ten years.[6] In an effort to minimize fraud, the 1996 INS rule required that all permanent residents holding the old form I–151, Alien Registration Receipt Card, which was issued before 1979, must apply in person as soon as possible for a new card, Form I–551, Alien Registration Receipt Card, to demonstrate satisfactory proof of permanent resident status and work eligibility in the United States. The third explanation for the increased naturalization rates contends that the decision to naturalize was a strategic political act in reaction to the enactment of the Personal Responsibility and Work Opportunity Reconciliation Act of 1996, denying welfare benefits even to legal immigrants.

The first three explanations for the increase in naturalization among Latinos all have to do with policy changes at the national level. These explanations, however, fail to account for the larger increase in naturalizations in California. Both scholars and policy analysts have cited the unique political context in California in 1994 as a fourth explanation for the increase in naturalization among Latino immigrants (Pantoja, Ramírez, and Segura 2001; Rytina 2002; Fix, Passel, and Sucher 2003; Tactaquin 2004; Barreto, Ramírez, and Woods 2005; Wong 2006; Ong 2011).

Similar to HR 4437, in 1994 California's statewide Proposition 187 sought to deny undocumented immigrants access to public education, social services, and health care and required public officials to report suspected undocumented immigrants to the Immigration and Naturalization Service (Wong 2006).[7] Although most provisions of the proposition were subsequently struck down by a federal court in 1999, the successful passage of Proposition 187 and the political rhetoric during the 1994 general election created an anti-immigrant political context where citizen-eligible immigrants became more aware of immigration as salient issues. Paul Ong refers to "the act of seeking citizenship in response to increasing anti-immigrant sentiment" as "defensive naturalization" (2011). Ong's study of Chinese immigrants concurs with earlier assessments that, "because Proposition 187 was seen as a move against Latino immigrants, a large number of Latino non-citizens . . . made the decision to begin the naturalization process" (Pantoja, Ramírez, and Segura 2001:731). "Defensive naturalization" as discussed by Ong (2011), in conjunction with Pantoja, Ramírez, and Segura's (2001) findings in California during the 1990s, is consistent with the overarching concept of reactive mobilization as it is one form of political activation and reaction to political context.

Naturalization statistics do provide some evidence for the notion that low rates of naturalization among Latino immigrants were disrupted in the mid-1990s in reaction to California's anti-immigrant political context. A simple comparison of the three-year period before and after Proposition 187 passed is very instructive (that is, 1992–94 versus 1995–97). The average number of annual naturalizations nationally was 329,680 between 1992 and 1994. During this same period, immigrants who resided in California constituted an average of 23.6 percent of those who successfully naturalized. There was a noticeable increase in the average annual naturalizations nationally between 1995 and 1997, as the figure more than doubled to 710,334. California's share of the annual naturalizations also increased as evident by fact that more than a third (34.2 percent) of new citizens resided in the state.[8] Latino immigrants were largely responsible for this growth in naturalizations in California. The average number of Latino immigrants naturalizing in California per year before Proposition 187 (1992–94) was 9,828 and grew tenfold to 107,580 (1995–97). Given the numeric increase, it makes sense that the proportion of all new citizens residing in California who were Latino also increased from an average 13.2 percent annually to 43.4 percent.

Clearly, something unique took place in California during the 1990s. Unfortunately, it is not possible to pinpoint the causes of attitudinal and behavioral changes among Latino immigrants because of the confluence of policy changes and state-specific political context that served to mobilize Latino immigrants. In order to determine the extent to which political context changed the attitudes of citizen-eligible Latino immigrants, one would need reliable attitudinal measures among immigrants before and after Proposition 187. There is no such state or nationally representative data, leaving scholars and analysts with the only option of inferring causality. As I discuss below, I am able to overcome these deficiencies in available data for the surge in naturalization between 2007 and 2009.

Turning back to 2006, the great expectations among immigrant rights activists was that the demonstrations would serve as a catalyst for immigrants to want to naturalize throughout the United States. At the start of 2007, an estimated 8,150,000 legal permanent residents were eligible to naturalize (Rytina 2009).[9] However, as was the case in the mid-1990s, anti-immigrant legislation and protest demonstrations were not the only relevant issues to consider. Policy changes affecting citizenship were enacted that could impact immigrants' decision to pursue naturalization. In January 2007, for example, the United States Citizenship and Immigration Services (USCIS), the federal agency that oversees the naturalization process, announced plans to raise the cost of the naturalization application from $330 to $595, an increase of 561 percent since 1990.[10] Eight months later, USCIS announced that the naturalization test would be redesigned, significantly increasing the requirement of civics and geography knowledge and requiring greater English-language competency than before.[11] Immigrant rights advocates were understandably concerned that these two policy changes would add to the existing disincentives to naturalize such as the backlog of applications[12] and the historic rate of denials of citizenship petitions since 1993.[13]

Given the above-mentioned political context and policy changes, is there any indication that political context can impact the number of Latinos who apply for citizenship *or* the profile of Latino immigrants who initiate the process of naturalization? This is a very straightforward question with no straightforward answer. The same factors that made it difficult to disentangle the effects of political context from citizenship policy changes and efforts by Spanish-language media and Latino organizations to increase applications for citizenship in the mid-1990s also apply to any such analysis after the 2006 immigrant rights protests. It could be that rather than depress naturalization rates, policy changes that threaten to increase the financial costs and make the naturalization process more difficult may instead lead more citizen-eligible immigrants to apply for naturalization before the policy changes take effect. Because of the lag between when the policy changes were announced and when they would be implemented, it is difficult to know when immigrants became aware of these changes and whether they impacted their decision to begin the naturalization process. Ideally, there would be a nationally representative longitudinal study tracking Latino LPRs to identify when they decided to pursue U.S. citizenship, their motivation for doing so, and whether the announcement of policy changes, the mobilization of immigrants to take part in protest politics, or a combination of these factors impacted their attitudes toward the citizenship process.

To identify the discernible effects of a contentious political context, the immigrant protest marches, and the increased media coverage on immigrant attitudes, I use a natural experiment that took place in the data collection of the 2006 Latino National Survey (LNS). About half of the survey responses took place before the March 25 protest marches in Los Angeles, and the remainder were collected after the demonstrations. Subsequent coverage about the immigration debate, HR 4437, and the planned demonstrations in Spanish-language radio and television significantly increased after the Los Angeles demonstration. Beyond the natural experiment, the LNS is ideal because it is the largest survey of Latino citizens and noncitizens in the United States and was completed prior to any announcement of policy changes in the naturalization process.[14] This provides a unique opportunity to consider the effect of the anti-immigrant political context, the mass mobilization of Latinos nationally, and the increased media attention.

I make the case that, irrespective of whether immigrants actually participated in or lived in a city where large demonstrations took place, there was increased interest in naturalization and the predictors of who is more likely to be interested in applying for citizenship. I do find a link between the marches and interest in naturalization, as 49.3 percent of immigrants indicated they were interested in naturalization after the protest marches compared to 45.2 percent before the demonstrations. This difference is statistically significant at the 0.05 level (Pearson Chi Square 6.342). Whether or not these Latinos actually applied for citizenship and were approved is beyond the scope of the survey. At this point, I am more interested in identifying whether the predictors of interest in naturalization changed because this is able to identify whether distinct segments of Latino LPRs were mobilized to naturalize, or whether the impetus for naturalization simply expedited existing trends.

Table 2 compares the predictors of intention to naturalize (dependent variable) before (Model 1) and after (Model 2) the immigration marches took place. The independent variables include individual level characteristics that have been identified as important in the naturalization literature cited above. These include age, gender, marital status, socioeconomic status, homeownership, political interest, trust in government, residential stability, length of time in the United States, and English-language proficiency. I also include the frequency of watching television news because of the increased role of Spanish-language media in the discussion of the immigration debate and in the mobilization of protest participants and account for the possible effects of living in a city where a protest took place to account for variation in news coverage.

As a testament to the increased media attention about the protest marches and the immigration debate on Spanish-language television, Latino immigrants who indicated that they watch television news with more frequency were more likely to indicate a desire to initiate the citizenship process. Not surprisingly, before the marches, the statistically significant predictors of intent to naturalize are consistent with the expectations in the existing immigration literature. Women, homeowners, the residentially stable, those with greater self-reported English-language fluency, and those who pay more attention to politics are more likely to report intent to naturalize. There is a noticeable change in the strength of these predictors after the marches. The effect of homeownership is smaller, and the effect of political interest is bigger. Gender, residential stability, and English fluency are no longer statistically significant, but two resource-based variables, education and income, gain statistical significance after the protest marches. Two additional variables also reach statistical significance, one that is not surprising and one that is. Immigrants who have higher trust in government demonstrated greater levels of intent to naturalize. While many families were mobilized to participate in the immigration protest marches, it was Latino immigrants who are not married who indicated greater interest in U.S. citizenship. Finally, while HR 4437 and the related political controversy led to the massive mobilization of protest participants in select cities, living in one of those cities that experienced an immigrant rights demon-

Table 2 Predictors of intention to naturalize, Spanish-speaking noncitizen Latinos

Independent variables	Model 1 Pre-Immigrant Marches		Model 2 Post-Immigrant Marches	
	Logit	% Chg.[a]	Logit	% Chg.[a]
Age	0.004	0.0651	−0.004	−0.0698
	(0.006)		(0.007)	
Male	−0.175*	−0.0431	0.133	0.0331
	(0.121)		(0.138)	
Married	0.013	0.0033	−0.190*	−0.0472
	(0.128)		(0.146)	
High school graduate	0.094	0.0232	0.251**	0.0624
	(0.126)		(0.137)	
Homeowner	0.462***	0.1145	0.187*	0.0465
	(0.133)		(0.143)	
Residential stability (in years)	0.022*	0.261	0.015	0.1528
	(0.015)		(0.015)	
Television news frequency	−0.04	−0.0298	0.097*	0.0719
	(0.061)		(0.071)	
Political interest	0.24**	0.1188	0.341***	0.1688
	(0.091)		(0.099)	
Trust in government	0.072	0.0536	0.093*	0.0692
	(0.058)		(0.067)	
Resident in 2006 protest city	0.037	0.0092	0.031	0.0077
	(0.126)		(0.137)	
$25,000–$44,999	0.084	0.0207	0.510***	0.1269
	(0.149)		(0.166)	
$45,000–$64,999	0.237	0.059	0.874**	0.2115
	(0.282)		(0.309)	
Over $65,000	−0.145	−0.0353	0.657*	0.1614
	(0.397)		(0.501)	
Income missing	−0.152	−0.0372	0.046	0.0114
	(0.174)		(0.174)	
"Very well" spoken English	0.94***	0.2288	0.139	0.0346
	(0.281)		(0.286)	
U.S. resident (in years)	0.01	0.1496	0.002	0.0376
	(0.008)		(0.009)	
Constant	−1.21***		−1.54***	
	(0.344)		(0.408)	
N	1,487		1,219	

***p < 0.01 **p < 0.05 *p < 0.1 one-tailed

[a] Change in expected intention to naturalize produced by change from lowest to highest observed value of a predictor, holding others at their mean. If dichotomy, change in expected intention to naturalize produced by change from zero to one.

stration was not a significant predictor of intentions to naturalize. This is consistent with the notion that even among Latinos who did not attend a protest, there was a noticeable increase in group solidarity (Barreto, Segura, and Woods 2009). Clearly, changes in attitudes about citizenship are directly and indirectly impacted by political context, rhetoric, and media coverage.

In addition to changes in the predictors of intent to naturalize, there is a noticeable change in the views about why naturalization is important. The phenomenon of "defensive naturalization" is prevalent in the responses to the question, "What would you say is the main reason for becoming a citizen of the United States?" Before the immigration marches, only 2.2 percent of non-citizen Latino immigrants responded: "legal, political rights or civil rights/so people would not treat me unfairly." This dramatically increased to 18.1 percent after the marches. While more modest, the percentage of immigrants for whom being able to vote is the main reason to become a citizen also increased from 24.6 percent before the marches to 28.7 percent after the marches. Additionally there is one response that ties in with the slogan "We Are America." There is an increase in those who say it is important to naturalize to "become more American." Should these immigrants with heightened interest in the naturalization process become U.S. citizens, and then register to vote, this could have implications in electoral politics and policy making. It is to this question of the effect of political context and Latino organizational efforts on patterns of naturalization between 2007 and 2009 that I now shift my attention.

Catalysts for Naturalization after the 2006 Marches

The effects of the political context induced by HR 4437 (reactive mobilization) or the mobilization by organizations and Spanish-language media (proactive mobilization) will be more fully explained as more data become available. While it is possible that several factors played a role in the decision of these Latinos to begin the process of naturalization, the legacy of the immigration marches on the Latino organizations is more palpable. The 2006 marches prompted groups that work on immigration and civic organizations at the national, state, and local level to come together as the We Are America Alliance to advocate for comprehensive immigration reform. Recognizing the importance of helping eligible immigrants become U.S. citizens, national partners of the We Are America Alliance and Spanish-language media came together and, in January 2007, launched the Ya Es

Hora (YEH) ¡CIUDADANIA! (It's time, citizenship!) campaign.[15] Building on the momentum generated by the immigration marches to promote citizenship and civic participation, the campaign provided eligible immigrants with materials, information, and assistance. The campaign sought to increase the number of eligible Latinos pursuing naturalization, an important step toward full political participation.

The YEH model was centered on three pillars: (1) strategy, coordination, training, and technical assistance through national civic organizations; (2) a Spanish-language public-awareness campaign via national media companies; and (3) community education and support from local nonprofits and service providers. The campaign carried out its work through a series of public-service announcements, advertisements, and earned media; a national bilingual hotline and website; local naturalization assistance workshops; distribution of reference materials; and centros de ciudadanía (citizenship centers) for one-on-one citizenship assistance. Activities were designed to educate the public about the requirements, process, and cost of becoming a citizen and provide assistance to those who were eligible to do so. At workshops and centers, applicants received direct support with the naturalization application and were provided legal referrals when necessary.[16]

In fiscal year 2007, USCIS received almost 1.4 million petitions for naturalization (Yearbook of Immigration Statistics 2008). The tremendous influx of applications overwhelmed the USCIS processing system, causing a significant backlog and longer processing times for many applicants. According to congressional testimony from the former USCIS director Emilio Gonzalez: "Historically there have been increases in naturalization filings in advance of fee increases, Presidential elections, immigration debates, and new legislation. Still, none of these past increases compare to the magnitude of the surge we experienced this summer [of 2007]" (Gonzalez 2008).

In addition to the immigration marches and increased outreach undertaken by YEH, a number of different factors contributed to the surge of naturalization applications in 2007, including the proposed increase to the naturalization application fee and the introduction of a redesigned citizenship exam (Medina and Torres 2009). While all of these factors played a role in the surge, it is important to analyze the extent to which the YEH campaign led to measurable increases in the number of naturalizations. The presence of all these variables begs a number of important questions: Which of these factors, or combination of factors, were most salient for the increased rates of naturalization? Moreover, which had the greatest impact on Latinos' decision to initiate and/or complete the naturalization process? Finally, for those who didn't complete the process, what were the primary barriers?

In order to examine these questions, I present an analysis of aggregate USCIS statistics on the number of naturalizations in the top fifty metropolitan reporting areas for which USCIS gathers data. These data provide an initial assessment of the geographic patterns of change in naturalization rates before and after the immigrant marches in 2006 and the subsequent YEH efforts. I also consider the catalysts and barriers faced by individuals who have or have not completed the naturalization process and provide the results of a survey of Latinos who received assistance in the naturalization process from participating YEH organizations. These responses provide important insight into the motivating factors that can be credited for increased naturalization rates, voter registration, and voter turnout among Latinos.[17] These findings may have strong implications for composition of the citizen-age population and evolving Latino electorate. An analysis of increased Latino naturalization in the context of these factors could also have significant implications for electoral participation, particularly considering the concentration of Latinos in large electoral states (New York, California, Texas, Illinois, Florida), as well as key battleground states (New Mexico, Arizona, Colorado, North Carolina, and Florida).

I examine data derived from the Yearbook of Immigration Statistics for the top fifty metropolitan statistical areas of naturalizations from 2003 to 2008 and included the top forty-two that remained consistently in the top fifty throughout this period. The unit of analysis is the reported number of naturalizations in each metropolitan statistical area.[18] After standardizing the data collected, I calculate the percentage increase of naturalizations for Latinos and non-Latinos and calculate the percentage of Latino composition of the total number of naturalizations in a given year. I compare these two measures for 2003–6 against the same measures for 2007–8.[19] These comparisons help identify whether or not there was noticeable growth in the number of naturalizations for Latinos following the immigration marches of 2006 and the corresponding YEH campaign and to question whether this was part of a general trend toward increased rates of naturalization across various races and ethnicities, or something unique to Latino LPRs.

Figure 7 presents the metropolitan areas plotted based on the compiled calculations. The y-axis displays the level of growth in Latino naturaliza-

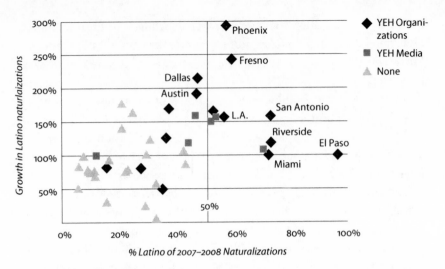

Fig. 7 Growth and presence of Latino naturalizations in top 43 metro areas, 2007–2008

tions between 2003–6 and 2007–8. The x-axis identifies the percentage of Latino naturalizations out of the total number of naturalizations in 2007–8. Additionally, I indicate the organizational and media presence across the metropolitan areas.[20] By classifying the reporting metropolitan areas in this manner, I am able to examine the relative impact of the YEH campaign on Latino naturalizations.

Between 2003 and 2006, there were only 5 metropolitan areas where Latinos constituted the majority of those who naturalized. After 2006, however, there were 11 metropolitan areas where Latinos constituted a majority of successful naturalizations.[21] Of the 42 metropolitan areas that were consistently in the top fifty areas for naturalization, 23 experienced at least 100 percent growth of the number of yearly Latino naturalized citizens in 2007–8, compared to the average number of Latino naturalized citizens in the preceding four years.[22] Latino organizational strength, in combination with Spanish-language media, is crucial to our understanding of when Latino LPRs are seen as a mobilizing opportunity. Sixty-four percent of metropolitan areas with strong YEH media and organizational presence experienced at least 100 percent growth in the number of Latino naturalizations and were also places where Latinos constituted the majority of all naturalizations. Overall, metropolitan areas that had either YEH organizational or media presence had consistently higher levels of growth in Latino naturalizations than metropolitan areas with no YEH presence.

The aggregate data are useful for identifying a relationship between the

YEH campaign on the naturalization rates of Latinos. A survey of a representative sample of 823 YEH participants, collected between October 16 and October 28, 2009, allows for a better understanding of the motivating factors that encouraged individuals to apply for citizenship, as well as the barriers that they faced. The sample was limited to five regional locations: northern Virginia, Houston, Chicago, New York, and Los Angeles. These areas were selected to provide a reasonable cross-section of the United States and the experiences of YEH participants. A random sample from the five metropolitan areas was selected and individuals were contacted by phone. The survey was conducted in either English or Spanish, based on the language preference of the participant, and all calls were conducted by bilingual Latino interviewers.

Based on the bivariate survey results, there is evidence that the YEH workshops had a positive effect on the number of Latino LPRs who pursued and were granted citizenship. With respect to successfully navigating the naturalization process, 92 percent of the respondents reported that they had completed and submitted their application to USCIS, of whom 92 percent were first-time applicants for citizenship. More importantly, 79 percent of respondents had been granted citizenship. The crucial role of Latino civic organizations in helping to expand the pool of citizen voting-age population should not be underestimated, as 20 percent of respondents said they were "somewhat or very unlikely" to apply without the assistance provided by YEH.[23]

Clearly, the capacity to help legal permanent residents navigate the bureaucratic process of applying for citizenship is an essential but insufficient component to change the composition of the citizen population. Spanish-language media proved to be a necessary complement to be able to seize on the opportunity to mobilize an activated segment of citizen-eligible Latino immigrant community. The partnership with Univision, impreMedia, Entravision, and La Opinión was key to the success of the YEH citizenship application workshops. Television, radio and print media accounted for 49 percent of the sources of information about the citizenship assistance workshops. In addition to the role of Spanish-language media and Latino organizations in mobilizing opportunities, when asked about their own decision to naturalize, 49 percent of survey respondents indicated that the immigration debate was "the main reason" or "an important reason" for naturalizing. When asked more generally about the most important reason to naturalize, 26 percent cited voting eligibility and 22 percent made reference to legal, political, or civil rights. It appears that the "defensive naturalization" legacy of the anti-immigrant context of 2006, evident in the LNS data, continued to be relevant for Latino immigrants who initiated or completed the naturalization process by October 2009. Moreover, 85 percent of Latino immigrants who had been granted citizenship had registered to vote, and 67 percent had voted at least once. Whether or not this shapes immigrant political attitudes as they register to vote is a different question.

Convergence of Proactive Mobilization and Reactive Mobilization

Taken together, there is evidence that Latino immigrants were not only activated into protest politics by the political context, but that there were lasting effects on predictors of interest in naturalization and successful citizenship-acquisition patterns. Moreover, aggregate naturalization statistics suggest that YEH played a role, and in some cities a particularly significant one, in increasing Latino naturalizations where the campaign carried out its work. On the whole, areas where YEH had an organizational and/or media presence experienced higher levels of growth in the number of Latino naturalizations than areas with no campaign activity. The involvement and presence of Spanish-language media complemented community-based assistance in filling out the complex citizenship application. It is very possible that other like-minded organizations not currently affiliated with YEH could repeat the efforts that have been shown to be effective. Depending on the state context, it is also possible that there are countermobilization efforts aimed at minimizing the role of new citizens.

Analysis of USCIS data also revealed an important finding about the percentage of Latino naturalizations among the top metropolitan areas. There was a notable increase in the number of metropolitan areas where Latinos composed a majority of completed naturalizations between 2003 and 2008. This notable change occurred within two years, showing that the Latino community was highly motivated to pursue naturalization in the aftermath of the 2006 immigration marches and the launch of the YEH campaign. Two-thirds of metropolitan areas with a YEH organizational and media presence were places where Latinos constituted the majority of all naturalizations, suggesting that the campaign's targeted efforts toward the Latino community may have contributed to this change.

More importantly, this finding illustrates the great potential of mobilizing this community not only in response to exogenous contextual factors, but also through campaigns such as YEH, which provide Latinos with essential information and assistance on the naturalization process.

The change is notable when considering the implications of this increase on Latino electoral participation. In particular, California, Texas, Arizona, and Florida were states with metropolitan areas where the growth of Latino naturalizations and the Latino share of overall naturalizations were particularly pronounced. All of these states have sizable Latino populations, hold significant electoral influence at the national level, and are places where issues concerning the Latino community are especially salient. With the focus that has been devoted to the political impact of Latinos in recent years, it is increasingly plausible that demography will signal destiny as Latino voters in each of these states will play a major role in shaping the nature of elections and associated policy outcomes.

The survey of YEH participants delved further into the various factors that affect an individual's decision to pursue citizenship and experiences with the naturalization process. While the vast majority of survey respondents had completed the process, high application costs,[24] English proficiency levels, and administrative delays continue to affect applicants' naturalization experiences. Thus, while many Latino immigrants are willing and eager to pursue naturalization, the lack of institutional support to help overcome some of the barriers may be slowing down the pace of naturalization to pre-2006 levels.

While YEH was undoubtedly instrumental in yielding successful results among survey respondents, the immigration debate was another major factor driving their motivation to apply for citizenship. For these applicants, the high level of activity surrounding immigration impelled them to pursue citizenship, a status that affords them full protections and rights in the United States, which can only be secured by going through the naturalization process. The survey results suggest that while the immigration debate served as a powerful impetus for individuals to naturalize, the YEH campaign provided many with the information and assistance needed to complete the intimidating process of becoming a citizen. In this respect, the campaign served as a means of enabling respondents to achieve their goal of attaining citizenship.

The aggregate data and survey responses suggest that the YEH campaign positively contributed to the increase of Latino naturalizations following the 2006 immigration marches. While there were a number of factors that contributed to the spike in applications in 2007, YEH organizational and Spanish-language media presence helped to maximize the number of Latinos applying for citizenship and successfully completing the process. These data do not allow for an analysis of the full scope of factors that affected

Latinos' decision to pursue citizenship. However, the survey results of individuals who participated in YEH reveal that proactive mobilization from within the Latino community had profound effects on the composition of new citizens and demonstrate that through targeted outreach and assistance, Latinos can be motivated to pursue naturalization beyond the levels expected as a result of reactive mobilization.

4

THE CHANGING CALIFORNIA VOTER

A Case Study of Mobilizing Opportunities and Latino Participation over Time

Perhaps more than any other state, California witnessed many demographic and political changes in the 1990s. The convergence of these dramatic changes makes it increasingly complex to predict what lies ahead for California. Yet, despite these complexities, there are some patterns that help explain California's current social and political landscape. First, the release of the 2000 Census indicates that California became the third majority-minority state—joining Hawaii and New Mexico.[1] These demographic changes were largely the result of an increase in Latino and Asian immigration, as well as births to minority and immigrant women. The presence of Latinos and Asians is likely to continue to increase in the decades to come. The diversification of the state and the electorate is even more apparent in the 2010 Census, but for the purpose of this case study, I focus on the changes from 1990 to 2000. Latinos made up three-fourths of California's 4.1 million population growth from 1990 to 2000 and represented one in three Californians, up from one in four in 1990.[2] The white population constituted 57 percent of the total population in 1990. By the year 2000, the percentage of whites dropped to 46.7. During this same period, the Latino share of the population increased from 25.8 percent in 1990 to 32.4 percent in 2000.[3] The younger age distribution among Latinos, immigration trends, and birth rates suggest that Latinos will be the largest segment of the entire population in the near future. It appears that population in California already looks like what the U.S. population is projected to become.

Clearly, California's demographic composition changed significantly in the ten-year period between 1990 and 2000. With such changes in the state's social landscape, one might assume that the political landscape also witnessed significant changes. Will the population changes translate to changes in the composition and behavior of the electorate? One of the consequences of an increasingly older white population and younger nonwhite population is that despite their declining presence in the population, whites would continue to be overrepresented among the state's electorate due to the higher voting rates among older eligible voters. The combined effects of population change and voter propensity by age ensured that the "California voter" also changed, albeit at a slower rate than the population. In 1992, percentages of whites, Latinos, African Americans, and Asians in the electorate were at 82, 7, 6, and 3, respectively. By the year 2000 these percentages had changed to 71, 14, 7, and 6 for the above groups, respectively. While the "demography is destiny" scenario discussed in chapter 1 is more likely to take place in California before other states, naturalization patterns and age distribution are factors that are sure to play a role.

Beyond demography, California serves as an excellent case study because the contentious national politics related to race and immigration since 2006 have many similarities to what took place in California between 1994 and 1998. Long before HR 4437 in the U.S. Congress in 2005 or Arizona's SB 1070 in 2010, there was a political context that served as a mobilizing opportunity for California's Latino population and electorate. The factors creating this context in 1994 were the passage of Proposition 187, a ballot initiative banning undocumented immigrants from most social services; the reelection of Governor Pete Wilson; and a shift in party control in the state assembly. Pundits and scholars attribute much of this change to the mobilizing effects of the political context on new Latino voters, who are said to be younger and to have less education and income than other racial/ethnic groups or previous waves of Latino voters. In this chapter, I seek to demonstrate empirically when and how context structures the nature of the political behavior of the Latino electorate in California.[4]

I assess the continued relevance of models of participation that focus on individual-level characteristics, while ignoring the effects of political context. One way to conceptualize the intersection of the individual and political context is by testing for the possibility of unique generational/cohort effects. If participation among a cohort is temporal in nature, it limits the discussion to one election cycle. However, if it is not temporal, these findings can highlight the possibility that political context can serve as a catalyst for changes in the electorate and the turnout among a cohort of voters. Utilizing the 1997 Tomás Rivera Policy Institute postelection survey, this chapter considers how the effects of this context become evident by analyzing the patterns of mobilization and participation among Latinos in California.[5] In particular, I compare naturalized and native-born Latinos across several elections in the 1990s, examining the extent to which electoral participation can be explained by political context, nativity, and registration cohort. I assess the hypotheses that there are significant differences in the rate of electoral participation between native and naturalized Latinos in California, as well as between those who first entered the electorate in a politically charged environment and those who did not.

In this chapter, I discuss the effects of social and political context on the political behavior of Latinos, the fastest-growing segments of the California electorate. I begin by drawing on the insights of the participation literature and the "cohort" literature to explain voter-turnout fluctuations among naturalized and native-born Latinos in registration cohorts. I assess the hypothesis that California's politicized climate in the 1990s had a mobilizing effect on Latino political participation. A nuanced account of Latino electoral participation requires an understanding of the impact of nativity on turnout given the significant presence of naturalized voters. Because there may be significant differences in the rates of electoral participation between native-born and naturalized Latinos in California, I turn to the Latino politics and immigrant literature. There is disagreement in the literature, both theoretical and empirical, about the effects of nativity on voting. Early works argue that the socialization into electoral politics is slower among immigrants because they are not as familiar with the political system as are the native-born citizens; these works therefore find that naturalized voters are less prone to participate. Conversely, recent analysis of the effects of nativity suggest that Latino immigrants, after naturalization and registration, are more likely to vote because they have to undergo a two-stage process of political socialization in order to gain access to the ballot box and are therefore more appreciative of the importance of voting. I consider the impact of nativity, in combination with socioeconomic status (SES), and simultaneously incorporate the possibility that political context can impact Latino participation rates.

Using validated survey data, I find that Latinos who first registered to vote during the height of the politicized context, between 1994 and 1996, had higher rates of turnout in 1996 and exhibit greater propensity to participate in subsequent elections. However, among those in this registration cohort, naturalized Latinos are most likely to continue voting. Two important findings may be predictive of what will happen nationally. First, context matters more than previous scholars have recognized. In the cases that I consider, context is determinative of political behavior in ways that elude individual-level explanations. Second, there are differential effects of context on subgroups of Latino voters. Latinos subgroups are not monolithic, so we should not expect uniform effects of context on them.

The remainder of the chapter is divided into five sections. In the first section, I discuss the political context during the 1990s and its relation to the California electorate. I then review the existing models of participation, including the cohort and life-cycle literatures, and consider their relevance to the study of Latino participation. In the third section, I discuss the changing California electorate and the "Latino participation puzzle," as well as present a series of testable hypotheses. I argue that the "changing California voter" was shaped by demographic changes and the political context of the 1990s, which led to the mobilization of a certain segment of the Latino population. The fourth section describes the data and presents the results, and the final section concludes with implications from the analysis.

Tyranny of the Majority? Statewide Ballot Propositions and California's Electorate

Early in 1994, the stage had been set for Proposition 187 in the preceding legislative session by the efforts of Republican assemblyman Richard Mountjoy, who had sponsored ten mostly unsuccessful immigration bills in the state legislature. Unable to get restrictive immigration bills past the Democratically controlled state House or senate, he was the self-proclaimed spokesman for a loose network of newly formed local grassroots organizations that tapped into fear and discontent among the state's white voters. Although the authors of the ballot initiative were not Republican Party officials or legislators, the primary list of endorsements, spokespersons, and campaign donors included then governor Pete Wilson, Republican assemblyman Richard Mountjoy, and the California Republican Party. The GOP helped bankroll the pro–187 campaign, contributing well over half of the $484,188 raised,[6] and Wilson ran a series of tough pro–187 TV ads (Morain 1994). It is likely that the levels of support for Proposition 187 would not have reached their actual levels if the California GOP or Pete Wilson had not supported the initiative. "Wilson's endorsement lent Proposition 187 the legitimation it needed, especially because of its prior association with fringe grass-roots organizations[,]and provided the resources necessary to mobilize the voters' fears and resentment with him and not against him" (Smith and Tarallo 1995:665).

Despite clear signs of the changing state demographics, especially the increased presence of Latinos, or perhaps because of these changes, Governor Pete Wilson and many GOP assembly candidates strongly supported pro-187 efforts and played on the state's economic and social fears to promote their reelection campaigns. Thus, the GOP and "Wilson gambled on California Latinos' lack of political integration, low voter turnout and hence inability to stem the tide of Proposition 187. And it worked" (Smith and Tarallo 1995:669). This resulted in contentious politics that would transform the political landscape. Not only was Wilson's reelection campaign successful, but Republicans became the majority party in the state assembly for the first time in more than twenty years and subsequently used direct democracy for other race-targeted efforts (for example, anti–affirmative action and anti–bilingual education).[7]

An overview of the electoral influence of the state's racial and ethnic groups from 1990 to 2000 highlights the significance of the 1994 general election. Despite strong opposition to Proposition 187 from mainstream religious, labor, and community groups and negative recommendations by every major newspaper in the state, Wilson's use of Proposition 187 as the cornerstone of his campaign led to the largest bloc vote by white voters for any candidate during this ten-year period. Moreover, enough white voters supported Wilson and Proposition 187 to overwhelm the combined white and racial/ethnic bloc of voters who voted against Proposition 187, and those who supported Democrat Kathleen Brown for governor. Scholars and pundits attribute this "bloc vote" of white voters to their perception of social, economic, and political threat caused by the many changes California experienced during this period.

California's Democratic Party incurred electoral losses as a result of the levels of white vote support for Pete Wilson and Proposition 187. The politicized climate initiated by Proposition 187 was followed by the successful passage of Proposition 209 to eliminate affirmative action in 1996 and Proposition 227 to end bilingual education in 1998. However, the consequence of these propositions was Latino reactive mobilization as evidenced by the increased rates of naturalization and voter registration among Latinos in California. This mobilizing opportunity for Latino voters subsequently was instrumental in ensuring that Democrats in the state capital would consolidate their legislative power, first by recapturing the state House of Representatives, and then the governor's office.[8]

While Latinos and other racial/ethnic minorities and the Democratic Party were adversely affected by the initiative process, the latter effects proved more damaging to the Republican Party (Bowler, Nicholson, and Segura 2006). Latinos, the primary target of Proposition 187, were largely responsible for the damage incurred by the GOP. By 1996, Democrats regained control of the state assembly. A Latina, Sally Havice-Morales, was one of four Democrats who won in districts held by Republicans in 1994. The number of Latino state assembly members increased from seven prior to 1994 to fourteen in 1996.[9] Similarly, Latinos grew in their share of the statewide electorate, increasing from 7 percent in 1992 to 14 percent in 2000. Journalistic accounts of the general election in 1994 suggest that Latinos did not mobilize effectively to defeat Proposition 187 or Pete Wilson's reelection campaign (Weintraub 1994). Although Latinos proved unable to defeat Proposition 187, their electoral mobilization began during, although was not fully realized until after, the 1994 election. These gains are notable given that 1994 was not a presidential election year.

As suggested above, changes in the political landscape do not solely reflect the demographic changes. They are also impacted by the partisan politics and a reaction to political stimuli. The suggestion, based on analysis of a white voter preference for ballot propositions, Latino electoral and legislative gains, and change in partisan control, that contentious politics targeting Latinos changed the partisan context in California is useful to a certain degree but is not sufficient. Instead, this descriptive account of election results, partisan competition, and white and Latino political behavior must be supplemented by an analysis of what caused these changes and their impact on the evolving Latino electorate.

¿Quien Vota? (Who Votes?)

Latinos, particularly in California, have been plagued with the label "the sleeping giant," implying that despite the growing number of Latinos, their electoral participation has not awakened to its numerical potential. However, these characterizations oversimplify the dynamics of the actual numerical increases, failing to account for the fact that many Latinos are not eligible for citizenship. The key to an analysis of whether Latinos are realizing their potential is to focus on Latino citizens of voting age and ask, Of those eligible, why do so many fail to register and turn out to vote? To this end, I consider literature that explains determinants of turnout in general, as well as Latino-specific determinants.[10]

Among the various models that have been developed to account for differences in participation, socioeconomic status (that is, education and income) is widely cited as the best predictor of turnout regardless of race or ethnicity (Verba and Nie 1972; Wolfinger and Rosenstone 1980; Rosenstone and Hansen 1993; Verba, Schlozman, and Brady 1995). Given the lower socioeconomic status of Latinos,[11] it is no surprise that Latinos have lower rates of participation compared to most other racial and ethnic groups. Although complicated by the lack of adequate national data on Latinos,[12] low turnout among Latinos, compared to other groups, has been explained by demographic characteristics (Wolfinger and Rosenstone 1980; Lien 1994; DeSipio 1996). In particular, education has been significantly associated with lower participation among Latinos (Leighley and Vedlitz 1999). Although the SES model explains why the turnout gap between Latinos and whites is eliminated once standard demographic variables are held constant, it does not shed light on the differences among subgroups of Latinos.[13]

Consideration of differences in participation among Latinos has resulted in a "mixed bag" of approaches and explanations. For example, the explanation of why participation among naturalized Latinos is lower than that of U.S.-born Latinos has been largely based on comparing the experience of Latinos to that of previous waves of immigrant groups. According to the traditional literature on immigrants' political mobilization, political machines and partisan organizations served as mediating institutions between naturalization and the political system (Banfield and Wilson 1963; Glazer and Moynihan 1963; Dahl 1961; Allen 1993). More recently Erie (1988), Jones-Correa (1998), Wong (2005), and Abrajano and Alvarez (2010) assert that mobilization of newer immigrant cohorts is not happening, possibly because these groups could threaten existing power structures.

Rather than emphasizing the lack of external mobilization of Latinos, others have expanded on the SES model to account for differences between naturalized and native-born Latinos. For example, DeSipio found differences among Latinos in the electoral participation, based on national origin, during the 1988 election,[14] and that the "addition of naturalization status to the model for voting . . . indicates that naturalization has a negative impact" (DeSipio 1996:157). Similarly, Tam Cho (1999) suggests that, controlling for socioeconomic status, turnout among the native-born is higher than that of naturalized Latinos in California because the socialization process into the political system is slower and longer for immigrants than for the native-born. However, it would be problematic to use this characterization of Latinos today given that Tam Cho used survey data from 1984 and DeSipio used the Latino National Political Survey, which was conducted between 1989 and 1990. Both data sets were collected well before the surge in naturalization, registration, and electoral participation among Latinos beginning in the 1990s.

Using data from the November 1996 Current Population Survey (CPS), Bass and Casper (1999) found that native-born citizens have higher rates of participation than naturalized citizens and that, among immigrants, the length of residence in the United States increases the likelihood of voting. However, they caution against ignoring the effects of country of origin, as there was variation in voting rates among naturalized citizens depending on country of birth. One exception to the generalization that the native-born vote at higher rates was among naturalized Latino citizens, who reported voting at a higher rate than their native-born counterparts. Emphasizing their multivariate model, they conclude that "Hispanic naturalized citizens continue to be more likely to vote than native-born Hispanics even when other factors in the model are controlled for" (Bass and Casper 1999:13).

Highton and Burris (2002) draw on the strengths of earlier models to explain differences in turnout between Latinos and non-Latinos, as well as differences among Latinos. Using CPS data from 1976 to 1996, they test for inter- and intragroup differences, standard socioeconomic factors, and length of residence to get a more complete perspective on Latino turnout. They find that naturalized Latinos reported turnout increases with length of time living in the United States.[15] Highton and Burris's persuasive hypotheses of the relevance of length of time and group origin does not account for why trends in California have been markedly different. The strength of their argument could be further diminished if we consider that while California has seen an increase in Latino naturalization, registration, and turnout, the rates for Texas Latinos were stagnant or declining in the 1990s. Given these contrasting trends and the fact that over half of the Latino population (and the majority of the United States' Mexican-origin population) live in these two states, it is possible that their model of voter turnout does not capture state-specific effects. Similarly, using in-depth interviews with Mexican-origin Latinos in Los Angeles and New York, Wong (2005) finds that as immigrants spend more time in the United States, both their rates of electoral and nonelectoral participation increase. Wong's qualitative case study of Latinos in New York and Los Angeles complement the patterns suggested by Highton and Burris (2002), although we cannot generalize to the overall Latino population because of the inclusion of noncitizens in the analysis and the geographic-specific patterns.

As stated earlier, among the most consistent predictors of voting are income, education, and age. The relationship between the aging process and participation captures the effects of distinct life stages such as early youth, adolescence, and adulthood, as well as parenthood and marriage (Jennings 1979; Beck and Jennings 1982; Stoker and Jennings 1995). One of the critiques of this life-cycle approach and its socialization effects on participation is that it may neglect the possibility of cohort politics and political generations whereby historical and social conditions impact the formation of civic orientation. According to Braungart and Braungart (1986), political "cohorts" and "generations" are distinct in that cohorts refer to persons of the same age group maturing during the same time period, while a generation has a distinct age-group consciousness. Moreover, "a cohort becomes transformed into a political generation when many of its members become aware that they are bound together by a shared age-group consciousness and mobilize as an active force for political change" (217). One example of this age-group consciousness is that of the 1960s "protest generation." Jennings (1987) finds that over a span of several years, the protest generation remains distinctive, especially in their attitudes. [16]

Closely related to generational effects, period (historical) effects refer to specific historical events that shape ideology and behavior across the sociopolitical continuum. One example of such period effects is discussed by Beck and Jennings (1979). According to the authors, "the late 1960s and early 1970s were a deviant period where participation in American politics was concerned. During this time, the young were more active politically than their elders, substantially increasing their participation from previous years, and Americans on the ideological left participated more than those at other positions along the ideological continuum" (737). Similarly, Miller (1992) tests for period effects among pre- and post–New Deal voters and finds distinct political behavior over time.

Studies on Latino participation have largely neglected the concepts of generations, cohort, and period effects. Pantoja, Ramírez, and Segura (2001) develop a model of Latino electoral participation that captures fluctuations in Latino voter turnout using the naturalization cohort and political periods as analytical tools to explain unique patterns participation of Latinos. They are the first to explore the possibility that year of naturalization, in conjunction with the political environment, affected voter turnout.

Their comparison of Latinos in California, Texas, and Florida finds that California Latinos who naturalized between 1992 and 1996[17] have substantially higher rates of validated voter turnout in the 1996 general presidential election than native-born Latinos, those who naturalized in an earlier period in California, or those who naturalized at any point in Texas and Florida. They attribute this mobilization and increased turnout to the high-profile ballot initiatives and polarizing rhetoric in California.

Beyond issues of nativity, does it matter when people first enter the electorate? In general, the year of entry into the electorate has not been considered to be as important as other factors. Among the few to consider registration cohort as relevant, Nie, Verba, and Petrocik (1976) examine the impact of voter generation, and its effects on partisan realignment and turnout. They found that "the New Deal realignment represented a gradual process of consolidation of Democratic support based on the mobilization of new voters rather than on permanent conversion of Republicans" (Nie, Verba, and Petrocik, 1976:85). Higher turnout among Democrats between 1932 and 1944 can be largely explained by the high turnout among newly mobilized groups of young, substantially female, urban, working-class, and foreign-born.[18]

Interestingly, despite the relevance of when a particular set of voters first entered the electorate to turnout patterns and its effects on party realignment, previous research on minority voter turnout has largely overlooked registration cohort effects. More recently, Barreto and Woods (2005) test for turnout rates of Latinos who first registered to vote between 1994 and 1998 in Los Angeles County. Using registrar of voter data, they find that Latinos who first entered the electorate during this politicized climate have higher turnout than non-Latinos entering the electorate during the same period. The partisan implications among these newly mobilized Latinos who first registered between 1994 and 1998 in Los Angeles County make the advantage gained by Democrats during the New Deal realignment pale in comparison. According to Barreto and Woods (2005), of those Latinos in this registration cohort who voted in 1998, 75 percent are registered Democrats, whereas only 7 percent were registered Republicans.[19]

No research has been done to simultaneously look at the effects of nativity and registration cohort on voter turnout primarily because these characteristics were not as salient in earlier periods. Additionally, information on these factors is hard to collect and measure. Given the above insights into determinants of turnout, we must revise the way in which we examine political participation, especially among Latinos in California. This chapter examines the extent to which electoral participation across several years can be explained by political context, nativity, and registration cohort.

The Latino Participation Puzzle

Several pundits and scholars have suggested that the politicized climate, as a result of the passage of three consecutive ballot initiatives (Propositions 187 in 1994, 209 in 1996, and 227 in 1998)[20] had immediate and potentially lasting effects on the nature of California's electorate and the pool of Latino eligible voters. [21] In 1992, Latinos comprised 7 percent of the electorate in California, 12 percent in 1996, and 14 percent in 2000 (Los Angeles Times Exit Poll 1992; CNN Exit Polls 1996 and 2000).[22] The Field Institute estimates that, as of May 2000, Latinos constitute 1 million of the net increase of 1.1 million new registered voters in California during the 1990s (Field Institute 2000:1).

The change in the composition of the electorate is impacted by the influx of new voters, but could also be impacted by turnout rates. Before examining current patterns of participation among Latinos in California, we must first examine citizenship as the greatest obstacle to Latino electoral participation (Calvo and Rosenstone 1989; DeSipio 1996; Uhlaner 1996). Naturalization rates among all immigrants declined from the 1970s to the early 1990s (Johnson et al. 1999). The increase of foreign-born,[23] among all Latinos, inherently exacerbates the citizenship hurdle for voting eligibility among Latinos. Although immigration accounts for the number of foreign-born, low naturalization rates among legal residents depress the size of the Latino electorate.[24] As I demonstrated in chapter 3, Latino naturalization rates increased significantly in the mid–1990s. A study of naturalization by the Public Policy Institute of California (PPIC) indicates that California has had among the lowest rates of naturalization, but that California experienced faster growth than national rates. Simultaneously, according to the study, "the propensity to naturalize increased even more dramatically for particular groups of immigrants: better educated immigrants, Latino immigrants, and immigrants in California" (Johnson et al. 1999:60–61).

In and of itself, increased naturalization rates do not inherently provide evidence that that the politicized climate led to higher registration and turnout rates among Latinos. However, the Public Policy Institute of California data suggest that compared to other Californians, Latinos are younger and have less education and lower incomes—all characteristics that have historically been associated with low levels of electoral participation (Johnson et al. 1999). Moreover, despite the fact that recent Latino registrants have more of these characteristics than Latinos who registered prior to 1994 (Field Institute 2000:1), Latino political participation is on the rise. The combination of an increasing number of Latinos registered to vote, higher turnout, and the corresponding socioeconomic characteristics mentioned above suggests that the Latino electorate is increasingly complex. Clearly, a theory of Latino turnout must account for this twist in the "participation puzzle."[25] I suggest that the "Latino participation puzzle" in California came about during the 1990s, as evidenced by the steady increased turnout, while the levels of Latino voters' socioeconomic indicators (for example, age, education, income) have decreased.

The inability of socioeconomic variables to explain these patterns of participation among Latinos suggests that something else affected turnout. Context and other social and political considerations allow for a nuanced approach to explain this transition from high levels of inactivity in electoral politics to a defining role in California's governance. The successive increase of population, registration, and participation among many Latinos, who are transforming the pool of Latino eligible voters, can be traced to their politically motivated response to three consecutive election cycles in California (1994–98) with ballot initiatives that were largely perceived as an attack on Latinos and in particular Latino immigrants. Moreover, among naturalized Latinos, the politically charged environment was the driving force behind the significant rise among Latinos to go beyond naturalization and become part of the electorate.

Hypothesis 1: Socioeconomic status indicators (specifically age and education) will predict participation, although both will do so at lesser degrees than the participation literature suggests.

Hypothesis 2: Latinos who first registered to vote between 1994 and 1996 will have higher rates of turnout in the 1996 general election, even after controlling for socioeconomic status.

Hypothesis 3: Among those in the 1994–96 registration cohort, naturalized Latinos will have the highest rates of turnout in the 1996 general election, after controlling for SES.

Hypothesis 4: After controlling for SES, patterns of participation in elections after 1996 will be similar to the expected findings in hypotheses two and three.

I argue that subsequent levels of political participation are endogenous to those characteristics that drove Latinos to register to vote in a period of perceived threat or animosity.[26] While I expect to find that the political context in California mobilized Latinos in this registration cohort to vote at higher levels than previous registration cohorts, I anticipate that naturalized Latinos in this registration cohort are even more politically motivated because they underwent a two-step process of naturalization and registration. The decision to register to vote in response to a politically charged environment, despite the added hurdle of naturalization, is a testament to their commitment to engage in electoral participation and gives us strong signals about fluctuations of voter turnout among and between Latinos. For example, I do not expect substantive differences between native-born Latinos and naturalized Latinos who entered the electorate before the political context existed. However, I expect naturalized Latinos in this registration cohort to be more motivated than either native-born or naturalized Latinos in previous registration cohorts and to therefore vote and vote often.

The context that led to the New Deal realignment had a generational effect on partisan identification and political participation rates of specific cohorts of voters. Similarly, I expect the political context of feeling politically targeted by state referendums to have a unique and lasting impact on long-term voter turnout rates of newcomers to the electoral process during this climate, especially those Latinos who experienced the two-step process of naturalization and registration.

Latino Cohorts

The Tomás Rivera Policy Institute conducted a three-state study of the Latino electorate in California, Texas, and Florida in 1997. An overall sample size of 1,324 respondents was drawn based on Latino-surname citizens. The California share of the sample was 452, or 34.1 percent of the entire sample. To facilitate a multivariate analysis of attributes and behavior of Latino voters, the sample included an intentional oversample of Latinos who self-reported being registered to vote. Among the forty-seven demographic and political questions in the survey, respondents were asked if they were native-born or naturalized citizens, the year they naturalized, whether they were registered to vote, and if they voted in the 1996 general election.[27] The self-reported registration and turnout were then subject to external validation, using voter rolls and records, to determine whether these retrospective reports of registration and voting were accurate. While this gave an accurate snapshot perspective of Latino voting behavior, very little could be said about patterns of participation before or after the election. Subsequently, voter rolls and records were used to determine whether respondents were registered and voted during the period of 1992 through 2000.[28] This analysis, therefore, is afforded the enviable opportunity to select validated voter turnout as the dependent variable, in any primary or general election included in the observed years.[29] The dependent variable in the analysis presented, regardless of year selected, is coded (1) for an actual vote, and (0) for a nonvote.[30]

A respondent's source of citizenship was coded as (1) if naturalized, and (0) if they were native-born. In addition, naturalization year was grouped together to test for naturalization cohort effects. The demographics of the sample are demonstrated in table 3. Native-born Latinos constituted 48 percent of the sample, and naturalized Latinos comprised 52 percent. Among the naturalized, 21.7 percent gained citizenship status in 1985 or earlier, 14 percent between 1986 and 1991, and 44.7 percent during the five-year period 1992–96.[31] This supports the notion that there was a surge in naturalization in the early to mid–1990s, especially in 1996, but does not tell us if this increase has translated into increased propensity to register to vote.

If the naturalization did lead to an expansion of the pool of registered voters, and a pattern of when Latinos first registered to vote emerges, then mobilization can be said to have occurred. In fact, a pattern emerges among naturalized and native-born Latinos when they entered the electorate (registration cohort or political baptism). Latinos, irrespective of nativity, registered to vote in greater numbers in 1996. Interestingly, those who naturalized before 1985 behave very similarly to native-born Latinos, and those who naturalized between 1986 and 1991 behave more like those who naturalized between 1992 and 1996. However, these "newly naturalized" Latinos appear to have been more mobilized in 1996, as 63 percent registered that year. This pattern of increased registration exhibited among all groups, but particularly the newly naturalized, suggests that something motivated them to take the first step in the electoral process.

Still, joining the electorate in large numbers does not guarantee greater turnout. Do patterns of registration translate into trends in voter turnout? It appears then, that in addition to naturalization cohort, we must take into account the registration cohort to determine whether when Latinos first registered to vote impacted their voter turnout, even when controlling for individual-level characteristics. Drawing upon the literature on individual-level characteristics, I estimate the effects of eleven independent variables on voter turnout. The key independent variables to test for nativity and registration cohort effects are Naturalized and 1st Registered 1994–96 and are operationalized as dummy variables that identify those Latinos who are naturalized citizens and those who first registered to vote between 1994 and 1996.[32] Given the previous conflicting accounts of the effects of naturalization on voter turnout, I included an interaction variable, Naturalized*1st Registered 1994–96, so as to isolate the behavior of naturalized Latinos who first registered during the politicized climate between 1994 and 1996. I expect the coefficients on 1st Registered 1994–96 and Naturalized*1st Registered 1994–96 to be positive and significant while that of Naturalized is negative, because naturalized Latinos in other registration cohorts are less likely to be motivated to participate by the hostile political climate.[33]

The results of the multivariate analysis, Model 1, support the expectation of hypothesis 1 about the relevance of the individual-level characteristics and SES model. Older Latinos and those with more education are more likely to have voted in the 1996 general election. Both of these variables are significant predictors of turnout. In addition, strength of partisanship is positively associated with the likelihood of voting. However, the size of the coefficient of the three significant variables, above, is not as large as that of the key variables testing for effects of a political context.

There is also compelling support for hypothesis 2, that those who first registered during this politicized environment (1st Registered 1994–96) are more likely to have turned out to vote in the 1996 general election than those who were already in the electorate prior to this period. Particularly important is the performance of the interaction variable, Naturalized*1st Registered 1994–96, that accounts for naturalized Latinos who are in this registration cohort. As predicted by hypothesis 3, this reaffirms the salience of political context as a key determinant of turnout among naturalized Latino citizens who first registered during the politicized climate.[34]

Considering each model individually is important but is even more important to identify patterns across election cycles. In general, the political implication of a mobilized Latino registration cohort is that the effects of negative rhetoric continue into other elections. Six years after Proposition 187 was passed,[35] Latinos in that registration cohort, especially naturalized Latinos, continue to show a greater propensity to vote than other Latinos. This finding supports the predictions of hypothesis 4. Other interesting

Table 3 Logistic regression results for predicting vote

Variables	Model 1 1996 General	Model 2 1998 Primary	Model 3 1998 General	Model 4 2000 Primary	Model 5 2000 General	Model 6 "Super-voters" (turnout ≥ 75%)
Naturalized	−.902***	−.530**	−1.389***	−.413*	−0.35	−0.088
	(.315)	(.310)	(.326)	(.302)	(.280)	(.311)
Registered	1.495***	0.426	.485*	.680**	.441*	0.26
1994–96	(.382)	(.350)	(.342)	(.348)	(.340)	(.365)
Naturalized*1st	2.011***	1.444***	1.719***	0.328	1.058***	.938**
Reg. 1994–96	(.559)	(.475)	(.481)	(.464)	(.462)	(.478)
Strength of	.233*	0.153	−0.019	−0.048	.226*	0.088
partisanship	(.180)	(.166)	(.165)	(.162)	(.157)	(.167)
High school	.819***	.559***	.754***	.613***	.503**	.563***
graduate	(.283)	(.255)	(.257)	(.248)	(.244)	(.254)
Age	.036***	.031***	.031***	.035***	.019***	.022***
	(.009)	(.008)	(.008)	(.008)	(.008)	(.008)
Constant	−3.514***	−2.336***	−2.836***	−2.095***	−1.961***	−2.836***
	(.757)	(.662)	(.668)	(.642)	(.609)	(.684)
PPC	76.72%	69.12%	66.67%	66.42%	67.65%	68.87%
Sample size	408	408	408	408	408	408

***Significant at p≤ .01   **Significant at p≤ .05   * p≤ .10 (one-tailed tests)
Note: Other control variables were: political interest, Democrat, Mexican origin, Hispanic contact, group mobilization, and church attendance.

patterns emerge in the longitudinal perspective. First, socioeconomic characteristics have positive and significant effects across all elections. Second, literature on partisanship suggests that strong partisans are more likely to vote than weak identifiers. It appears that this is the case for Latinos in presidential elections, but not in nonpresidential elections. Although membership in organizations that called prior to the election, Group Mobilization, was not significantly related to turnout in the 1996 general election, organizational membership had a positive and significant effect in three of the next four elections. Finally, regardless of election, the percentage predicted correctly by the multivariate model ranges from 66.42 percent, in the 2000 primary election, to 76.72 percent in the 1996 general election.

Model 6, which predicts 68.87 percent of the cases correctly, brings a new perspective to the debate about the consequences of a political climate on Latino turnout. The dependent variable in this case is "super-voter," coded (1) if the proportion of elections that the respondent voted, out of

Table 4 Latino voter turnout, changes in predicted probabilities, minàmax

Variables	Model 1 1996 General	Model 2 1998 Primary	Model 3 1998 General	Model 4 2000 Primary	Model 5 2000 General	Model 6 "Super voters" (turnout ≥ 75%)
Naturalized	−.21***	−.13**	−.32***	−.09*		
First registered 1994–96	.33***		.10*	.17**	.12*	
Naturalized*1st Reg. 1994–96	.41***	.34***	.41***		.22***	.21**
Political interest		−.13*				
Strength of partisanship	.17*				.16*	
Group mobilization		.12*	.14*		.15**	.09*
High school graduate	.19***	.13***	.19***	.15***	.12***	.13***
Age	.48***	.44***	.42***	.48***	.28***	.31***

***Significant at p£ .01   **Significant at p£ .05   * p£ .10 (one-tailed tests)
Note: All predicted probabilities and confidence intervals are calculated holding all other predictors at their mean value, and based on logit estimates in Table 1 using CLARIFY software (Tomz, Wittenberg, and King 1999).

the total eligible, is greater or equal to 75 percent, and coded (0) for lower proportional turnout. This dependent variable captures the intensity of the mobilization and of other determinants of ideal levels of participation. The results indicate that only four variables meet conventional levels of statistical significance. Interestingly, the interaction variable, Naturalized*1st Registered 1994–96, has the biggest coefficient. Education and age continue to have a statistically significant effect on higher proportional levels of participation across several elections. Finally, the composite measure, Group Mobilization, of being contacted prior to the election by an organization to which the respondent belongs helps to predict high levels of turnout.

Considering the estimates in table 3, Latinos who first registered between 1994 and 1996, especially those who were naturalized, were more likely to vote. The substantive effects of the variables presented can be estimated via the change in predicted probability of voting as the independent variable moves from the minimum observed value to the maximum observed value while holding other variables at their mean. These estimates are displayed in table 4, only for the coefficients yielding significant effects. For example, it does appear that scholars of Latino participation were partly correct in suggesting that naturalized voters are less likely to vote than native-born Latinos. More interesting is the change in predicted probability as we look at those who first registered to vote in 1994–96. In all elections, except the 1998 primary, being a member of this registration cohort significantly increased the probability of voting. Finally, the interaction variable of being naturalized and in the 1994–96 registration cohort resulted in the most impressive change in predicted probability of voting.[36]

The effects of political context are noticeable by distinguishing between four cohorts: (1) Naturalized, Registered 1994–96; (2) Native-born, Registered 1994–96; (3) Native-born, not Registered 1994–96; and (4) Naturalized, not Registered 1994–96. Figure 8 examines the predicted probabilities of voting for the four cohorts across several elections, where I present the point estimates and the 95 percent confidence intervals. Three findings stand out. The mobilizing effects of political context had the greatest impact on the "Naturalized, Registered 1994–96" cohort of Latino voters, given that they have the highest predicted probability of voting in every election but the 2000 primary. This is even more significant if we consider the naturalized cohort that first registered to vote during a nonpoliticized context had the lowest predicted probability of voting.

Second, the rank order, in terms of predicted probability of turnout among the cohorts, is consistent across nearly all elections, with the "Naturalized, Not 1st Registered 1994–96" cohort having the lowest predicted probability of voting, followed by the "Native-born, Not 1st Registered 1994–96" cohort, then the "Native-born, 1st Registered 1994–96" cohort, and finally the "Naturalized, 1st Registered 1994–96" cohort.[37] Third, although the predicted probability of voting of both "1st Registered 1994–96" cohorts (native-born and naturalized) was initially much higher than the statewide turnout, the predicted probability of voting is increasingly similar to the statewide turnout with each successive election. The mobilizing effects of context appear to have reached a plateau that is closer to statewide turnout than the turnout of previous Latino voters.

In addition to the findings on different election cycles from 1996 to 2000, I include an additional measure of mobilizing effects of political context. Rather than presenting the predicted probability of voting, the dependent variable is "super-voter," or having voted in at least 75 percent of eligible elections. The predicted probability of being a "super-voter" among the "Naturalized, 1st Registered 1994–96" cohort is nearly double that of the other three cohorts of Latino voters. This composite measure of turnout more directly shows the extent of mobilization of this cohort.

Beyond SES Context, Nativity, and Registration Cohort

> These findings challenge the "conventional wisdom" about patterns of participation in America. They are best explained by recognizing that the opportunities for political action among the American citizenry are not fixed, but instead vary with changes in the political stimuli across different periods.
> —Paul Allen Beck and M. Kent Jennings, "Political Periods and Political Participation"

This chapter has made the case that, as was true for a segment of the electorate in the United States during the 1960s and 1970s, there is a segment of the California electorate whose patterns of participation challenge the "conventional wisdom." Latinos who first registered to vote during California's politicized climate in the mid–1990s, especially those who are naturalized, reacted to this political stimulus through their choices at the voting booth. Furthermore, these changes, as a result of reactive mobilization, proved to last beyond the immediate elections that were characterized by a politicized climate, but the effects eventually lessened among native-born Latinos.

This chapter introduces a new way to look at cohorts/generations of voters. Previously, scholars have relied on age as the noteworthy distinction between voters. This assumes that either all persons register to vote when they reach the age of eighteen or that, regardless of when a person first registered to vote, they underwent the same relative political socialization as others of the same age cohort. By focusing on when citizens first register to vote, as opposed to when they became eligible to vote, this chapter proposes a new way of looking at political cohorts/generations. Furthermore, unlike the cohort/generation literature that emphasizes the changing attitudes and behavior of the existing pool of voters, I argue that the California electorate was transformed during the 1990s by the influx of new Latino voters with distinctive demographic characteristics and motivations for voting, resulting in distinct patterns of participation.

The continued growth of the naturalized Latinos, as a percentage of the population and a percentage of the pool of Latino eligible voters, makes this population essential for Latino political incorporation.[38] Furthermore, how the political system responds to this growth and how Latinos react to perceived acceptance or rejection is sure to impact levels of Latino political incorporation. The findings reported here contribute to scholarship on the participation dimension of incorporation. The empirical results paint a picture where nativity, political context, and other individual-level charac-

Fig. 8   Probability of voting predicted by nativity and registration cohort

1996 general

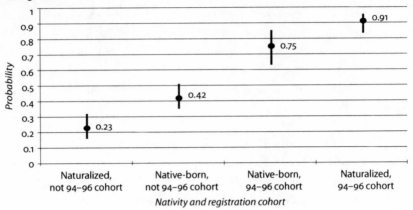

1998 primary

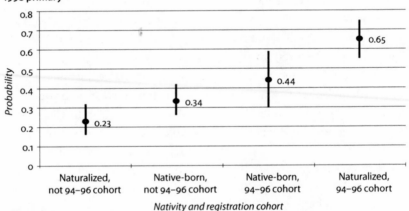

1998 general

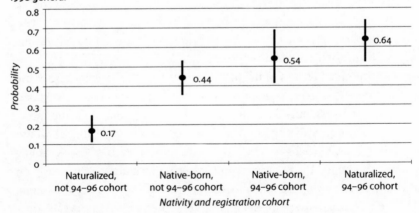

Note: Predicted probabilities and 95 percent confidence intervals are calculated holding all other predictors at their mean value, and based on logit estimates in table 1 using CLARIFY software (Tomz, Wittenberg, and King 1999).

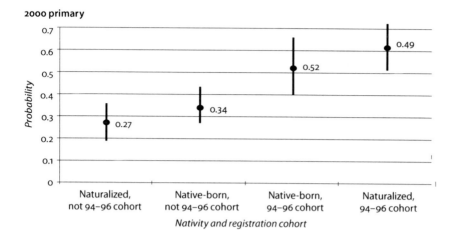

2000 primary

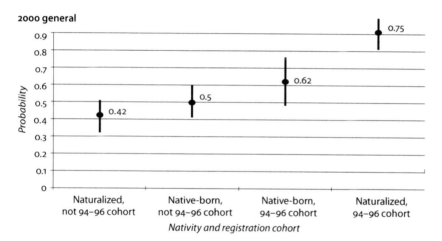

2000 general

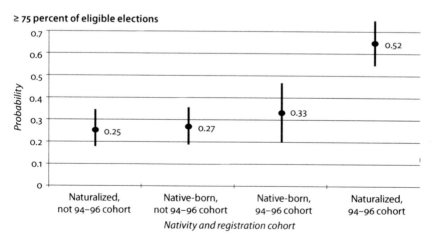

≥ 75 percent of eligible elections

teristics (for example, partisan strength, SES, organizational involvement) interact to affect voter turnout.

Research on Latino turnout emphasizes the role of socioeconomic characteristics on turnout. Will education and age continue to be significant determinants of Latino voter participation if an increasing segment of the potential pool of Latino voters is much younger and less educated than other racial/ethnic groups? In California, as of the year 2010, SES indicators continue to be relevant. Although they may not have the greatest effects on turnout, they are the most consistent predictors of turnout. They are also important characteristics associated with very high ($\geq$ 75 percent) turnout among Latinos. In addition, the positive effects of organizational affiliation and the noneffects of partisan affiliation on turnout suggest that either Latinos react more favorably to mobilization by nonpartisan organizations, or political parties have not yet made the necessary investment in Latino voter mobilization efforts. Given the increased percentage of labor union participation among Latinos,[39] and the increased role of labor in California elections and politics, the implications could be far-reaching.

While previous research on the patterns of participation of native-born and naturalized Latinos suggests that there are differences in participation, it does fully delineate these differences. The often-neglected variables that may be determinative of turnout among naturalized Latinos include national-origin differences, length of residence in the United States, and when Latinos first enter the electorate. This chapter makes the case that turnout in the 1990s in California can be largely explained by the latter variable. By utilizing unique measures of registration cohort, nativity, and their interaction, this chapter addresses the intricacies related to gauging the effects of a perceived and real anti-Latino political context on naturalized and native-born Latinos. More importantly, this innovative approach suggests that political context can have long-term mobilizing implications for Latinos entering the electorate in response to such a context, and that the mobilization is greater and longer-lasting among the naturalized within this cohort. This finding may be particularly relevant to future contexts of anti-Latino sentiment in other states, especially those that are going through rapid demographic transformation due to the influx of Latino immigrants.

Furthermore, although the surge in the number of naturalized Latinos in California may have been affected by (1) the increased pool of Latinos eligible for citizenship because of IRCA; (2) the INS Green Card replacement program; and (3) welfare reform and Propositions 187, 209, and 227, we must be skeptical of how and when these are used to explain the changing citizen population. In fact, the above explanations have been used interchangeably not only to explain the increased pool of naturalized Latinos but also the increased number of Latinos registered to vote and of those actually turning out to vote. While this assumes that the above factors impacted all Latinos in a similar way by mobilizing them to naturalize, register, and vote, consistent with the 2000 PPIC report (Johnson et al. 1999) and Pantoja, Ramírez, and Segura's (2001) findings, this chapter suggests that "the changing California voter" is largely the result of the influx of naturalized Latinos entering the electorate between 1994 and 1996 and voting at greater rates than other cohorts of Latino voters.

While the first and second factors may have impacted Latinos in California in their decision to become naturalized citizens, the third factor resulted in a mobilized segment of naturalized Latinos. Specifically, the politicized climate in California had a differential impact on naturalized Latinos (some were newly naturalized while others had naturalized several years before the politicized climate) who first registered in this political climate as opposed to those who are U.S. native-born. With the understanding that we must not assume uniform effects of the above-mentioned factors on all Latinos, we can begin to explore questions of long-term mobilization effects among and between Latino subgroups. By understanding that Latinos are not a homogeneous group, and that registration cohort and nativity do matter, we can specifically address the potential differences between Latinos and their short-term and long-term political participation.

5

VOICE OF
THE PEOPLE

The Evolution and Effectiveness
of Latino Voter Mobilization

The transformation of the electorate is among the most significant changes that have accompanied the demographic change that has occurred in the United States during the last twenty years. Many questions remain as to what role Latinos have played in this transformation, and the consequences of this change. As the preceding chapters have argued, demographic change alone does not always yield immediate and discernible consequences for American politics. It is necessary to first identify how and when Latinos have become activated to take part in the civic and political life of the United States. Politically, however, it is not their nonelectoral civic engagement that will capture the attention of the political elite, but rather the extent to which naturalized Latinos and their native-born children participate in elections. In 1980, there were 2.5 million Latino voters in the United States. It is estimated that by the year 2012, this figure will have grown nearly five-fold to more than 12 million voters (NALEO Educational Fund 2012).

The growth in the electorate is important, but the relevance of Latinos for American politics cannot be fully understood simply by focusing on the potential aggregate number of Latino voters in presidential elections. How, when, and where there has been growth is also important. Chapters 3 and 4 illustrate that an important and substantial segment of the citizenship-eligible Latino immigrant population has been mobilized by both political context (reactive mobilization) and more intense Latino organizational efforts (proactive mobilization) to encourage Latinos to pursue U.S. citizenship than ever before. These same mobilizing opportunities have altered the rate at which the activated native-born and naturalized immigrants turned out to vote in California during the 1990s. But, as I have argued, the contemporary and future significance of the Latino electorate must be understood within particular electoral contexts. The vast majority of Latinos do not live in the competitive or swing states in presidential elections. Instead, more than half of the Latino population is concentrated in California, Texas, and New York, three populous states that very reliably vote for one party or another. Conventional wisdom posits that mobilization increases participation, but also that lower socioeconomic status (SES) and noncompetitive election contexts depress turnout and likely impact campaign strategies. This conventional wisdom, however, would not have predicted that the antagonistic political context in the mid-1990s and the middle of the first decade of the twenty-first century would result in a mobilizing opportunity that brought these newly activated Latinos from the streets to the ballot box. Nor would it have predicted the emerging role of Latino organizations in this transformation.

The combination of Latino demographic characteristics and their concentration in these noncompetitive states helps explain why both Democratic and Republican presidential campaigns have largely focused on symbolic outreach rather than particularized mobilization.[1] This lack of direct mobilization of Latinos by political parties, therefore, is consistent with theoretical expectations that political elites focus their attention on likely and influential voters (Rosenstone and Hansen 1993). Despite the relative neglect of the Latino electorate by political parties, its growth necessitates a clearer understanding of existing patterns of Latino electoral participation, as well as identifying the group's receptiveness to electoral mobilization efforts. This is not an easy task given the diversity of the Latino electorate, the uneven expansion of the Latino electorate across states, and the variation in voter turnout across electoral contexts over time.

In this chapter, I focus on three questions: (1) How has the influx of new Latino voters changed the political calculus among partisan and nonpartisan elites?; (2) Can Latino organizations seize on these opportunities to mobilize Latinos to vote, as they did when they mobilized Latinos to take to the streets in 2006 and pursue citizenship in the subsequent years?; (3) Will all demographic segments of the Latino electorate, across all state contexts, be equally responsive to their appeals? As I have illustrated in the preceding chapters, not all Latinos react in the same way to exogenous stimuli from a politically threatening environment. There are direct and indirect effects of mobilizing opportunities on participation in political protests, naturalization rates, and voter turnout. It therefore makes sense that elite mobilization may be differentially effective across segments of the Latino electorate.

The first section of this chapter examines the leading theoretical frameworks regarding the role of mobilization on participation, the segmentation of voters, and their applicability to Latino voters. The second section describes the contemporary efforts by presidential campaigns to reach out to Latino voters and the consequences of segmentation or microtargeting of voters for election-specific partisan mobilization efforts. The third section shifts the focus to the changes in nonpartisan Latino mobilization efforts. In particular, I discuss the evolution of nonpartisan elite mobilization of Latino voters from localized and broad efforts to sophisticated and coordinated efforts. I also contrast the voter segmentation among these Latino mobilization efforts geared to long-term political incorporation efforts of low-propensity Latino voters who are largely neglected by partisan campaigns. The fourth section presents the outcomes of these "get out the vote" (GOTV) efforts across multiple electoral contexts from 2000 to 2010 and offers an explanation, based on a combination of voter-specific characteristics and contextual effects, for the wide variation in the effectiveness of similar efforts. Each of these sections aims to illustrate that while political mobilization can be critical to incorporating the Latino population into the United States electorate, political campaigns and organizations should not assume that a single approach to political mobilization will be effective across the entire Latino population. Rather, attention to context and voter-specific characteristics (such as voting history or nativity) is the key to understanding whether or not a political mobilization effort will be successful. The final section of this chapter reviews how the findings emphasize this point.

Mobilization, Voter Segmentation, and Political Participation

Socioeconomic status (SES) is not the only determinant of voting, but the utility of the SES model, which focuses on individual-level characteristics, for explaining levels of participation is well-established. As important as the personal characteristics of voters is the extent to which they are asked to participate (Caldeira, Clausen, and Patterson 1990; Caldeira, Patterson, and Markko 1985; Crotty 1971; Huckfeldt and Sprague 1992; Rosenstone and Hansen 1993; Verba, Schlozman, and Brady 1995). The consensus about the importance of mobilization is complicated by the need to disentangle the effects of participation and mobilization when the same personal characteristics that explain participation also explain the likelihood of being mobilized (Leighley 2001).

Given the relevance of mobilization for participation, it is important to understand what accounts for differential rates of mobilization among subgroups. Rosenstone and Hansen (1993) argue that levels of participation are reflective of mobilization activities by elites. More specifically, they argue that efficiency and outcome-driven concerns lead political elites to be very selective in deciding which voters to mobilize. It is rational for political elites to be selective in their mobilization strategy because "they want to get the most effective number involved with the least amount of effort" (Rosenstone and Hansen 1993:30–31). Accordingly, differences in mobilization are largely determined by whether the groups or individuals fall into one or more of the four categories of citizens whom leaders are likely to target. These include (*a*) people they already know, (*b*) those centrally positioned in social networks; (*c*) influential individuals; and (*d*) those likely to respond to mobilization. Unfortunately, because Latinos have been historically marginalized and excluded from traditional circles of influence, they are often neglected because they do not fit neatly into one of these four preferred categories.

The practical politics and political-marketing literatures also shed light on how political elites a priori target segments of the electorate based on key voter-specific characteristics such as age, gender, lifecycle, previous voting history, and registered party affiliation (Baines 1999; Bowler and Farrell 1992; Butler and Ranney 1992; Lees-Marshment 2001; Mancini and Swanson 1996; Mauser 1983; Smith and Hirst 2001). According to Baines (1999), "segmentation of voters becomes an important process in political marketing because the voter market is not homogeneous and different voter groups contribute more or less to different [electoral] campaign outcomes" (404). It is also clear that the segmentation of voters by specific characteristics, or microtargeting, has evolved significantly with technological advances and greater access to consumer information that can be manipulated for campaign strategies. "Since 1990 the development of segmentation has seen a shift in emphasis from the traditional (geographic and demographic) methods of segmentation towards an increased use of psychographic/attitudinal bases to segment political markets" (Smith and Hirst 2001:1059).

Although the concept of voter segmentation (microtargeting and even nanotargeting) can shed light on one of the components of the modern campaign, it does little to identify the link between mobilization and participation as political behavior scholars have emphasized. On the other hand, scholars of political participation largely assume that all forms of contact have similar positive effects on turnout and that mobilization efforts are equally effective among all voters. These assumptions can be problematic for several reasons. It is well documented that voter-mobilization efforts disproportionately target likely voters (Gershtenson 2003). Therefore, to the extent that there is a relation between contact and turnout, the apparent causal relation may be spurious if contact is endogenous (Green and Gerber 2004). This has normative consequences if mobilization efforts largely neglect Latino voters (Wong 2006; Ramakrishnan 2005; Ramírez 2005; Wielhouwer 2002; Shaw, de la Garza and Lee 2000; Verba, Scholzman, and Brady 1995). Also, by failing to distinguish between the effects of contact via mail, phone, and in person, the conclusions drawn about the effects of voter-mobilization efforts are incomplete at best (Green and Gerber 2001; Bennion 2005).

Studies utilizing randomized field experimental methods can, by design, address the above concerns. Specifically, field experiments tackle the uncertainty underlying the relation between mobilization and participation by manipulating whether a person is mobilized to vote, randomly assigning different modes of contact, and verifying turnout with voter rolls. This experimental tradition in political science is exemplified by early works on the impact of GOTV efforts (Gosnell 1926, 1927; Eldersveld 1956). Since 2000, there has been a renewed interest in using field experiments to distinguish the effects of the different forms of GOTV campaigns on voter turnout (Gerber and Green 2000; Green and Gerber 2004; Ramírez 2005; Wong 2005). In addition to their contribution to the understanding of the effectiveness of different voter-mobilization efforts, these studies serve to caution against broad assumptions that pervade the literature on the positive effects of all GOTV efforts. Beyond the general effects of GOTV, Green and Gerber (2001) have shown that the varying effectiveness of phone contact from one experiment to another may depend on the message being conveyed to the treatment population and/or who administers the contact. Specifically, they claim that a conversational approach of phone canvassing of young voters by young volunteers and workers in the Youth Vote 2000 coalition may have helped make the phone canvassing more successful than it was in previous field experiments. In addition, it is possible that certain modes of voter mobilization can be more effective in certain types of elections (for example, presidential versus off-year) and among those less likely to vote or be contacted (for example, youth). It is possible that the reason why recent, but not older, studies find phone canvassing to be effective in raising turnout among youth is precisely due to the experiment's targeting of a group with greater possibilities of increased turnout.

Another concern is that the failure to control for contextual and demographic factors that may affect turnout makes it hard to identify possible differential effects of mobilization on turnout. While randomized field experiments have a methodological advantage over observational studies in addressing some of these concerns, there has been little work to determine whether certain segments of the electorate are more responsive than others to mobilization. In other words, there may be greater effects among segments of the electorate with distinct demographic traits or who are uniquely impacted by particular political contexts (for example, youth, naturalized citizens, senior citizens, racial and ethnic minorities). Survey research attempts to account for this through the use of multivariate regression analysis, while field experiments utilize a two-stage least-squares approach. While these methods are useful, neither is able to directly test the relative effects of the same mobilization effort across segments of the electorate that one believes may behave differently.

The comparison of young and mature voter responsiveness to GOTV appeals by Nickerson (2006) and Bennion (2005) represent the first efforts among field experiments to seriously consider the effects of contextual and demographic factors. Both studies find that young voters may be more responsive to mobilization efforts precisely because they tend to be neglected by political elites and thus respond to the novelty of being asked to participate. However, testing this hypothesis is difficult because conducting separate models for young and older voters significantly reduces the sample size and, therefore the robustness of the findings. Bennion's analysis of GOTV efforts in a hotly contested congressional race is reduced from 2,178 voters in the combined sample to just 401 when considering the effects of mobilization only on young voters. In his meta-analysis of six randomized controlled experiments, Nickerson (2006) is forced to pool together the data from the six experiments because none of the individual experiments contained "sufficient numbers of young people to determine if they react differently to the treatment" (2006:50). Although their studies have not been replicated by others, there is value in their initial findings that responsiveness to similar mobilization requests may vary across segments of the electorate. Later in this chapter, I take up this theme by analyzing whether the effectiveness of political mobilization efforts varies across different segments of the Latino electorate.

Symbolic or Substantive? Latino Outreach in Presidential Campaigns

With the Latino electorate perceived as an untapped resource of possible votes and support, the popular media often suggests that both partisan and nonpartisan organizations must target Latino voters through specific Latino events or campaigning in Spanish. This sentiment is well-captured by the headline "Obama Spanish Language Ad Blitz Aims to Wrap up Latino Vote" (Bravender 2012). According to this news story, the Obama campaign spent more than $2 million on Spanish-language television and radio ads from April to June, and the pro-Obama super PAC "Priorities USA Action" and the Service Employees International Union have committed to spending $4 million through the summer on Spanish TV and radio ads attacking Romney in Colorado, Nevada, and Florida (Bravender 2012). Given the dramatic growth in the amount of money raised by presidential campaigns and super PACs, it makes sense that there is an overall saturation of television and radio ad markets and that this should lead to more being spent on Spanish-language media. The proportion of campaign money being spent on Spanish-language media, however, has not kept up with the growth in mainstream media ad buys despite evidence that there is an increase in the number of Latino voters who watch and listen to Spanish-language media. Irrespective of the adequacy of spending on Spanish-language political ads since 2000, presidential campaigns have made other overtures to attract the Latino electorate with targeted Latino outreach efforts such as "Juntos Con Romney," "Latinos for Obama," "Hispanics for McCain," "Unidos Con Kerry," and "Viva Bush" featuring high-profile Latino surrogates.

Increased use of Spanish-language political ads and campaign-related outreach to Latino voters should not be confused with voter-mobilization efforts. The distinction between these two strategies comes down to the emphasis given to persuading undecided voters compared to mobilizing potential supporters. When faced with this dichotomy about Latino voters, political campaigns have typically opted for the former strategy, as evident by the increased political advertising but low levels of contact by political campaigns (Leighley 2001; Wong 2006; Verba, Schlozman, and Brady 1995; de la Garza and DeSipio 1992). In 1989–90, Latinos reported being asked to participate at a lower rate (25 percent) than African Americans (40 percent) and whites (56 percent) (Verba, Schlozman, and Brady 1995).[2] According to the 2008 Collaborative Multiracial Political Study, 31 percent of Latinos reported being contacted, compared to 34 percent of black voters and 37 percent of white voters. The gap in contact by campaigns between Latinos and other racial groups had closed significantly because more Latino voters *and* fewer black and white voters report being contacted. A closer look at the 2008 data also reveals that not all Latinos throughout the United States reported being contacted at the same rates. More than half of Latino registered voters living in four battleground states—Colorado, Florida, Nevada, and New Mexico—reported being contacted during the 2008 election cycle compared to 29 percent of Latinos in uncompetitive states. Beyond electoral context, the disparity of contact between white and Latino voters can be partly explained by individual-level characteristics. Latinos are more likely to be young and have lower levels of education and income, characteristics that are negatively associated with partisan mobilization efforts (Gershtenson 2003; Leighley 2001; Verba, Schlozman, and Brady 1995; Rosenstone and Hansen 1993).

An understanding of uneven rates of partisan mobilization not only gives us a glimpse into the logic and nature of partisan campaign strategies, but it also expands what we know about the causes and consequences of uneven turnout. Hajnal (2009) makes a compelling argument as to how and when uneven turnout at the local level leads to biased outcomes in American politics. A natural extension of this argument is that voter segmentation creates biases in mobilization. This then leads to the uneven rates of participation and subsequently "America's uneven democracy," as discussed by Hajnal (2009).

To turn nonvoters into voters, political elites will likely have to move away from the "air-war" campaigns to expend resources on mobilization and contacting activities that do not have an immediate pay-off, are cost-intensive, and require a personalized approach. Luckily, technological innovations now allow political and organizational campaigns to draw on a wealth of consumer data. It is now possible to precisely target voters using direct and personalized voter mobilization, which has been shown to be a more effective tool than more general outreach methods to motivate people to vote. Given this increased capability, there is growing sentiment that mobilization efforts on the "ground level" will gain more prominence in future political campaigns (Franke-Ruta and Meyerson 2004).[3] Many credit the increased levels of direct mobilization by the George W. Bush campaign in 2004 and the Obama campaign in 2008 with their respective wins. Evan Thomas went so far as to claim that "the Obama campaign ran the biggest, best-financed get-out-the-vote campaign in the history of American politics. It wanted to turn out minorities and the young, groups that traditionally stay away from the polls" (2010:189). Clearly, this renewed interest and the innovations in targeting voters have the potential to impact voter turnout, as well as existing theories of voter mobilization.[4]

Voice of the People and the Latino GOTV since 2000

Despite the increase in both Spanish-language political advertising and in the percentage of Latinos who report being contacted, neither has kept up with rate of growth among Latinos voting in presidential elections. Doubts remain about the relationship between Spanish-language media advertising or partisan mobilization efforts and the increase in Latino voter participation. Instead, many Latinos were mobilized to register and vote at higher levels in reaction to a contentious political context, as was the case among California Latino voters between 1996 and 2000 (Pantoja, Ramírez, and Segura 2001; Barreto, Ramírez, and Woods 2005; Barreto 2005). Given the persistent presence of low-propensity Latino voters, it is evident that a significant number of Latinos were not mobilized by exogenous political shocks. Therefore, to the extent that political campaigns spend more time and money on persuasion of likely voters, through voter segmentation/ microtargeting, Latinos who were already mobilized by the political context are likely to be targeted by candidates and campaigns while low-propensity Latino voters may continue to be neglected. Even with the growth of particularized mobilization of Latinos in 2008, it is unclear whether this was a single-election phenomenon or the start of a new era where Latinos become a sought-after bloc of voters and where outreach is more substantive than the symbolic efforts that characterized the 2000 and 2004 elections (de la Garza and DeSipio 2005; de la Garza, DeSipio, and Leal 2010).

Nonpartisan organizations have a different goal than political campaigns. Their aim is to increase the electoral presence of Latinos at the polls, and Latino nonpartisan organizations can do this either through voter-registration efforts or by ensuring that those who are registered make it to the polls on election day. Latino voter-registration efforts have been around since the 1960s and were credited with helping John F. Kennedy win the Electoral College votes in Texas. The prominence of this approach is evident in the continued efforts by Latino organizations such as the Southwest Voter Registration and Education Project (SVREP). As important as these efforts have been to encourage more Latinos to register to vote, they do not improve turnout rates of those who are already registered to vote. A long-term strategy, on the other hand, focuses on those who are not voting regularly to make their voices heard. In general, political parties and other political organizations do not pursue this long-term strategy and instead focus on the most proximate election and selectively target particular segments of the electorate to mobilize during each election cycle.

It is not surprising that political elites focus on likely voters, or that Latino voters living in areas with large minority populations are often overlooked by partisan organizations because they are perceived to be harder to mobilize. If partisan campaigns have not engaged in Latino voter mobilization, is there evidence that nonpartisan organizations have stepped in to fill this void? A Tomás Rivera Policy Institute (TRPI) report assessing Latino voter-mobilization efforts in 2000 in the United States among Latino civic organizations found that voter-registration efforts were the most common mobilization strategy (de la Garza et al. 2002). Based on in-depth interviews, this report found that very few organizations in 2000 got involved in GOTV initiatives, and among the few that did, none were able to confidently indicate how many voters they turned out. The TRPI report concluded with a particularly gloomy assessment: "Overall, there is little to be said about Latino GOTV efforts. In California, which we consider to have the most effectively organized Latino communities in the nation, those few Latino mobilization campaigns identified were episodic, under-funded and dependent on volunteers" (de la Garza et al. 2002:7). Beyond funding issues, one of the most significant hurdles in conducting large-scale GOTV drives before 2000 was the difficulty in acquiring and working with voter-registration files across jurisdictions.

The 2000 general election was not a fully lost cause, as a new model of GOTV emerged and provided a glimmer of hope for Latino mobilization efforts in subsequent elections. In particular, the National Association of Latino Elected and Appointed Officials (NALEO) attempted to break the cycle of neglect by partisan campaigns and the relative absence of Latino-led efforts. NALEO's Civic Engagement division initiated its own GOTV effort focusing on geographic concentration of unlikely Latino voters or "low-propensity" voters. With time, this would transform existing Latino voter-mobilization efforts from what I characterize as "mom-and-pop shops" to voter-mobilization efforts that would rival better-funded labor and partisan mobilization efforts. Below, I describe the expansion and evolution of this effort from 2000 to 2010.

During the 2000 general election, NALEO contracted with Leading Edge Data Services, a political data company, to identify all precincts in Los Angeles where Latinos comprised at least 70 percent of registered voters. Of the 188 precincts identified, 96 matched the second criterion, which identified less than 50 percent of these Latinos as likely voters.[5] In total, 59,460 Latino voters were targeted for treatment by phone canvassing, regardless of partisan registration, previous voting history, nativity, gender, or age. In total, there were ninety-five bilingual paid volunteers involved in the NALEO GOTV effort. The sum of the logged hours worked was 2,017.32 hours spread over the period from October 28, 2000, through November 6, 2000. Short training sessions were conducted prior to the phone canvassing. Each phone canvasser was given a "scripted message" to follow but was encouraged to conduct the call in a more conversational style. In practice, this conversational approach was the norm among phone canvassers. They were also given short descriptions of important ballot propositions with short pro and con statements to facilitate the dissemination of information and answer basic questions about these propositions. Callers were instructed to record the call outcome on preformatted paper call sheets. A sustained and well-funded voter engagement initiative grew from this initial GOTV drive in the 2000 election. In 2001, the NALEO Educational Fund launched Voces del Pueblo (Voice of the People), with one primary programmatic goal: to increase Latino voter participation.

2002 Voces del Pueblo

NALEO learned two important lessons from the effort in 2000, and one question remained. The first lesson was how to logistically implement an ambitious large-scale mobilization effort. The second lesson was that while it was possible to gauge some proximate measure of effectiveness (described in the results section), they would have to look to outside evaluations to determine more precise measures of the program's effectiveness. One important question heading into the 2002 election was whether other forms of contact beyond "live calls" could prove effective. In 2002, Voces del Pueblo was launched in six sites: Los Angeles County, Orange County (California), Harris County (Texas), Denver Metropolitan Area (Colorado), New York City, and the state of New Mexico. The selection of these sites was based primarily on NALEO's presence in these communities and access to potential funders of the mobilization effort. Voces del Pueblo was significantly more ambitious than the mobilization effort in 2000, utilizing three types of voter contact—mail, automated "robo-calls," and live calls—and incorporating field experiment procedures and analysis. The greatly expanded voter-mobilization effort targeted 465,134 registered Latino voters across five states and represents the largest such experiment of Latinos to date.

It is important to note that NALEO not only sought to understand whether they could effectively get out the vote, but months before the GOTV effort, a paid consultant conducted focus groups in each site to identify the most important issues, as well as helping to refine and customize the message, images, and even colors of the mail pieces that would be mailed in the final weeks of the campaign. In addition to the direct-mail component of the GOTV effort, automated robo-calls featuring national or local celebrities were incorporated because automated dialers can deliver thousands of calls, thereby increasing the capacity to reach more Latinos quickly. Finally, because of greater infrastructure and resources in California, Orange County and Los Angeles County were the only sites selected to receive "live calls." This part of the GOTV effort was staffed by fifty-one bilingual paid volunteers who placed calls to both counties between October 24 and November 4, 2002. During this period, callers attempted to contact 52,315 Latino voters who lived in the targeted precincts.[6]

2004 Voces Del Pueblo

In 2002, the targeting strategy could be classified as macrotargeting, given that it was based on aggregate concentrations of Latino voters (precincts with heavy concentrations of Latino registered voters), but where fewer than half could be classified as likely voters. The commissioned evaluation of the 2002 Voces del Pueblo campaign found that direct mail and robocalls had little to no effect, whereas the effect of live calls was more encouraging. By 2004, there was a desire for more precision during the targeting stage. Rather than using aggregate precinct characteristics, the Voces del Pueblo GOTV effort began the process of voter segmentation and microtargeting. Rather than focus on Latino likely voters, the Civic Engagement department at NALEO decided to focus only on targeted "low-propensity" Latino voters in New York City, Harris County (Texas), and Los Angeles, Orange, and Alameda Counties in California. In addition to low-propensity Latino voters (Voces-eligible), a "non-low-propensity" group of Latino voters (Non Voces-Eligible) was added to the Los Angeles sample to determine whether Latinos with greater voting propensity were comparably receptive to mobilization efforts.

The evolution of Latino voter mobilization began to take shape as NALEO took steps to increase efficiency and capacity at all stages of the voter mobilization effort. Rather than produce printed call sheets to record the call outcome and then transfer these outcomes into an electronic database, the Voces del Pueblo team developed a networked electronic program that would allow for data to be input directly to record the call outcome. The anticipated growth of the Voces del Pueblo in subsequent elections required infrastructure investment in database management. In order to ensure consistent quality of calls across sites, all live calls originated in the Los Angeles office. Finally, rather than contract with a political data vendor, NALEO opted to build data-management capacity internally and purchased the voter files directly from county registrars. The challenge was that the voter-registration data in New York and Harris County did not have telephone numbers and had to be acquired through commercial data vendors.

While the target population for the 2004 Voces del Pueblo effort was 250,000 voters nationally, more than 380,000 records were sent to a commercial data vendor to cross-reference the records with consumer data and update any information that appeared incorrect or missing.[7] Even with the oversample of 130,000 records, there was a lower than expected yield rate of recorded matches. Only 29 percent of the 179,000 voter files for Harris County and New York City were enhanced with a telephone number. Given this loss of data, both of these sites were excluded from the field experiment because a control group would reduce the total actual attempted contacts.[8] One of the challenges in conducting field experiments in the context of a real-world effort is that organizations must be accountable to their funding sources. In this instance, NALEO had stipulated that a baseline number of voters would be contacted in each site and therefore could not exclude certain voters from treatment in Harris County and New York. The California sites did have enough voters to select a control group that would be used to determine the relative effect of the GOTV campaign.

In total, the 2004 phone-bank operation attempted to contact 79,385 Latino voters over the span of twenty days, beginning on Friday, October 9, and ending Friday, October 29. The 2004 GOTV effort was the first time that the Voces del Pueblo program implemented a centralized live-call operation targeting all five communities simultaneously.

2006 Voces del Pueblo

In 2006, NALEO's GOTV drive consisted of live calls to Los Angeles, Riverside, and San Bernardino Counties in California, as well as New York City and Houston. Having already demonstrated a commitment and capacity to engage in voter mobilization, NALEO was well positioned to obtain funding from the Irvine Foundation's newly established "California Votes Initiative" with the goal of increasing "voter participation rates among infrequent voters, particularly in low-income and ethnic communities" (James Irvine Foundation). The challenge was to continue to grow the Voces del Pueblo effort, benefiting from economies of scale in database management, while maintaining a centralized phone-bank operation to assure consistent quality control across communities. Two key changes that took place in 2006 were the development of a Web-based user-friendly system for phone-banking that would prove instrumental in the next phase of Latino voter mobilization and a refinement of voter segmentation to differentiate between low-propensity voters that would be targeted. These included (*a*) youth, (*b*) new registered voters, (*c*) infrequent voters, and (*d*) nonvoters.

2008 Ya Es Hora: ¡Ve y Vota! (It's Time: Go and Vote!)

One of the consequences of the 2006 immigrant protests was the increased collaboration between local, regional, and national Latino and other civic organizations through the We Are America Alliance. The national partners included the Center for Community Change, the National Council of La Raza (NCLR), Mi Familia Vota, and NALEO. The coalition involved dozens of organizations across eighteen states. The We Are America Alliance solidified existing partnerships and developed new ones allowing NALEO's Voces del Pueblo mobilization effort to evolve once again as part of the The "Ya es hora ¡Ve y Vota!" campaign, described as "the non-partisan voter engagement segment of the *ya es hora* comprehensive civic participation strategy, designed to remove the barriers to full Latino electoral participation" (Ya es Hora). This joint effort was led by NALEO, Mi Familia Vota, and NCLR, in collaboration with media partners Entravision Communications, ImpreMedia, and Univision Communications.

In 2008, NALEO moved away from centralized phone-banking to localized phone-banking with centralized data management and training. It built relationships with affiliates in multiple states and conducted volunteer training and other logistical assistance. NALEO's mobilization effort expanded dramatically in 2008. It included six counties in California, and Las Vegas, Denver, Long Island, New Mexico, Harris County, El Paso, Dallas, Miami, and Phoenix. This new approach to live calls greatly expanded the number of Latinos it attempted to contact to more than 100,000 low-propensity voters.

2010 Ya Es Hora: Ve y Vota (It's Time: Go and Vote)

In 2010, NALEO outreached to voters from eighteen distinct communities in five different states: Arizona, California, Florida, New York, and Texas.[9] In each community, the program targeted "low-propensity" Latino voters.[10] These voters received multiple contacts from the NALEO and partner organizations, encouraging them to vote on Election Day, November 2, 2010. In total, this GOTV drive attempted to contact 235,000 Latino voters through live calls. Without a doubt, Latino voter mobilization has greatly evolved from what de la Garza and his colleagues deemed to be sporadic and underfunded in 2000 to sophisticated, systematic, and better-funded voter-mobilization efforts. Not only has NALEO's own GOTV efforts evolved, but the increased interaction and collaboration across Latino organizations after the 2006 immigrant protests has influenced the nature of other efforts to mobilize Latino voters.

From Voter Segmentation to Segmented Mobilization

Is it possible that the few GOTV campaigns that targeted Latino voters had differential effects on distinct segments of the electorate? Borrowing a phrase from Portes and Zhou's work on patterns of immigrant assimilation and adaptation, I make the case that rather than uniform effects of mobilization, the confluence of individual-level characteristics with context has led to "segmented mobilization," where the same GOTV efforts have differential effects on the participation of Latinos with different voter-specific characteristics.

Portes and Zhou (1993) reject the "straight-line assimilation" model of immigrant adaptation, which assumes that immigrant groups will become more "American" with length of residence or with each successive generation that is born in the United States. Instead, they propose an alternative "segmented assimilation" model, which posits that patterns of assimilation vary by immigrant group and that the immigrant group's path to assimilation and incorporation is dependent on favorable factors including location, skin color, and occupational opportunities, which then determine whether the outcomes are favorable and conducive to assimilation. Similarly, I argue against the assumption that mobilization efforts will have equivalent, positive, and homogeneous effects on voter-participation rates among all voters because the existing patterns of voter turnout of distinct segments of Latino voters are dependent on key individual characteristics.

These characteristics can range from nativity, to age, to when Latino voters first entered the electorate, to unique electoral contexts. Moreover, the political socialization of Latinos is so heavily influenced by these variables that the effectiveness of mobilization efforts are significantly impacted, over and above the effects of political party affiliation. Note that "segmented mobilization" is very different from the "voter segmentation" discussed here. The former focuses on the heterogeneous effects of mobilization efforts on different segments of the electorate, whereas the latter addresses the strategic decision to devote resources targeting certain segments of the electorate rather than others.

It is hardly a novel idea that time of political socialization can have significant cohort effects. It has been well established that exogenous political events can serve as catalysts for pre-adult socialization (Sears and Valentino 1997) and that being involved in the 1960s protest movement had long-term effects on rates of participation and political attitudes (Jennings 1987). Similarly, the case has been made that higher turnout among Democrats, between 1932 and 1944, can be largely explained by the high turnout among newly mobilized cohorts of young, substantially female, urban, working-class, and foreign-born (Nie, Verba, and Petrocik 1976).

Despite the relevance of political socialization and cohort effects for party realignment, only a small subset of research on minority voter turnout has simultaneously operationalized both political socialization and cohort analysis to explore contemporary patterns of participation of racial and ethnic minorities, particularly Latinos. Given that not all Latinos were mobilized to participate in political protest, pursue citizenship, and vote, I argue that distinguishing between levels of effectiveness of mobilization is a useful approach to identify the key differences among Latinos in the United States. First, Pantoja, Ramírez, and Segura (2001) develop a model of Latino electoral participation that captures fluctuations in voter turnout among native-born and naturalized Latinos across naturalization cohorts. They are the first to fully explore the relationship between the time in which Latinos obtained citizenship, in conjunction with the political environment, and voter turnout. Their comparison of Latinos in California, Texas, and Florida finds that California Latinos who naturalized between 1992 and 1996 have substantially higher rates of validated voter turnout in the 1996 general presidential election than native-born Latinos, those who naturalized in an earlier period in California, or those who naturalized at any point in Texas and Florida. They attribute this mobilization and increased turnout to the high-profile ballot initiatives and polarizing rhetoric in California.

Barreto (2005) reaffirms the continued significance of nativity as he finds that Latino naturalized voters had higher turnout rates in the 2002 general election in California than native-born Latino voters.

It is also the case that the highly charged political context in California during the mid–1990s discussed in chapter 4 has been found to have had important impact on the political socialization of Latinos in the state. Barreto and Woods (2005) test for turnout rates of Latinos who first registered between 1994 and 1998 in Los Angeles County. Using validated voter-registrar data, they find that Latinos who first entered the electorate during this politicized climate have higher turnout than non-Latinos entering the electorate during the same period. The partisan implications among these newly mobilized Latinos who first registered between 1994 and 1998 in Los Angeles County make the advantage gained by Democrats during the New Deal realignment pale in comparison. According to Barreto and Woods (2005), of those Latinos in this registration cohort who voted in 1998, 75 percent were registered Democrats, whereas only 7 percent were registered Republicans.

Two cross-sectional studies have focused on the influx of Latinos into the electorate, investigating whether they are distinct from Latinos who were already part of the electorate prior to 1994. Barreto, Ramírez, and Woods (2005) find that the heightened political context explains most of the increase in voting among naturalized voters since 1996 beyond what would be expected with normal influx of Latino immigrants eligible for naturalization. As I argue in chapter 4, the date of first registration (or their "political baptism"), in conjunction with nativity, can serve as a useful tool to identify four cohorts of Latino voters. Among Latinos in California, those who first registered to vote during a politically charged climate (1994–96) turned out at higher levels in five statewide elections between 1996 and 2000 than did Latinos who first registered at any other time. Furthermore, among this mobilized group of Latinos, and contrary to the findings of previous empirical studies, those who were naturalized citizens had the highest levels of participation. Conversely, among those Latinos who were not mobilized by the political context, the native-born cohort had higher rates of participation than the naturalized. These findings confirm the mobilizing effect of a state's political context and further add a conceptual tool to differentiate the effects among subgroups or segments of Latino voters. These findings suggest that not all Latinos react to the same negative political context[11] and in particular suggest that an analysis of Latino mobilization and participation must consider nativity and date of first registration, when relevant, as important intervening variables. That is, these voter-specific characteristics matter for mobilizing Latinos.

The concept of segmented mobilization is important because it goes beyond racial and ethnic intergroup comparisons of the rates of mobilization experienced by population subgroups. Instead, it recognizes that a separate analysis is needed to capture intragroup receptivity to mobilization requests. In addition to the theoretical significance of expanding GOTV field experiments to racial and ethnic minorities, results from these experiments can have profound normative consequences. Given both parties' increased interest in Latinos, any insights into this population's receptiveness to mobilization can transform the changing perceptions of Latinos as an inactive electorate (Fraga and Ramírez 2004).

The evolution of NALEO's mobilization efforts, as described above, allow for the consideration of the effectiveness of similar mobilization by one organization in multiple electoral contexts because the organization was willing to incorporate embedded, randomized field experiments in their mobilization efforts. The challenging case is the GOTV drive in 2000, because it did not utilize this method. Without a control group, one cannot directly estimate the effects of phone contact on turnout. It is necessary to identify and implement a post-hoc method for measuring the effects. The decision to target only precincts with less than 50 percent Latino likely voters was not based on a scientific formula or on any particular theoretical expectation by NALEO. This arbitrary cutoff point allows for a comparison of the precincts that barely met the inclusion criteria with those that barely missed being included. The precincts in the 49–50 percent likely voter group were assigned to the treatment group, and those precincts in the 50.01–51 percent likely voter group were assigned to the control group. In other words, I compared those in the first group, who were assigned to receive a phone call from NALEO, to those in the second group, who were very similar to the first group, but were not assigned to receive a call. This process yielded 19 precincts in the treatment group and 23 precincts in the control group. In order to determine whether the 19 precincts in treatment group were in fact similar to the 23 precincts in the control group, Census data were appended to the respective precincts.[12] Based on independent samples tests, there was no statistically significant difference between the control and treatment groups. Thus, while not a "randomized" experiment, this real-world quasi-experimental approach allows us to make some cautionary estimates of the impact of phone contact on Latinos in Latino supermajority precincts, and whether certain cohorts or segments were uniquely receptive to the same mobilization effort.

One drawback to the quasi-experimental approach employed here is the reduced certainty of the treatment effects. Existing field experiments, however, are not large enough to determine whether it is possible that the same localized effort had different impacts on distinct segments of the Latino electorate. More specifically, the experiments by Michelson (2005) are too small and the experiments by Ramírez (2005) lack sufficient voters in the control group to produce robust findings beyond the overall effects on Latinos.[13] Thus, the quasi-experimental approach is the only option for testing the segmented mobilization theory.

Given the pattern of Latino participation in California discussed in chapter 4, we can generate hypotheses given the expectation that the existing voter propensity is inversely related to the effects of a single phone contact. While the contentious politics in California since 1994 generally showed little impact upon native-born voters and those who were already registered to vote, there is reason to believe that these existing Latino voters may still be receptive to coethnic mobilization appeals (Shaw, de la Garza, and Lee 2000). On the other hand, there is also reason to believe that it will be harder to significantly raise the levels of turnout among the segment of the electorate whose political baptism came as a result of a perceived attack on Latinos in California. It is not that these Latinos are disengaged from the political system and will therefore ignore requests to participate. On the contrary, because they are already participating at higher levels than one would expect given their SES levels, it will be harder to increase further the rates of participation with a single phone call. Thus, the overarching hypothesis is that successful phone contact will have a positive effect on voter turnout on the segments of the Latino electorate that were not already motivated by the political context in the mid–1990s.

The underlying logic of segmented mobilization is that the contextual factors that significantly altered the patterns of Latino participation in California since the mid–1990s also had an impact on the receptivity of other segments of the Latino electorate to mobilization requests. The unique political behavior of particular registration cohorts to different political contexts suggests the possibility that the effectiveness of direct GOTV messages may be masked if one lumps together all Latino voters, rather than considering the effects on distinct segments of the Latino electorate. As such, I present the general results of the quasi-experimental approach and then consider whether when a voter enters the electorate and/or the nativity of voters are important intervening variables to consider in studies of Latino mobilization. Several of the works cited above suggest that foreign-born Latinos reacted to California's politically charged context during the mid-1990s by increasing their voter registration and turnout rates. While native-born Latinos were less receptive to context-related mobilization, it is possible that they may actually be more receptive to particularized mobilization. A comparison of the effect of contact on turnout shows statistically significant effects only among native-born Latinos. The effect of contact on turnout is an increase in the probability of voting by 7.6 percentage points.

Furthermore, there are promising results from the phone contact when we further separate Latino voters into four cohorts or segments by nativity and date of registration. Recall that prior research found that Latinos who were newly registered to vote were more mobilized by the political context than the existing Latino electorate. NALEO's nonpartisan mobilization campaign actually has a relatively large effect on those Latinos who were registered to vote before the highly charged political context. According to the regression results, phone contact had no real effect on voters who registered to voter since 1994. Conversely, phone contact boosts the probability of voting among the *native born, pre-1994* and the *naturalized, pre-1994* cohorts by about 14.2 and 13.9 percentage points respectively. As large as these findings are, why should we have expected differential effects of GOTV efforts on Latino subgroups? As stated earlier, there is existing evidence that the political context in California mobilized segments of the Latino electorate (Pantoja, Ramírez, and Segura 2001; Ramírez 2002; Barreto and Woods 2005; Barreto, Ramírez, and Woods 2005; Barreto 2005). All of these scholars agree that Latinos in California were mobilized to participate because of the racially charged political context in the mid-1990s and likely resulted in a cohort effect. While native-born and naturalized Latinos who were already part of the electorate may not have responded to the indirect mobilization by the political context at the outset, it appears that they were primed to respond positively to phone contact as a mobilizing tool. This is not to imply that those who first registered to vote during the politicized context are not receptive to recruitment; rather, it is to highlight the difficulty in finding significant mobilization effects of one phone call among a group of voters who were already considerably mobilized by the political context.

As we shift to measuring the effects of mobilization as NALEO's GOTV efforts beyond 2000, it is not possible to differentiate between native-born and naturalized segments of the electorate because these variables are not available in the data that I analyze. Moreover, as NALEO became increasingly focused on only those voters who could be classified as "low-propensity," this inherently excluded large segments of the California electorate that were mobilized by the political context. I therefore present the overall effects of mobilization and identify segmented mobilization effects based on other targeting characteristics such as young voter, new voter, nonvoter, etc.

In the first randomized field experiment, the 2002 Voces del Pueblo campaign had a greater effect on turnout with more personalized contact method. Live calls raised turnout by 4.6 percent, which is comparable to other studies of voter mobilization efforts using live phone-banking. There is some evidence that context matters, as direct mail had a very small (0.2 percent and 0.3 percent) but statistically significant effect in Colorado and Harris County respectively. This same mobilization effort, however, had no statistically significant effect in New Mexico or Orange and Los Angeles Counties in California. The randomized field experiments in 2004 and 2006 were largely set aside, as issues arose due to low yield rate of available voters with telephone numbers during the targeting stage, or significant subsequent low yield rates in the postelection efforts to measure the effectiveness of the GOTV drives.

In 2008, I was able to measure the overall effectiveness of the mobilization efforts and identified differential rates of receptivity to such appeals based on individual voter characteristics and electoral political context. First, in 2008, I find that electoral context does matter. Of all of the GOTV sites, low-propensity Latino voters in Las Vegas were more likely to respond to voter-mobilization efforts. There was a 3.7 percent turnout effect of live calls. Because NALEO not only targeted individuals, but all members of a household who are classified as "low-propensity," I was able to further consider segmented mobilization based on household composition. I don't find any measurable positive effects of mobilization on the turnout of mixed households (for example, households where, based on one target category, one voter is classified as one type of low-propensity voter and one or more additional household members were classified as another type of low-propensity voters). There were positive and statistically significant effects on homogeneous households that were infrequent (voted in one of four elections), with a turnout effect of 4.11 percent. Homogeneous Latino young-voter households appear to have been more receptive to mobilization in 2008. There was a 9.8 percent turnout effect of mobilization among young-voter households.

In 2010, a unique opportunity existed to measure the effectiveness of mobilization across a larger universe of low-propensity Latino voters in various electoral contexts. The design and analysis of NALEO's GOTV efforts in 2010 required a more complex approach to delineate whether the same mobilization appeals resulted in segmented mobilization. Given the heterogeneous nature of the low-propensity voters and households in the sites, the randomized field experiment used sample stratification to ensure that treatment and control groups in each respective site was commensurate to the presence by household size and household composition at each site. The sample stratification resulted in 70 separate strata or 70 smaller experiments. A fixed-effects regression accounts for the 70 different strata and allows one to pool all the sites together to measure the effect in all the sites.

Overall, the comparison of the treatment and control groups indicates that, after controlling for contact rate in each of the strata, the estimated overall effect is a statistically significant increase in turnout of 2.34 percent among those who were contacted. Unlike 2008, there were no statistically significant effects of household composition in 2010. Because so many of the low-propensity voters were in single-voter households, I consider the effects of mobilization only on single-voter households. The comparison of strata is much more straightforward because voter classifications and contact rates are for individual voters as opposed to multiple-voter households that could be mixed. Once we account for contact rates, the estimated treatment effect is 3.85 percent among those voters who were contacted.

The question remains as to whether the diverging patterns of statistically significant effects on turnout are due to contextual effects that determined site-specific turnout. A close inspection of the eighteen communities suggests that turnout is definitely impacted by local forces. Turnout in the respective counties during the 2010 general election varied greatly, ranging from 23.3 percent in El Paso County to 64.3 percent in San Diego County. Likewise there is great variation in the turnout among single-voter households in the randomized field experiment ranging from 21.3 percent in El Paso County to 53.1 percent in Riverside County. The dramatic difference in turnout across sites, as well as the differences between targeted low-propensity voter turnout and countywide turnout, helps make the case that simply pooling together all of the sites where NALEO (and partner organizations) conducted GOTV drives could yield misleading findings.

If democracy is to be preserved, partisan elites must look beyond short-term electoral goals that neglect low-propensity voters and those who reside in uncompetitive contexts, and must expand personalized mobilization efforts similar to those employed by political machines in the past. What are the theoretical and normative implications of the above findings? First, theoretically, there is sufficient evidence to suggest that voter-mobilization efforts have positive effects on Latinos, particularly low-propensity voters. Historically, Latinos have not been the target of voter-mobilization efforts by political campaigns. The analysis in this chapter suggests that nonpartisan organizations have stepped into the void, building massive Latino voter-mobilization efforts over the past decade. Further, these efforts have yielded more refined information about the conditions under which Latinos respond to voter-mobilization efforts. Nonpartisan voter-mobilization efforts by NALEO have revealed that phone contact is more effective than mail, for example.

More specifically, there is evidence that a "one size fits all" approach to mobilizing Latino voters may not be the most effective in generating sustained turnout. Rather, it is clear from the results of NALEO's field experiments that the effectiveness of voter-mobilization efforts depends on voter-specific characteristics. Whether Latinos are low- versus high-propensity voters, their date of registration, and whether they are naturalized versus native-born citizens—all of these factors matter a great deal when it comes to whether or not a phone call will get them to the polls. In addition, in line with the overall theme of this book, it is clear that the degree to which Latino voters respond to mobilization efforts depends on place and geographic context. The relevance of the segmented mobilization hypothesis to the political behavior literature and to those seeking to reach a growing number of Latino voters is that mobilization efforts do not have equivalent, positive, and homogeneous effects on participation rates among all Latino voters. Outreach efforts should be designed accordingly.

6

THE EVOLVING LATINO ELECTORATE AND THE FUTURE OF AMERICAN POLITICS

The story of how and where Latino voters will matter, I contend, is not a story of revolutionary change. Instead, it is a story about evolutionary change in the Latino electorate and the factors that propel the growth in the pool of Latino eligible voters. The tremendous growth in the number of Latino voters is not the endpoint. More Latinos will be eligible to vote in the next eighteen years than the total number of current Latino registered voters. Just as the Latino electorate is evolving, so is the perception of it by pundits and scholars. It didn't take long after the November 6, 2012, election for political pundits to revise their commentary about Latino voters or their role in the 2012 presidential election and beyond.[1] A day after the election, the *New York Times* touted the record Latino turnout and their solid support of Barack Obama. "Defying predictions that their participation would be lackluster, Latinos turned out in record numbers on Tuesday and voted for President Obama by broad margins, tipping the balance in at least three swing states and securing their position as an organized force in American politics with the power to move national elections" (Preston and Santos 2012). Similarly, a CNN news story proclaimed: "Latinos not only helped Obama win in key battleground states, but they made up 10% of the electorate for the first time ever" (Rodriguez 2012). The theme of "unprecedented presence" of the Latino vote and the electoral consequences reverberated in most mainstream media outlets. In reporting based on Fox News exit polls, it was remarked that "Latino voters have never had a greater and more significant impact on a presidential election in history" (Llenas

2010). A day later, a *Los Angeles Times* editorial announced "Tuesday's Winner and Losers." The editorial's assessment was that Latinos were "winners" because "their overwhelming backing of Obama and other Democrats is widely regarded as a key factor in Tuesday's results, prompting much soul-searching by Republicans about how they can better appeal to this growing demographic" (*Los Angeles Times,* November 8, 2012).

But not all pundits were as quick to concede that the presidential election had made Latino voters "winners." Allison Kopicki, the polling editor at the *New York Times,* and her coauthor, Will Irving, dissected exit polls to determine if the outcome of the election would have been different without any Latino voters or through manipulated changes in Latino voter preference.[2] According to this analysis, Latino voters were inconsequential in Iowa and New Hampshire. Barack Obama also could have won Ohio, Virginia, and Pennsylvania with substantially lower levels of Latino support. Even before acknowledging that Mr. Obama did need a majority of Latino voters to emerge victorious in Colorado, Florida, or Nevada, Kopicki and Irving (2013) largely write off the Latino vote because with the wins in Iowa, New Hampshire, Ohio, Pennsylvania, Virginia, "along with the safe Democratic states that Mr. Obama should have carried regardless of the Hispanic vote, the president would have reached 283 electoral votes, winning the Electoral College without needing to win a majority of the Hispanic vote in each state." They further warn that Republicans interested in winning back the White House in 2016 need to reexamine the exit poll results if the intended strategy is crafted solely focused on Latino voters or immigration policy.

Tempting as it may be for academic analyses of the role of Latino voters in national party politics to be dismissive of the punditry noted above, it is important to highlight the similarities to the two scholarly approaches to the study of Latino politics noted at the beginning of the book. The skeptical journalistic interpretation that Latinos were not crucial to the outcome of the presidential election parallels academic accounts that have applied the "pivotal vote" thesis in previous election cycles and concluded that the role of Latinos has been largely muted by non-Latino voting preferences and contextual factors beyond their control (de la Garza and DeSipio 1999, 2005). The less sanguine view that Latinos are rarely "pivotal voters" neglects the many ways in which this electorate has impacted election dynamics beyond the ballot box. By helping shift some states from competitive to safe Democratic or by enlarging the Democratic advantage in expensive media markets, Latino voters have allowed for election resources to be spent in more competitive state contests and have therefore shifted campaign strategies. The shortsighted view that influence is tied to single election outcomes fails to consider how other variables that are not easily measured can also impact levels of political salience.

Similarly, pundit accounts heralding the unprecedented nature of Latino electoral participation and their unified voter behavior as a sign of an expanding role of Latinos in American politics mirror the "demography is destiny" approach in academic studies. National Latino voter turnout was indeed higher than some predicted, and the 71 percent support for Barack Obama among Latino voters almost matched the previous record when President Bill Clinton was supported by 72 percent of Latino voters in his 1996 reelection bid. While comparisons to previous patterns of Latino voter preferences make for good headlines, it is more important to note that the unified vote in the 1996 election was of a significantly smaller national Latino electorate. According to the Current Population Survey (CPS), 4.9 million Latinos voted in 1996. Based on national exit polls, it is estimated that as many as 12.5 million Latinos cast ballots in 2012 (Taylor et al. 2012). While the tremendous growth is important, it is even more important to note that the new, much larger, Latino electorate reverted to previous patterns despite increasing diversity within the Latino community. Moreover, both the pundit and academic views of inevitable salience fail to explain the process by which Latinos will shape the future of American politics. Conventional wisdom, therefore, needs to be updated, and this is made more evident by taking a long-term view of the historical context.

Redefining American Democracy?

The population of the United States has changed dramatically since the start of the twentieth century. According to U.S. Census figures, the total population in 2010 was more than four times the population in 1900. The early 1900s witnessed the peak of the third wave of immigrants being admitted to the United States. These immigrants accounted for most of the population growth in the first three decades, only to be surpassed by the dramatic population growth during the baby boom period of the late 1940s to the mid–1960s. In particular, between 1950 and 1960, the population grew by almost 28 million people, and the rate of growth remained at more than 20 million in each of the subsequent decades. Until the end of the twentieth century, the lion's share of the immigrant population growth was a result of European immigrants, as evidenced by the fact that 75 percent of all foreign-born residents in the United States were born in Europe. After the removal of quota-based immigration policies and the rise of a preference system established in the Immigration Act of 1965, there was a rebirth of American immigration (Tichenor 2002).[3] Not only was there an increase in the number of immigrants coming to the United States, but the source of immigration significantly changed in the fourth wave of immigration. Most of the newer immigrants came from Latin America and Asia.

As a result of the composition of the most recent immigration wave, the share of the foreign-born population in the United States who were born in Europe declined to 60 percent in 1970, 37 percent in 1980, 22 percent in 1990, 16 percent in 2000, and only 12 percent in 2010. After the 1980 census, immigrants from Latin America and Asia comprised 49 percent of the foreign-born population, and this share has only gone up. In 1990, immigrants from these two regions comprised 68 percent of the foreign-born population, 78 percent in 2000 and 81 percent in 2010. Understandably, this had dramatic implications on the raw population growth in the United States. The twenty-year period between 1990 and 2010 experienced the single-largest population growth, from 248,709,873 in 1990 to 308,745,538 in 2010, an increase of 60,035,665. No two-decade period has experienced the same absolute growth in the history of the United States. Latin American and Asian immigrants *and* their U.S.-born children accounted for over 60 percent of the total U.S. population growth during this period.[4] The size and nature of the fourth wave of immigration has led to questions about the effects of the influx of immigrants from Latin America and Asia on the composition of the population and electorate, as well as the nature of representation in contemporary American democracy.

For some, the changing demographic composition of society poses a challenge for America's national identity, especially as it relates to immigrants from Latin America and the perceived inability of these immigrants to assimilate (Huntington 2004). Rather than focus on the cultural consequences of increased diversity for America's national identity, most political pundits focus on the impact of the new demographic reality for national politics. The 2012 presidential election demonstrated that when the white electorate is split among the two presidential candidates, common preferences among America's racial and ethnic minorities can prove consequential to election outcomes, especially if they prefer one candidate at a more than three to one ratio.[5] A coherent or unified nonwhite voting bloc has not historically been the norm, and only time will tell whether comparable levels of bloc voting can be replicated in future presidential and nonpresidential elections. Furthermore, it is not inherently true that political salience is solely derived from bloc voting for a particular candidate or party. The extent to which racial and ethnic minorities are deemed salient hinges on the current and projected composition of the electorate and distribution of voter preferences. Non-Hispanic white voters accounted for 72 percent in the 2012 election, continuing a downward trend since 1976, when they accounted for 89 percent of all voters. If this trend continues, the electorate is projected to become majority-minority through a gradual process spanning several decades. Why is the current pace of change in the composition of the electorate much slower than the population? According to the 2010 Census, the proportion of the population that is non-Hispanic white is 63.7 percent, 7 percent less than their proportion of voters in the 2012 election. The overrepresentation of whites in the electorate can be largely explained by race-related differences in age distribution, citizenship rates, and socioeconomic status.

Beyond the "Pete Wilson Effect": Changing Electorates, Changing Politics

Change is tied into the observable ways in which politics is a dynamic process of identifying who participates and what prompted them to become active. I have argued that this dynamic change is caused by proactive mobilization and reactive mobilization. Some would feel compelled to identify what has happened as the result of "change from within" and "change from without." However, this characterization of reactive mobilization as simply "change from without" fails to acknowledge that even in reaction to exogenous shocks, Latino residents, citizens, and voters demonstrate political agency in the various ways in which they respond to political threat. Catalysts for participation, by themselves, do not automatically lead to change and are instead necessary but insufficient conditions for mobilization.

As the preceding chapters demonstrate, understanding the aspirational role of a diverse electorate requires additional analytical rigor by focusing on when and where this change is likely to occur. As the largest ethnic minority in the United States, Latinos are redefining American democracy. They are doing this state by state, through change in presence among the state population, naturalization patterns, presence in the citizen voting-age population, and rates of voter participation. In chapter 2, I highlighted the dual roles of proactive mobilization and reactive mobilization in Latino participation in protest politics. This kind of political activity was not tied into any particular election cycle, yet the historic nature of the 2006 immigrant protest marches in reaction to HR 4437 exerted external pressure on legislative behavior of the U.S. Senate. This ensured the failure of any HR 4437–equivalent Senate bills and instead motivated the U.S. Senate's attempt at comprehensive immigration reform.

In chapter 3, I demonstrated that the enhanced visibility of Latino immigrants and their supporters in mass protests was followed by an increasing presence among immigrants seeking U.S. citizenship. Here, too, the convergence of proactive mobilization and reactive mobilization resulted in the largest effects. The naturalization process, as many have already noted, is a byzantine bureaucratic process that increasingly requires specialized legal understanding of the immigration system (Plascencia 2012; Félix 2008). This can ultimately be a disenchanting experience for many of the immigrants seeking U.S. citizenship. The perceived political threat among Latino immigrants may have been the catalyst, or a mobilizing opportunity, for greater interest in naturalization, but Latino organizations had already gained the necessary expertise to help immigrants navigate the citizenship application process. Had these Latino organizations not grown the institutional capacity in efforts to mobilize opportunities, it is unclear whether the increased interest in naturalization would have significantly changed the existing citizenship patterns. In other words, it is important to consider whether or not the activation of Latinos into politics and reduction in the citizenship hurdle was preceded by elite efforts to reduce the barriers to broad civic incorporation of immigrants.

The case study of the changing Latino vote in California during the 1990s, discussed in chapter 4, illustrates the consequences of when the primary, but not exclusive, source of electoral mobilization is a political threat. The effects of perceived and real anti-Latino political context on naturalized and native-born Latinos is notable but also suggests that the response to the same stimulus varies within the Latino population. By tracking the validated turnout of Latinos over multiple elections, I found that political context can affect the behavior of Latinos beyond one election cycle among those Latinos who enter the electorate in response to such a context, and that the mobilization is greater and longer-lasting among the naturalized within this cohort. However, as the perceived political threat subsided, the effect of reactive mobilization also moderated. In this case, the "Pete Wilson effect"[6] decreased over time among U.S.-born Latinos, but the effect among newly registered naturalized voters lasted longer and remained distinct from the existing base of naturalized voters. The variance in participation rate within the Latino communities in the same state suggests that it is unlikely that reactive mobilization will be constant among Latino voters within or across states.

One of the keys to understanding the patterns across states is to look at the extent to which Latino civic infrastructure allows for proactive mobilization to reduce the barriers to citizenship and voter turnout. In chapter 5, I focused on the evolution of voter-mobilization efforts across place and time. I found that while the established organizational presence and experience in voter-mobilization are important, there are also additional community-specific factors that affect low-propensity Latino voters' responsiveness to such appeals.

State Contexts, Responsive Capacity, and Two-Party Competition

My state-centered approach of the sources of mobilization more concretely captures the transformation of Latinos' civic and political reality and the engines of the evolution of the Latino electorate. However, I did not address the other likely downstream consequences such as descriptive and substantive representation in legislative institutions. Will the influx of a new electorate translate into a change in the nature of the existing two-party structure or have meaningful consequences for who gets elected? My approach is not inherently at odds with a perspective that sees the diversification of the electorate as likely to have consequences for party electoral fortunes. However, recognizing that a population shift, as an input, can have consequences on the composition of the electorate, partisan voter preferences, and election-specific outcomes is only an initial step to assessing the potential for Latinos to impact American democracy. Change is not occurring uniformly throughout the United States. Some states with similar demographic diversity have witnessed greater increase in the rates of Latino political participation, while change has lagged behind in other states. It is also true that change in Latino turnout is more consequential for election outcomes in states where partisan preferences are more evenly divided.

The potential for America's racial and ethnic minorities to influence the political environment is rooted in the notion that demographic changes can lead to sequential change in the composition of the eligible voter population, the pool of registered voters, those who vote, and those who get elected. This change, however, is neither linear nor path-dependent. Instead, transformation requires some form of collective action to ensure that the distinct preferences and needs of Latinos are considered by the existing political majority. Why, despite the noticeable transformation of the population in certain states, have these numbers not translated into commensurate change in the electorate or descriptive representation?

To begin to answer this question requires that we recognize that at the core of American democracy is a two-party system. What this two-party structure means for emerging groups is a source of some debate. Bowler and Segura's (2011) positive outlook on the potential of demographic changes to have significant political consequences is based, among other things, on analyses measuring the political effects of identity, the Democratic Party's reliance on minority voters, and party identification and two-party voting among minorities. This, however, stands in stark contrast to two earlier accounts of the political relationship between racial and ethnic minorities and the two-party system. In *Uneasy Alliances: Race and Party Competition in America*, Paul Frymer (1999) challenges the notion that two-party competition results in more democratic and inclusive politics. Frymer makes a compelling case that the two-party system has structured competition around white voters and that the established pattern of African American support for the Democratic Party has led to its electoral capture (1999). Thomas Kim (2007) similarly makes the case that in order to understand how competition affects racial and ethnic minorities, one must consider the degree to which partisan strategies and party elites value racial and ethnic minority interests. Not only are they valued differently, according to Kim, but he argues that as a result of a campaign finance controversy between 1996 and 1998, Asian Americans found themselves as an "isolated minority facing a decidedly hostile bipartisan majority" (2007:4).

There are clear differences of opinion about the consequences of party competition; these range from assertions of the Democratic Party's electoral capture of African Americans to hostility toward Asian Americans by both political parties, to more recent views that minorities not only can, but will shift American politics. How do we reconcile such diverging perspectives about the role of racial minorities in a two-party system? Specifically, what is the likelihood that the assertion that demography is destiny will come to fruition? The key to reconciling this debate comes from a close look at the Latino population as the largest racial/ethnic minority, the state political contexts in which they live, and the sources of change in the potential and actual electorate.

The extent to which Latino voters are perceived to be politically relevant beyond one election cycle hinges on three factors related to the community's responsive capacity. First, it is important to consider the scope, size, and consistency of growth of Latino voters across election cycles. Second, as I have argued throughout the book, the nature of the growth should coincide with proactive mobilization or reactive mobilization. Finally, it is important to determine the effect of the first two factors on party competition across states and nationally. My focus has been on the first two factors, but it is possible to return to some of the findings to discuss the third factor. Chapter 4 provides a compelling case study of California's Latino community and its responsive capacity. In this case, the surge in naturalization, voter registration, and turnout rates can be traced to the reactive mobilization of voters in response to political threat, as well as the established proactive mobilization consisting of naturalization workshops and GOTV drives. Did the mobilization of an often-overlooked Latino electorate lead to noticeable change in California's two-party competition? The answer is a qualified yes. Over a span of sixteen years, Democrats have consolidated power, which included winning every statewide office, obtaining a supermajority in both chambers of the state legislature,[7] and over 70 percent of the congressional delegation. The last time that either political party held a supermajority in both chambers of the state legislature was in 1933, when Republicans controlled the legislature.[8] It is widely accepted that the influx of Latino voters helped to expedite this difficult feat. According to Mark DiCamillo, director of the Field Poll, "California would not be a blue state if it wasn't for the growing number of ethnic voters" (Challet 2012). While Latinos are the largest segment of the ethnic voters that DiCamillo references, they were not alone. The Latino vote, by itself, is rarely decisive, but it does give the Democrats a much larger lead in the polls to win statewide races, thereby changing the election dynamics.

Throughout the book, I have argued that three critical changes took place with respect to the proactive mobilization efforts that increased the pool of potential Latino voters. First, the evolution of this electorate can be traced to significant changes in the political roles of Spanish-language media and Latino civic organizations. In particular, I noted the increased willingness of Spanish-language media to serve in an advocacy role, which led to its involvement in mobilizing those who participated in the immigration protests and the naturalization process. Second, there was also a significant change in the extent to which Latino organizations broadened their collaboration with Spanish-language media to seek to expand the pool of potential voters (that is, targeting the "recruits"). This unprecedented and sustained relationship between civic organizations and Spanish-language media assisted many eligible immigrants in navigating the cumbersome process of naturalization by reducing some of the information costs. As I noted in chapter 2, the 1960s civil rights movement experienced something similar with respect to black radio and African American newspapers and information diffusion, but what was unique and unprecedented was the role of non-English-language use, multicity coordination, and collaboration within and across multiple radio stations for both reactive mobilization and then proactive mobilization of legal permanent residents to pursue U.S. citizenship. Finally, I noted that there is still a significant segment of Latinos who are registered to vote but are less likely to go to the polls on election day. Their infrequent appearance at the polls can be a sign that they are "reticent"[9] and therefore not vested in the political system or that they are "neglected" because the political system has failed to do for them what political parties did for earlier waves of immigrants.[10] Irrespective of the cause of low turnout, Latino voter-mobilization efforts also evolved. Latino civic organizations had the foresight to target and expand efforts outreaching to low-propensity Latino voters. The growing willingness of national and local Latino organizations to embrace technological innovation in voter-outreach methods and the need for increased collaboration across organizations is a prime example of the necessary civic infrastructure that can be changed only through proactive mobilization. These three components of proactive mobilization help to determine the extent to which population growth yields growth in the electorate.

Beyond 2012: Outlook for Latino Political Salience in the States

At the start of the book, I proposed a typology of states based on their Latino population and electoral presence and growth. With respect to the electorate, California was one of three states classified as "Dynamic" because both the Latino voter-registration presence in 2010 and the rate of its growth from 1990 to 2010 were above the mean among the ten states I considered. The pace at which California shifted from a competitive two-party state in the mid–1990s to an overwhelmingly Democratic state in 2012 was not altogether expected. This transformation was primarily driven by two factors: moderation in white voter preferences; and the influx of new Latino voters who had previously not participated in politics. After the state's voters demonstrated a willingness to support a variety of statewide initiatives between 1994 and 1996 that targeted unauthorized immigrants, affirmative action, and bilingual education, a shift to the ideological center occurred, with voters demonstrating an aversion to extreme positions pursued by the right wing of the Republican Party (Bowler, Nicholson, and Segura 2006).[11] When combined with the influx of a more liberal bloc of new Latino voters, California's partisan outlook has shifted decidedly in favor of the Democratic Party. California demonstrates that the evolving Latino electorate can be politically salient not simply because it grew, but because of the changes in the composition, motivations, and preferences of the newly registered Latino voters. It is important to assess, based on incidence of proactive and reactive mobilization, whether other states are likely to experience similar transformations. I therefore focus on the outlook for Latino political salience in select states based on the four typologies: Dynamic, Emergent, Moderate, and Established. Three states—Florida, Arizona, and Nevada— deserve special consideration as they are the most likely cases, after California, where the evolving Latino state electorates will help shape the future of two-party politics. I also provide brief accounts of the evolving Latino electorate and state contexts in Colorado, New Mexico, and Texas.

Dynamic: Great Expectations in Florida and Arizona?

It is not surprising that Florida should be the center of attention with regard to the role of Latino voters in the future of party competition. There are key similarities between the Golden State and the Sunshine State. Like California, Florida is a large state, has a history of two-party politics, and is currently undergoing significant demographic change. Numerically, less than half as many Latinos are registered to vote in Florida than in California, but it is important to consider the proportion of the state electorate that is Latino. With this comparative metric in mind, the Latino electorate in Florida is slightly smaller than in California,[12] but has established a significant presence because of its broad support for Republican candidates and a willingness to support Democratic candidates in select elections. The 2008 and 2012 presidential elections reflected this pattern. However, questions remain as to whether Barack Obama's ability to win the majority of Latino voters in Florida for two consecutive elections is ephemeral behavior or if this portends a gradual change in party politics in the Sunshine State. The evolution of the Florida Latino electorate is not simply taking place on the state level, but also in local elections. As a result of the election in 2012, for example, a Latino Democrat represents the Miami area in Congress for the first time.

The evolution of Latino voters in the Miami area and the state of Florida is due to the proactive mobilization of non-Cuban Latinos who moved into the state, as well as the notable shift in voter preferences among second- and third-generation Latinos, including Cuban Americans. It is not just that civic organizations have helped immigrants through the naturalization process or sought to register new Latino voters, but also that the transmission of voter preferences between established Cuban American voters and their children has not been sufficiently robust to maintain the levels of support for Republican candidates.[13] The proactive mobilization has been complemented by further changes among the existing Latino voters. In particular, there is some evidence of reactive mobilization as evidenced by the response to perceived political attacks of the pan-ethnic Latino community among established Latino voters. For example, Republican leaders attempted to pass voter ID laws and state immigration legislation similar to Arizona's SB 1070. In reaction to these efforts, a Spanish-language radio campaign targeted Senator Anitere Flores and Representative Carlos López-Cantera, Latino Republican members of the state legislature who supported these immigration bills.

It is conceivable that the recent shift in support for Democrats among new and existing segments of Florida's Latino electorate can be partially attributed to candidate-specific appeals by Barack Obama. However, this explanation is incomplete because it fails to account for the notable Latino community reaction to perceived political threat. The prominence of Latino civic organizations in key population centers in the state facilitates greater capacity for proactive mobilization, as well as a possible synergy with a sense of Latino pan-ethnic solidarity around immigration policy and voter-access issues.[14] Greater Latino pan-ethnic identity and solidarity could prove even more consequential given the continued influx of voter-eligible Latinos from other states, the coming of age of U.S.-born Latinos, and the increasing number of Latino immigrants who naturalize. However, the issue of partisanship is more complicated in Florida because the partisanship of new Latino voters who have moved to Florida, such as Puerto Ricans, diverges significantly from established Latino voters in that they are more likely to identify with the Democratic Party. Young Latinos and new citizens have also demonstrated more affinity for the Democratic Party than the established Latino electorate, which previously consisted of a plurality of Cuban Americans. Combined, these new partisan proclivities could dilute (or mute) the effect of the Latino community's presence and pivotal-vote status if Latino voter preferences are more divided than the state as a whole.[15]

Arizona has been the epicenter of reactive mobilization in the United

States since 2006. Arizona's Latino community has responded not only to the immigration bill SB 1070, but also to efforts being made to disband raza studies (that is, Mexican American studies) in the Tucson Unified School District. This has led to even greater than expected solidarity and mobilization among both immigrants and U.S.-born Latinos. This sense of solidarity, however, has not resulted in increased political salience comparable to that witnessed in California in the mid–1990s. Arizona serves as a strong reminder that reactive mobilization is essential but not sufficient to transform the electoral relevance of Latino voters in a state. The civic infrastructure Latino organizations offered before the contentious political context was less established than in other states like California, Texas, Florida, and New York. As such, the level of proactive mobilization by well-resourced Latino organizations like Mi Familia Vota only began to establish firm ground after the 2006 immigration protest marches and subsequent elections.[16] Arizona's experience is distinct, and the lines between proactive and reactive mobilization may appear to be somewhat blurred. Since the 1990s, in other states with greater Latino civic infrastructure, the proactive mobilization by organizations gets a boost from the reactive mobilization. In the case of Arizona, not only did the Latino proactive mobilization get a boost, but it proved to be the catalyst for proactive mobilization to develop. This more closely parallels the experience in California, Texas, Illinois, New York, and Florida decades earlier, where many contemporary established Latino civic organizations that engage in proactive mobilization originated in the reactive mobilization of the late 1960s and 1970s.

In addition to Arizona's lack of well-resourced Latino organizations, Spanish-language radio has not had and does not have comparable presence in the state or in its most populous metropolitan areas. Whereas Spanish-language media played a significant role elsewhere in both the proactive mobilization of Latinos and capitalizing on the catalyst of reactive mobilization in the Latino community in 2006, this has not been the case in Arizona.[17] As of 2012, there are fewer than thirty Spanish-language radio stations in the state, and neither of its largest metro areas is ranked in the top ten media markets in the country. Phoenix does make it into the top fifteen media markets, but none of the three Spanish-language radio stations in the Phoenix metro area garners enough audience share to break into the top ten radio stations. However, this might not be as bleak as it might appear. As I indicated in chapter 2, in the years after the 2006 immigration protests, there was an increase in "corporatization" of the DJs because of the syndication to many cities. This has had a negative effect on the collaborations between local organizations, local stations, and local communities across many cities. Because KNAI ("Radio Campesina") is directly linked to the Cesar Chavez Foundation, its longevity and effectiveness may supersede Univision's KHOT.

Without all of the perceived population and organizational capacity advantages of Latinos in California, Florida, New York, and Texas, there are still great expectations that Arizona is likely to be the next state where Latinos can impact two-party competition at the state level. This process can be expedited if national Latino organizations work with local Latino organizations to enhance the civic infrastructure through proactive mobilization. There is a good foundation upon which a local-national collaboration between Latino organizations can build. Relative to other states, the growth in the Latino CVAP has kept pace with the growth in population since 2001. Whereas Latino populations in other states fare worse in rates of naturalization of the citizenship-eligible Latino population, this is less the case in Arizona. Increased availability of citizenship workshops would help maintain the current rates of naturalization once the perceived and real political threat associated with lack of citizenship in the state subsides. It is important to note that while the eligible pool of Latino voters is comparable to the proportion in California, the strong Republican preferences among the state's white voters often overwhelm the Democratic preferences among Latino voters in statewide elections.

The proactive mobilization by Latino organizations is essential to the vitality of Latino electorate because it plays an important role in reducing the barriers to participation.[18] However, two other factors are critical to determining when Latino voters in Arizona will be more politically relevant with respect to partisan competition. The first has to do with the demographic reality of young Latinos in an aging state. According to the latest population estimate, 37 percent of Latinos in Arizona are under the age of eighteen, which is significantly higher than the 18 percent among non-Hispanic whites. Conversely, only 8 percent of Latinos in Arizona are older than sixty years, which is much less than the 27 percent of non-Hispanic whites. Older Americans are more likely to vote than the younger citizens. Irrespective of income and education levels, it should therefore not be surprising that Latinos have lower rates of participation given that Latinos account for 43 percent of the population under eighteen but only 12 percent of those over sixty. In the short term, this means that non-Hispanic whites are more likely to vote, but it also means that the size of this segment of the electorate is contingent on the mortality of these aging white voters. The second critical factor that will affect the relevance of the Latino vote for elections outcomes has to do with whether there will be any moderation in the political behavior of the state's aging white population. The temporal nature of these two critical factors should encourage, rather than discourage, Latino organizations to pursue proactive mobilization because these will be more important to the long-term salience of Latinos once the political threat and subsequent reactive mobilization dissipate.

Emergent: Betting on Nevada's Latino Population?

More than any other state considered in this book, Nevada represents the state that has witnessed the most dramatic evolution of the state's Latino population and electorate with respect to trajectory and political salience for two-party competition since 1990. Recently, Nevada has leaned Democratic in presidential elections, and Latinos are credited with this dynamic outcome. However, the congressional delegation is split at both the House of Representatives and U.S. Senate. There is also a split within state politics as Democrats control both chambers of the state legislature, but there is a Republican governor (who is Latino).

In 2010 and 2012, many pundits and political campaigns were skeptical about the relevance of the state's Latino electorate or the significance of issues deemed important to the Latino community such as immigration. The "Emergent" label for the Latino electorate in Nevada is apt because there is a lot of untapped and nascent potential. Few analysts recognize that there are more Latino registered voters in Nevada than in New Mexico. It is also the case that the proportion of the state population that is Latino (27 percent) is greater than that of other states such as Colorado, Florida, Illinois, and New York. However, there is a lot of untapped potential as only 34 percent of the Nevada's Latino population is comprised of adult U.S. citizens. This is the lowest proportion of CVAP in the ten states considered.

The state partisan context further highlights the potential for Latinos to help shape party politics in Nevada. Given the contested nature of statewide elections in 2010 and 2012, the pivotal role of Latinos in specific elections was made apparent. Some of this was due to organized interest betting on the Latino electorate. There is some evidence of proactive mobilization, largely from labor unions and national pan-ethnic Latino organizations, but these have primarily focused on voter turnout. Long-term political salience will be more likely if proactive mobilization by civic organizations expands to address citizenship rates and voter registration of Latino CVAP, both of which lag behind other states. There is a lot of uncertainty about whether organized interests will continue to bet on the Latino community and invest in their long-term growth. The four-year period between 2008 and 2012 demonstrated that when mobilizing opportunities congeal, there can be greater effects. The antagonistic, anti-immigrant context ushered a mobilizing opportunity for Latino immigrants and their supporters. While the reactive mobilization spurred more interest in naturalization, it dissipated after Sharron Angle's failed bid to unseat U.S. Senator Harry Reid in 2010 and the election of the Nevada's first Latino governor. It is up to Latino organizations, including labor unions, to mobilize opportunities through greater proactive mobilization.

Moderate: Essential, yet Tenuous Nature of Latinos in Colorado

In their analysis of Colorado in the 2000 election, Hero and Jaramillo (2005) posed a significant question regarding Latino voters: Was the influence of Colorado's Latino voters in the elections more apparent than real or more real than apparent? Drawing on Guerra and Fraga's (1996) list of strategic and contextual conditions necessary for Latinos to be influential in statewide elections, Hero and Jaramillo conclude that Latino voter influence in Colorado was more real than apparent, but that it was more noticeable in state senate elections. They predicted that "the typically essential, yet frequently tenuous, nature of Latinos in Colorado politics is thus likely to become increasingly significant" (148). This essential, yet tenuous nature continues to describe the role of Latinos in the state two decade after the 1992 election. Rather than focus on strategic or contextual conditions necessary for impacting specific election outcomes, it becomes necessary to consider the relevance of proactive and reactive mobilization and the consequences for the distinct demographic profile of the state's Latino population and electorate.

Colorado is unique among southwestern states with respect to the proportion of the Latino community born in the United States. Nearly nine in ten of the state's Latino citizen voting-age population (CVAP) was born in the United States, a notable difference from the 75 percent average across the ten states considered throughout this book. The only state with a higher proportion of native-born Latino adult citizens is New Mexico at 92 percent (Motel and Patten 2012). One takeaway point from the analysis of the Latino CVAP is that the barriers to civic engagement among Latinos in Colorado are not primarily driven by immigrants and the citizenship hurdle. This claim is further substantiated by the fact that only about 92,000 Latino immigrants in Colorado have obtained legal permanent residence status since 1985. Of these immigrants, more than 21,000 had naturalized by 2010. This means that three in four LPRs have yet to pursue citizenship.

Proactive mobilization of citizen-eligible Latino immigrants may reduce the barriers to full participation, but Latino civic organizations should recognize that voter registration appears to be a larger hurdle for the evolving Latino electorate in Colorado. Less than half of the estimated 455,000 Latino CVAP population is registered to vote. Voter registration and voter mobilization, therefore, remain as politically promising mobilizing opportunities. The history of proactive mobilization in Denver and other cities has had episodic results with respect to presence and growth of the Latino electorate.

There is less history of reactive mobilization in response to political threat in Colorado. There have been isolated cases, such as efforts by former congressman Tom Tancredo to scapegoat immigrants and occasional efforts to use the statewide initiative. However, the state's elected officials have largely remained centrist with respect to immigration, and the state's voters rejected a statewide ballot initiative that would have done away with bilingual education. With reactive mobilization as an unlikely scenario, voter-registration drives and GOTV efforts will likely be the center-pieces of Latino civic organizations. Given the likely continuation of a competitive two-party context, proactive mobilization is more important in Colorado. Modest but steady growth in Latino voter participation has the potential to enhance their essential, yet tenuous role in party politics.

Established: The Unintended Consequences of Partisan Incorporation in New Mexico and Texas

Less than a decade ago, New Mexico was a very competitive two-party state. Latinos have helped turn this purple state into a trending blue state at the presidential level. Similarly, the congressional delegation is dominated by Democrats, with the lone Republican representing New Mexico's Second District. With respect to the state's party politics, there are more Democrats in both chambers of the state legislature, but there is a Republican governor. New Mexico is a particularly notable case in that there is a long history of political incorporation of Latinos in state politics. Latinos have served at every level of office, including governor, lieutenant governor, secretary of state, U.S. Senate, U.S. House of Representatives, and leadership in both state legislative chambers. Since 2010, Latinos represent the state as governor, lieutenant governor, House Speaker, majority leader of the state senate, and majority leader of the state House.[19] It is important to note that Latinos hold these leadership positions as Democrats and Republicans. In no other state have Latinos experienced the same level of descriptive representation.

Not only have Latinos achieved success in getting elected to New Mexico's highest offices, but the citizenship barrier for electoral participation is significantly lower than other states. As was the case in Colorado, a relatively small proportion of the state's Latino population is foreign-born. As such, proactive mobilization should be more straightforward, focusing on voter registration and voter mobilization. Although more than 500,000 Latino adults are eligible to register to vote, only 48 percent are actually registered, whereas this figure is almost 59 percent among non-Latinos. It is important to note that of the ten states considered, the rate of voter registration among non-Latinos is the lowest in New Mexico. Why Latino and non-Latino voter registration is lower there than other states is not readily apparent. Perhaps because Latinos have been embedded within the state's power structure, pan-ethnic Latino organizations have not flourished as much as they have in other states. While this relative lack of civic infrastructure outside of the party organizations helps explain why there are fewer organizations engaged in proactive mobilization of Latinos, it does not explain why there are lower rates of voter registration among non-Latinos.

It is difficult to forecast how the evolution and continued presence of the Latino electorate will impact two-party competition because New Mexico is so different from the other nine states. The lower registration rate of Latinos suggests the need for more proactive mobilization by Latino civic organizations. If proactive mobilization has not been robust, how likely is it that an exogenous shock will serve as a mobilizing opportunity and lead to reactive mobilization? Given the strong presence of Latino elites within the two-party system, it is not surprising that the political context in New Mexico has been less antagonistic toward Latinos. Moreover, because there is a smaller presence of immigrants and no statewide initiative process, there have also been fewer opportunities for legislation targeting immigrants as has been the case in California and Arizona.

In 2011, this established pattern changed when Republican lawmakers sought to change the law that allowed undocumented immigrants the opportunity to obtain driver's licenses. Having campaigned on a promise to change this practice, Susana Martinez, the first Latina governor in the United

States, has used her office to get a bill passed through the state House, despite Democratic control of the chamber. The state senate blocked this bill, with some pressure from immigrant rights activists. At the start of the new legislative session in 2013, Paul Pacheco, a Latino Republican state House representative, sponsored the measure backed by Governor Martinez, but it faces opposition by Democrats in both chambers and has continued to energize immigrant rights activists. The unintended consequences of partisan integration may be lower rates of electoral participation among Latino eligible voters, but recent changes in the political behavior of Republican lawmakers may result in *new* unintended consequences that may lead to reactive mobilization among the Latino community and Latino elected officials. Recent immigration restrictionist efforts may serve as a catalyst to activate eligible Latinos who may not have participated in electoral politics. It may be that instead of modest growth, more Latinos will become politically activated. This could benefit Democrats if more Latinos register to vote in response to perceived political threat. After the 2010 election of Susana Martinez, it was believed that Republicans could make inroads with Latino voters in New Mexico. Rather than attracting existing Latino voters, efforts to change the existing driver's license law appears to be having the opposite effect and may even lead to the influx of new Latino voters who view Republicans in a negative light.

Texas is a particularly challenging case to forecast because of the state's partisan history and uncertain partisan future. While the state population has a proportion of Latino registered voters comparable to that of California, the degree to which Latino voters are perceived to be politically salient and the other relevant factors in two-party politics are both distinct. The transformation of party politics in Texas began in 1980, when Republican presidential candidates began to win the state. Like many other states in the American South, it would take several elections before the Republican strength in national elections translated into success in the legislature and governorship. Although not fully politically incorporated, Latino voters and elected officials benefited from Democratic control in that they were able to gain some leverage and influence that was lacking in all other states except New Mexico. Throughout the 1970s and 1980s, many questioned why, despite similar presence in the state population, Latino presence in the pool of voters and the number of state legislators in California did not match the levels witnessed in Texas. One of the unintended consequences of partisan integration within the Texas Democratic Party in the 1970s and 1980s was that the Latino electorate and elected officials were seen as largely inconsequential when the dominance of the Democrats in the state legislature and governorship began to erode quickly after Democratic governor Ann Richards lost her reelection bid in 1994.[20] The sudden top-down partisan change in Texas had secondary unintended consequences for the evolving Latino electorate in the 1990s and 2000s. The proactive mobilization that was needed when the pool of eligible Latino voters grew during this period could not benefit from earlier integration into the Democratic Party because it was a sinking ship with minimal resources to grow its base of support.

The question remains, Why have Latinos in Texas not witnessed the levels of contemporary political influence evident in other "majority-minority" states in the continental United States? The fact that African Americans comprise a larger share of the population and pool of eligible minority voters in Texas should suggest that the portrait of the actual electorate would be more diverse because fewer minority voters face the citizenship hurdle than in California with its larger Latino and Asian immigrant population. Texas is a prime example that demography does not ensure a political destiny. The first major difference between these two states begins with the fact that non-Hispanic white voters in Texas are significantly more likely to be registered Republican and ideologically conservative. A consistently unified white electorate can overwhelm minority voter preferences. Not only is the profile of the electorate different, but there are institutional differences and variation in civic infrastructure.

As demonstrated in chapter 4, shortly before California became a "majority-minority" state in 2000, the political context there became particularly hostile to Latinos and immigrants in the mid–1990s. Why didn't this same pattern emerge in Texas in the years before it became a majority-minority state in 2010? The key difference is that the state does not have a statewide initiative process. In California, restrictionist immigration legislation was initiated and subject to direct democracy because Democratic lawmakers blocked attempts to do this through the state legislature. Despite dominating state politics since the late 1990s, Republicans in Texas have not pursued anti-immigration laws in the state legislature, and both Governor George W. Bush and Governor Rick Perry took more centrist stances with respect to immigration and education. Counterintuitively, the rise of conservatives and Republicans in the electorate has occurred at the same time that elected Republican lawmakers in Texas have held the line on extremism with respect to immigration legislation. This quasi-moderation among Republican elected officials has kept levels of reactive mobilization low among Latinos. Without this additional catalyst for mobilization among established Latino organizations, their proactive mobilization efforts have been less successful with respect to increasing naturalization rates or participation in elections.

The partisan political future in Texas is less certain and is contingent largely on demography *and* the mobilizing opportunities for its Latino population. First, there is a large pool of young U.S.-born Latinos who have not become activated into politics. It would be hard to argue against the untapped potential of this segment of the population should mobilization of opportunities be realized. Reliance on this segment of the population, and assuming stability of current partisan preferences by race and ethnicity, it is possible to envision gradual change in partisan preferences akin to a rolling realignment in ten to twenty years, when a sizable portion of these voters reach middle age and vote at higher rates. Another demographic issue has to do with the need to address the large Latino citizenship-eligible immigrant population that has not initiated the naturalization process. The presence of both the native-born and LPR population presents the Latino community with an opportunity to mobilize and bring them into the electorate. There is an established civic infrastructure in the Latino community to help address the lower rates of naturalization, registration, and voter turnout. Spanish-language media also has a strong presence and has the potential to cultivate interest in politics, where civic organizations have been less successful. This may not be a burden that only Latino elites address. In January 2013, it was suggested that national partisan forces may become involved in mobilizing the nonvoting segment of the population. According to public radio, Battleground Texas—a Washington-based group composed of strategists from the President Obama's reelection campaign—intends to invest tens of millions of dollars to convert Texas from a red state to a purple or blue state, drawing on the growing Latino population. Sylvia Manzano, a researcher at the polling firm Latino Decisions, warns that such mobilization may lead to countermobilization of and by Republicans. "So we can actually have more Republicans turn out when more Latinos, or more African-Americans, or more Democrats [turn out]" (Diaz 2013). These dynamics are what make forecasting the partisan context in Texas particularly challenging. It is important to question whether or not Democrats can succeed in making Texas more competitive. It is equally or more important to note that national and state demographic change may have finally shifted away from the detrimental effects of party competition, as described by Frymer (1999) and Kim (2007).

American Democracy and the Lasting Imprint of Latino Political Activation

The selected state outlooks, from dynamic to established, paint a complex but realistic picture of the future of two-party politics and the varied role of Latino organizational proactive mobilization and Latino voter reactive mobilization. The Latino population and its electoral presence (measured by the estimates of registered voters in each state) are the barometer with which to assess its political relevance. But presence is not enough. States with incidents of reactive mobilization have been instrumental in the overall growth of the voting eligible Latino community. While external political threat has served as a catalyst, or "mobilizing opportunity," it is also the case that Latino organizations, Spanish-language media, and elected officials have sought to "mobilize opportunities" where Latinos as residents, citizens, and voters become active and engaged in the U.S. political system not simply as a reaction to immediate threat, but by transcending the obstacles to participation.

What makes the 1990s and the first decade of the twenty-first century unique is that the proactive mobilization, measured by Latino organizational efforts to enhance civic infrastructure, converged with the reactive mobilization of Latinos as residents, citizens, and voters in response to contentious political contexts. Organizational efforts to reduce the barriers to participation are conscious attempts to mobilize opportunities, and the outcome of these efforts can be amplified by opportunities to mobilize prompted by exogenous political threat. I argue that both of these mobilizing opportunities are equally important to consider when identifying patterns of growth in the Latino electorate. The deviation from expected electoral behavior is not simply relevant for individual election outcomes but also for how this changes the electoral calculus within parties. While Latino political power is not path-dependent, reactive mobilization can jump-start that process in response to mobilizing opportunities in the form of political threat. Absent the threat, proactive mobilization can mobilize opportunities to activate Latino political empowerment. The nature of political incorporation of Latinos in American politics will continue to face challenges from within and from without, but it is an unambiguous indication of the health of American democracy, as has been the case with previous waves of immigrants and other excluded groups such as African Americans. Those who would limit Latino political participation are inherently limiting the capacity of the American polity to evolve as it always has: slowly, painfully, at times unevenly, but always toward greater inclusion. Latinos, therefore, should be seen as the current barometer by which we might measure the health of American democracy. The state-specific forms that Latino political activation and incorporation will take will determine this evolving electorate's lasting imprint on American democracy in the twenty-first century.

Notes

1. State Contexts, Mobilization, and the Evolving Latino Electorate

1. "Super Tuesday" took place on February 5, 2008, when twenty-three states held the Democratic Party primary.

2. Mitt Romney used the phrase "binders full of women" during the second U.S. presidential debate with President Barack Obama in an attempt to highlight how he sought to hire more women for top positions while he was governor of Massachusetts. The phrase went viral and became an Internet meme that Romney's political opponents would use to attack him.

3. Days before the 2012 election, Matt Barreto of Latinos Decisions echoed earlier observations made by Pachon and de la Garza (1998) about "Why Pollsters Missed the Latino Vote—Again!" Barreto (2012) highlights the historical misrepresentation of Latino voters by pollsters due primarily to the undersampling of Latino voters generally, but particularly to the undersampling of Spanish-dominant Latinos or neglecting to have bilingual interviewers.

4. U.S. Census Bureau, Statistical Abstract of the United States: 2012.

5. As I note later in this work, a state-centered approach recognizes the heterogeneity of the Latino population and inherently recognizes that there is not one "Latino Electorate" but fifty Latino electorates.

6. There were also segments of the population who arrived as guest workers during the Bracero Program. Some of these guest workers returned to their home country while others eventually settled in the United States.

7. The endogenous thresholds are those whose change is driven by the Latino population, whereas the exogenous thresholds are those external conditions such as competitive elections.

8. Pastor and Sanchez (2012) argue that the gap between the potential and actual rates of naturalization may be due to inadequate civic infrastructure to help immigrants through the naturalization process. While citizenship is one barrier addressed by proactive mobilization, it is not the only one.

9. See Félix (2008) for examples of Latino organizations that help immigrants through English as a Second Language (ESL) classes and Civics Exam preparation.

10. I use the mean presence and mean percentage growth as the cutoff in the X and Y axes.

11. California alone accounts for 2.5 million unauthorized immigrants.

12. This is based on the immigrants who became LPRs since 1985 (Center for the Study of Immigrant Integration [CSII], University of Southern California, 2011, LPR Status and Naturalization Data).

13. It is unclear what factors are most responsible for why otherwise eligible Latinos do not register to vote.

14. This drop in Latino descriptive representation can be partly attributed to unfavorable redistricting, but also to the inability to ensure that outgoing Latino elected officials were replaced by co-ethnics.

15. It is also the case that while Latinos in Florida comprise a significantly smaller percentage of the population, they benefit from relatively more influence than Latinos in Texas. In some states like Colorado and New York, Latino electoral presence has witnessed relatively modest growth over time.

16. The term "Hispanos" is often used to describe the Latino or Hispanic population in New Mexico.

17. There is a long-standing debate as to what are the most significant engines of partisan transformation. The explanations include change in party affiliation of existing voters (Erikson and Tedin 1981, 1986); elite cues about issues and ideology (Carmines and Stimson 1989; Carsey and Layman 2004); and the influx of new voters (Campbell 1985; Andersen 1979). These explanations are not inherently mutually exclusive. To the extent that Latinos have the potential to transform American politics, we must look to all three, but I focus primarily on the mobilization of Latinos as new voters.

18. The increasing participation at the polls as a result of perceived political threat should not be viewed as a panacea for mobilizing Latino electoral participation. The reality is that there were still significant segments of the established Latino electorate in California during the 1990s and throughout the United States in the middle of the first decade of the twenty-first century that were not mobilized by the context, and even among those who were, the initial effect appears to have diminished over time.

19. Given party neglect of those who are perceived to either not vote or not be able to be mobilized, Latino organizations did the heavy lifting that political machines and party organizations once did for other new electorates.

20. While southern states have been required to collect the racial category in voter registration, there are no such mechanisms outside the South. The only mechanism for blacks outside the South is via geography. For Latinos, both geography and Spanish surname allow for targeted mobilization with a high degree of precision as is evident by the sophistication developed by Latino nonpartisan organizations well before the surge in interest among political parties and campaigns to seek out Latino voters.

2. Mobilization *en Español*

1. HR 4437 is also known as the Sensenbrenner Bill after its sponsor, Wisconsin republican Jim Sensenbrenner.

2. The list of Los Angeles–based disc jockeys/*locutores* who came together included: Eduardo "El Piolin" Sotelo, Rocio Sandoval "La Peligrosa," and Marcela Luevanos (KSCA La Nueva 101.9FM); Renán Almendárez Coello "El Cucuy" and Mayra Berenice (KLAX La Raza 97.9FM); Ricardo "El Mandril" Sanchez (KBUE Que Buena 105.5FM); Francisco Galvez Pacorro (KRCD Recuerdo 103.9FM); Colo Barrera and Nestor Pato Rocha (KSSE Super Estrella 107.1FM); Omar Velasco (KLVE K-Love 107.5FM); Humberto Luna (KHJ La Ranchera 930AM); Hugo Cadelago and Gerardo Lorenz (KTNQ 1020AM).

3. As quoted in Uranga 2006. "March Against Immigrant Bill Expected to Attract Thousands," *Daily News of Los Angeles,* March 24.

4. On May 1, 2006, for instance, immigrant sympathizers boycotted Walmart in Zacatecas, the capital of Mexico's largest traditional migrant-sending state. In large part, this was

the result of conferences coordinated by local academics, government officials, and media to demonstrate their solidarity with Latino immigrant protesters in the United States. The author thanks Professors Miguel Moctezuma and Rodolfo García Zamora of Universidad Autónoma de Zacatecas for providing information.

5. As well as needing to consider whether there are long-term consequences from the decision by Spanish-language media to become involved in a political controversy.

6. See Wang and Winn (2011) and Fox and Bada (2011) for more on this lack of consensus.

7. Some pundits questioned the influence of Spanish-language radio because of the lower turnout in subsequent years. However, they focus too much on perceived shortcomings of Spanish-language radio rather than on how the levels of participation among a largely invisible minority presents a challenge to conventional wisdom and theories of democratic participation.

8. See also Zepeda-Millán (2011).

9. In the case of Dallas, the April 9 march by some accounts was unique in that the main source of local DJ support was from Mauricio Reinoso (a.k.a. "Mean Mauri"), whose morning show on a popular Tejano radio station mixed Spanish and English.

10. Many nonsyndicated DJs such as KSCA's "El Mandril" and KHJ's Humberto Luna were also instrumental, but they were arguably secondary figures, whereas "El Cucuy" and "Piolin" were much more central to the initial frames in the March 25 protest march in downtown Los Angeles.

11. Several immigrant organizations obtained the necessary march permits from the City of Los Angeles, and paid for banners, posters, water, portable toilets, and the use of the microphones and speakers. While it is unlikely that the turnout would have been as great without the help of the disc jockeys, the actual planning and implementation of the march could not have happened without established organizations and their leaders.

12. The literature about alternative media questions the ability of mass media to avoid the pressures to corporatize and become disconnected from the community.

13. The critiques of Spanish-language radio extended to 2007, when the immigrant demonstrations commemorating the May 1, 2006, protests were not as large.

14. The top five Spanish-language radio stations had a combined 8.9 million cumulative weekly listeners in 2009.

15. Increasingly, the formats have expanded to include not just Spanish-language programing but also programs and DJs that use both Spanish and English.

16. Banda music is a brass-based form of traditional Mexican music.

17. Similar to Nielsen Media Research on television audiences, Arbitron collects listener data on radio audiences in the United States and reports the percentages of the radio market share garnered by radio stations.

18. The different formats include: Mexican Regional, Spanish Adult Hits, Spanish Contemporary, Spanish News/Talk, Spanish Oldies, Spanish Religious, Spanish Sports, Spanish Tropical, Spanish Variety, Latino Urban, Spanish Other, and Tejano.

19. These include New York, Los Angeles, Chicago, San Francisco, Dallas–Fort Worth, and Houston-Galveston.

20. Rachel Osterman of the *Chicago Tribune* reported in 2003 that for the first time, two Spanish-language stations made it into the top ten in the Chicago radio market (July 19, 2003).

21. The one possibility of fully becoming part of the mainstream is through bilingual stations, such as KXOL (Latino 96.3 in Los Angeles), whose disc jockeys broadcast mainly in English, with some Spanglish, and play a variety of English and Spanish-language music.

22. These will likely go down in history as some of the most significant moments of protest politics ever held in the United States.

3. Defensive Naturalization and the Opportunity to Mobilize

1. HR 4437 (Sensenbrenner Bill) had provisions that would allow local law enforcement agencies to turn over undocumented immigrants to Immigration and Customs Enforcement and build a 350–mile wall along the U.S.-Mexican border; it also would make it a felony to knowingly assist any individual with illegal status (Gonzales 2009; Ramírez 2011; Lazos 2007).

2. The "We Are America" slogan also appeared in Spanish, but it was more prominent in English.

3. Seventy-five percent of the IRCA population was born in Mexico (Rytina 2002:3).

4. Cuban-origin Latinos appear to be an exception to this. In fact, they have among the higher rates of naturalization and the least time lag between legal entry and citizenship, especially for those who immigrated before 1980.

5. This is now the Office of Immigration Statistics at the Department of Homeland Security.

6. Previously, this fee applied only to those who had to replace lost or stolen cards. From this point on, legal residents will incur the card replacement cost every ten years. The key point is simply that, one way or another, Latino legal residents had to pay a fee. Beyond the other benefits incurred by citizenship, a simple cost-benefit analysis would suggest a preference for a one-time fee versus recurring fees and time spent on the replacement process.

7. The contentious political context initiated by Proposition 187 was intensified by Propositions 209 and 227 in 1996 and 1998 respectively. See chapter 4 for specifics about Propositions 209 and 227.

8. See Balistreri and Van Hook (2004).

9. This is 100,000 fewer than the estimated 8,250,000 LPRs who were eligible to naturalize on January 1, 2006.

10. The citizenship application fee was $95 until December 1998 but is now $595.

11. The new citizenship test took effect for those who applied after October 1, 2008.

12. The average number of "pending" applications per fiscal year between FY 1993 and FY 2004 was 826,037. This is a significant increase from the 124,951 average per fiscal year between 1980 and 1992.

13. Of all identifiable outcomes per fiscal year, there is a noticeable increase in the percentage of applications that have been classified as "denied" since 1993. Between 1925 and 1992, the "denied" applications always comprise less than 10 percent, and the average for these fiscal years is 2.8 percent. The average rate of "denied" applications between 1993 and 2006 is 18.42 percent. It is noteworthy that this starts prior to 9–11.

14. There are other nationally representative surveys of Latinos, but they were collected more than five years before or after the demonstrations or tend to focus on Latino voters.

15. The Ya Es Hora campaign is a collaboration of civic organizations and Spanish-language media conglomerates that included the Mi Familia Vota Education Fund; National Association of Latino Elected and Appointed Officials (NALEO) Educational Fund; National Council of La Raza (NCLR); Service Employees International Union (SEIU); Entravision Communication Corporation; impreMedia LLC; Univision Communications; and approximately four hundred local civic organizations.

16. There was a limited fee of approximately thirty dollars.

17. The survey results are based on the responses of participants to questions about their attitudes toward the naturalization process. In order to determine actual naturalization rates, one must examine aggregate data. However, these data would not include all who initiated but failed to complete the process, nor would it include the total number of residents who were eligible to naturalize.

18. Aggregate data collected prior to 2003 were either incomplete or organized in a manner that did not allow for cross-year comparisons.

19. The average naturalization process takes over a year to complete. Since the majority of the marches took place between March 2006 and May 2006, the impact of the marches on completed naturalizations would not be evident until 2007.

20. The level of organizational and media presence was self-reported by YEH partnering organizations, prior to calculating the percentage of Latino naturalizations or levels of growth.

21. Between 2003 and 2008, the metropolitan areas with a majority of Latino naturalizations were El Paso, TX; Miami–Fort Lauderdale–Pompano Beach, FL; San Antonio, TX; Ventura-Oxnard-Thousand Oaks, CA; and Riverside–San Bernardino–Ontario, CA. By 2008, this list also included Fresno, CA; Phoenix-Mesa-Scottsdale, AZ; Los Angeles–Long Beach–Santa Ana, CA; San Diego–Carlsbad–San Marcos, CA; Houston–Sugar Land–Baytown, TX; and Las Vegas–Paradise, NV.

22. Only three metropolitan areas witnessed a greater than 55 percent increase in the average number of non-Latino naturalizations in 2007–8, as compared to the average in the preceding four years. In no instance did the non-Latino growth reach 100 percent.

23. Beyond the direct effects of political context and YEH Ciudadania on the naturalization rates, there appears to be a multiplier effect of mobilization. Over a third of respondents indicated that a friend or family had applied for citizenship since their own application for citizenship, and 97 percent of respondents indicated that they were "somewhat likely" or "very likely" to encourage family members or friends to pursue citizenship.

24. For many applicants, the high application fee continues to be a significant barrier to naturalization. The survey results showed that even individuals who were able to successfully complete the naturalization process had to find outside sources of financial assistance to pay for the process or save money in order to apply. Given the relatively lower incomes of Hispanic immigrants, high application fees have a disproportionately adverse impact on Latino naturalization applicants. The financial hurdles encountered by many immigrants who are eligible for naturalization make it imperative to provide potential applicants with information about the fee waiver process, administered by USCIS, so that citizenship does not remain an impossible goal for those with limited means. There is a fee waiver process administered by USCIS that is often overlooked.

4. The Changing California Voter

I am very grateful to the Tomás Rivera Policy Institute for use of the data. I am indebted to Rob Van Houweling for his assistance with the data and to Luis R. Fraga, Gary M. Segura, and Dominique Apollon for their helpful comments and suggestions.

1. By 2005, Texas had also become a majority-minority state.

2. State officials said births, not immigration, were responsible for more than 2 million of the new Latinos.

3. The percentage of Asian Americans in the state increased from 9.1 percent in 1990

to 10.8 percent in 2000. While the actual number of African Americans increased marginally from 1990 to 2000, their percentage of the population decreased from 7 percent to 6.4 percent.

4. As is the case with any explanation of political change, this chapter cannot fully account for all of the changes that have taken place. Rather, its purpose is to complement and supplement analyses of other changes, as well as other empirical explanations of nonelectoral political behavior that impacted California's Latino population.

5. California is an excellent choice for a case study for various reasons. First, it is the state with the greatest overall number of Latinos. Second, only in New Mexico do Latinos comprise a larger percentage of the state population (42.1%) or electorate (32%). For further discussion about why it is appropriate to focus on California when discussing the repercussions of increased population and electoral participation among Latinos, see Ramírez and Fraga (2008).

6. It was reported that the pro–Proposition 187 campaign had an outstanding debt of $297,691. In contrast, the anti–Proposition 187 camp (which included the California Teachers Association and Univision) raised and spent more than $1 million for their media campaign.

7. In 1994, the Republicans ran on a platform of scaling back government and tax reform, with the "Contract With America," which gave the GOP control of the U.S. House of Representatives for the first time in forty years. However, Democrats managed to retain the edge in California congressional delegation, 27–25.

8. Democrats recaptured a majority in the state assembly and the governor's office in 1996 and 1998, respectively. From 1998 until 2003, Democrats held majorities in both chambers of the legislature and the governor's office.

9. One of these new Latino legislators in 1996 was Republican Rod Pacheco. Three other Latino Republicans would join him in the state assembly in 1998.

10. There is no systematic body of literature on Latino political participation before the 1989 LNPS. There has been a dramatic increase in national surveys with a representative sample of Latinos, but as is the case among mainstream studies of political behavior, they are based on self-reported turnout. For notable exceptions, see Barreto, Segura, and Woods (2004), which is based on the universe of registered voters, but is only of Latino voters in Southern California.

11. The median age of Latinos is lower than the rest of the population. With regards to educational attainment, 44.5 percent of Latinos have less than a high school education compared to 16.2 percent for non-Hispanic whites (U.S. Census 1998).

12. See Highton and Burris (2001:3–4), for a more complete discussion of the inadequate sample of Latinos in national studies of participation and the resulting complications.

13. Standard theoretical literature on voting participation has focused very little on Latinos, in general, and even less on differences among Latinos like national origin, regional differences, and patterns among naturalized versus native-born, and registration cohort.

14. Those of Cuban origin had higher registration and turnout rates than other Latinos and even outperformed non-Hispanic whites.

15. See Fraga and Ramírez (2004) for a fuller discussion of California's exceptionalism as compared to other Latino-influence states.

16. Using a three-wave panel of young adults surveyed in 1965, 1973, and 1982, Jennings (1987) compares college-educated protesters ("protest generation") to college-educated nonprotesters.

17. They make reference to these years because this was when the greatest increase in naturalization and Latino electoral participation occurred, and they attribute this growth—

primarily in California—to the politicized climate instigated by Propositions 187 (in 1994) and 209 (in 1996).

18. There was increasing affiliation with Democrats among these groups during this time.

19. Although very insightful about actual voter behavior, especially about the turnout patterns of Latino registration cohorts, Barreto and Woods do not distinguish between native-born and naturalized Latinos. Also, only a longitudinal analysis of these voters over the next several election cycles could determine whether the Democratic advantage gained by this Latino registration cohort can be sustained.

20. Proposition 187 limited the access that undocumented workers had to public education, social services, and health care. It also imposed state penalties for the use, forging, and distribution of false residency documents. Proposition 209 severely limited the use of affirmative action programs. It outlawed the use of race and ethnicity in admissions to state colleges and universities, as well as in the awarding of contracts by state agencies and sub-state governments. Proposition 227 effectively eliminated the use of bilingual instruction in California public schools. Under this law, bilingual instruction was limited to one year for all students, regardless of language ability. Parents could petition for exceptions.

21. The causal relationship has been based primarily on anecdotes or aggregate-level analysis of increased naturalization and registration rates among Latinos. I argue in this chapter that the empirical analysis of individual voter behavior of Latinos does support the causal relationship between increased participation and salient political events.

22. See Alvarez and Butterfield (1998) for greater detail about the change in registration and participation rates among Latinos in California.

23. Among Latinos, 19.9 percent were foreign-born in 1970, 28.6 percent in 1980, and 35.8 percent in 1990 (Gibson and Lennon 1999).

24. DeSipio (1996:144–51) discusses the increasing bureaucracy and formal naturalization requirements involved in the administration and process of naturalization that may act as impediments for higher rates of naturalization. Prior to 1906, the process, guidelines, and administration were largely the responsibility of the states and local courts. The quest for a more standardized and fair process has centralized the process, greatly increasing the role of the national government and bureaucracy. The *Washington Post* reported that Latinos want to naturalize but were deterred by the cumbersome naturalization process (Pan 2000). Lower levels of educational attainment and lower incomes among Latinos compound the situation. Aside from the bureaucratic maze and the possible effects of SES, another source of delays among Latinos is the proximity of country of origin to the United States (see Bouvier 1996, especially the conclusion). Obviously, Latinos are not the only ones for whom naturalization does not appear to be an immediate necessity. Accessibility to the home country could be the reason why among all immigrants, Canadians are the least likely to naturalize, followed by those born in Mexico. Given that Mexicans constitute the largest segment of all Latinos, it is reasonable that their low rates of naturalization are largely due to the percentage they constitute of Latino legal residents.

25. First introduced by Brody (1978), this puzzle describes how turnout has steadily declined since the 1960s, yet "paradoxically, the best predictors at the microlevel—age, education, and income—have increased during the same period" (Tam Cho 1999:1140).

26. For a fuller discussion of the political context associated with Propositions 187, 209, and 227 and its impact on political participation of Latinos who naturalized in the 1990s, see Pantoja, Ramírez, and Segura (2001:10–12), who make a strong case for the effects of a politicized climate on naturalization and turnout rates. Although they agree that registration and turnout among Latinos has increased, Alvarez and Nagler contend that they "find

no clear sign that any of these proposition campaigns played a direct role in Latino voter mobilization during the 1990's" (1999:13). However, Alvarez and Nagler's analysis does not distinguish between native-born and naturalized, and neglects the possible differences in turnout between those who were already part of the electorate before the propositions and those who first registered during this political climate.

27. See Shaw, de la Garza, and Lee (2000) for more details on survey method and design.

28. Although registration dates were readily available, voting records in most counties went back to 1990, but records from the Los Angeles County Registrar of Voter went back only to 1992. Since about 40 percent of the sample was drawn from Los Angeles (to match the percentage of California Latino voters in this county), the longitudinal scope of this analysis was adjusted to 1992–2000, rather than the preferred span of 1990–2000. Still, this allows for a longitudinal perspective about Latino voting patterns that has been absent from previous research. In this analysis, I use turnout only from 1996–2000 because of the sizable increase in registered voters that took place after 1994, and because I wanted to test for lasting effects of the politicized climate between 1994 and 1996.

29. The resulting dataset is unique in that it allows me to simultaneously incorporate the advantages inherent to both surveys of political participation and panel surveys without the problems associated with these same studies such as misreporting of voter turnout (Shaw, de la Garza, and Lee 2000; Presser and Traugott 1992) and sample attrition (Aneshensel et al. 1990), respectively. In other words, this dataset allows for an accurate account of voter turnout over several elections. As I discuss in greater detail later, having knowledge of the date of first registration and current voting status (e.g., inactive, cancelled, new registrant, reregistered) allows for an understanding of proportionality of turnout (given the total years of eligibility) and even more innovation when selecting the dependent variable.

30. The only exception is when the dependent variable is a "super-voter," which describes those who voted in at least 75 percent of the elections for which they were eligible (for example, three of four, or six of eight elections). If this was the case, it was coded (1); and (0) otherwise.

31. The remaining 19.6 percent of naturalized Latinos did not report year of naturalization.

32. I chose to simply include the dichotomous variable of naturalization, as opposed to one that focused on naturalization cohort for two reasons. First, although Pantoja, Ramírez, and Segura (2001), using the same data, found that the turnout of newly naturalized Latinos outpaces that of long-term naturalized or native-born, I believe that the incorporation of registration cohort, and the interaction between the two variables, more directly captures the mobilization that they suggest occurred in response to Proposition 187 and Proposition 209. Furthermore, including naturalization as a dichotomous variable, without the naturalization cohort, increases the total number of cases observed because I was also able to include in the analysis those respondents who did not give date of naturalization. Furthermore, using registrar of voters information, I was able to determine nativity of those respondents who refused to answer the naturalization question, and therefore include them in the analysis.

33. Although Highton and Burris (2002) find that national Latino turnout among the naturalized must consider the length of residence in the United States, I do not feel that the predictive capability of this model is significantly compromised by the omission of the length of U.S. residence variable—which was not available in the Tomás Rivera Institute's 1997 survey.

34. None of the other control variables reached customary levels of significance.

35. See Ramírez and Fraga (2008) for details on the limits of Latino statewide influence.

36. Although "age" had the biggest change in predicted probability, this represents the increased likelihood of voting when increasing the age from 18 to 80 years old.

37. Once again, the one exception is the 2000 primary election.

38. Political incorporation has three descriptive dimensions: electoral, representational, and policy-based. It is defined as the extent to which group interests are articulated, represented, and met in public policy making. For more on the analytical conceptualization of political incorporation, see Ramírez and Fraga (2008); and Browning, Marshall, and Tabb (1984).

39. There is anecdotal evidence that Latinos now comprise a large percentage of the members in labor unions in California. Individual Latinos are also reaching the highest elective posts in powerful unions in California, but especially in Los Angeles County, as evidenced by the election of Miguel Contreras as the executive secretary treasurer of the Los Angeles County Federation of Labor in 1996.

5. Voice of the People

1. Particularized mobilization can range from self-reported contact by a political party or organization to "specific requests of individuals to participate in particular types of activities such as campaigning, contacting government officials, or getting involved in local politics" (Leighley 2001:102).

2. The 2001 Tomás Rivera Policy Institute postelection survey in California, Florida, Illinois, New York, and Texas found that fewer than one in three Latino registered voters reported being contacted.

3. Two related articles in the *New York Times Magazine* refer to the increased precision of targeting subpopulations based on consumer data as "microtargeting" (Bai 2004) and more recently "'nanotargeting'—microtargeting to the nth degree" (Edsall 2012).

4. Osborn, McClurg, and Knoll (2010) find that increased turnout, which they attribute to "mobilization" of voters, did help ensure Obama's victory. However, their analysis does not directly measure the effect of elite mobilization, but instead a "turnout effect" which does not distinguish between those who voted because of increased interest in the election.

5. Likely voters were defined as those who had voted in at least two of the last four elections. Unlikely voters would therefore be those who voted in only one or none of the previous four elections.

6. Of the total attempted, 35,853 Latino voters resided in Los Angeles County, and 16,462 resided in Orange County.

7. The commercial vendor was able to (1) update the addresses by cross-referencing against the National Change of Address registry (NCOA) and other consumer data-bank sources, therefore identifying individuals who had moved out of state; (2) correct any missing or incorrect address information such as address numbers, apartment numbers, or incorrect zip codes; (3) enhance the deliverability of the direct mail by appending Zip+4 numbers; and (4) verify phone numbers already in the voter files and obtain phone numbers for those records without a listed phone.

8. It is important to note that New York and Harris County did receive phone calls, but it was not possible to measure the effects of live calls on turnout because there was no control group.

9. The distinct sites were Maricopa and Pima Counties in Arizona; in California, it was Kern, Riverside, San Bernardino, San Diego, and Los Angeles Counties, as well as the cities of Garden Grove and Santa Ana; Orange and Miami-Dade Counties in Florida; Long Island and New York City in the New York; in Texas, this included the Dallas–Fort Worth Metro Area, El Paso and Harris Counties, and the Rio Grande Valley.

10. There are multiple factors driving the lower voting propensity among some Latino voters. Since, the year 2000, NALEO has sought to increase Latino likelihood of voting and makes a concerted effort to target these "low-propensity voters." For the descriptive characteristics of these voters, see the target universe selection criteria.

11. Discussions of California's politicized climate focus on the passage of two statewide ballot initiatives. In 1994, Proposition 187 limited the access that undocumented workers had to public education, social services, and health care. In 1996, Proposition 209 outlawed the use of race and ethnicity in admissions to state colleges and universities, as well as in the awarding of contracts by state agencies and substate governments.

12. These include percent Latino, percent white, percent homeowner, percent with at least a high school degree, household income, family income, percent below poverty line, percent monolingual English speakers, percent of the population 60 years or older, percent foreign-born.

13. Michelson's (2005) Latino sample was 764 (466 received treatment and 298 did not). While the live call experiments conducted by Ramirez (2005) included more than 50,000 voters, only 3 percent of the voters were assigned to the control group.

6. The Evolving Latino Electorate and the Future of American Politics

1. In the weeks leading up to the election, the *Guardian,* the *Washington Post,* and other mainstream media posited that enthusiasm about the election was lower among Latinos and would likely lead to lower voter turnout (Pilkington 2012). The Pew Hispanic Center also alluded to a possible drop in turnout based on lower levels of self-reported certainty about voting in the election among Latino voters (Lopez and Gonzalez-Barrera 2012).

2. In their analysis, Kopicki and Irving (2013) focused on vote totals in nine swing states, the estimated size of the state Latino electorate, and the reported patterns of vote choice among Latino voters.

3. This was also the moment when quotas were imposed on Western Hemisphere migrants—for the first time in history—disproportionately impacting Mexican migrants and leading to the era of undocumented migration (De Genova 2004).

4. Latinos and Asian Americans account for 46.84 percent and 13.39 percent of the total growth respectively.

5. According to exit polls in 2012, 80 percent of nonwhite voters reported voting for Barack Obama, whereas less than 20 percent supported Mitt Romney.

6. As discussed in chapter 4, Proposition 187 was seen as an anti-immigrant and anti-Latino statewide initiative that spurred greater rates of naturalization and participation among Latino voters who registered to vote during this contentious period. Because of Pete Wilson's strong association with Proposition 187, pundits and activists also referenced the mobilization that took place as the "Pete Wilson effect."

7. A supermajority, or two-thirds of each chamber, is needed to pass the state budget or overturn a gubernatorial veto.

8. The last time Democrats held a supermajority in both houses was in 1883.

9. According to DeSipio (1996), "reticents" are those Latinos who are registered but don't turn out.

10. A simple comparison of rates of reported contact over the last twenty years suggests that Latinos (and Asian Americans) have been overlooked by party and candidate campaigns.

11. The moderation was most robust among the state's white voters. Similarly, the expanded Latino presence impacted the political calculation of the centrist Republican elites.

12. Latinos comprise 16 percent of the registered voters in Florida and 22 percent of the registered voters in California.

13. Even some Cuban American personalities who had previously refrained from endorsing presidential candidates supported and endorsed Obama. These included the talk-show host Christina Saralegui and the singer and producer Gloria Estefan.

14. It is important to note that the civic infrastructure among Latino community varies throughout the state and is significantly stronger in the Miami-Dade Metropolitan Area.

15. It is unlikely that there will be a growth in the number of Republican-leaning Cuban Americans because newer cohorts of immigrants have not been as strongly supportive of Republicans, and second- and third-generation Cuban Americans are more similar to non–Cuban American Latinos. It is also possible that if there were a retrenchment and support increased for Republicans among white voters and the elderly, this would further dilute the salience of Latino voters.

16. There is a long presence of Mexican Americans in Arizona and a legacy of Chicano identity stemming from the 1960s and 1970s. This strong presence, however, did not result in large statewide organizations, as measured by monetary resources or membership. Moreover, national Latino organizations developed in California, Texas, New York, and Washington, D.C., because those had larger Latino populations or were more proximate to the headquarters of other civic and nonprofit organizations.

17. It would be unfair to the current status of Spanish-language radio in Arizona to be completely dismissive of KNAI "Radio Campesina," which does receive a significant share of the Spanish-language radio market. However, Spanish-language radio simply did not play as prominent a role in Arizona in 2006 as it did in LA, Chicago, Dallas, etc.

18. The three years leading up to the 2016 election will be determinative on the proactive mobilization side. It is more likely that the electoral presence of Latinos matters if sufficient organizational resources are expended to capitalize on the political activation of Latinos by increasing rates of naturalization, voter registration, and turnout.

19. There are more Latino elected officials in the Democratic Party, but there is an established record of Latino Republican leaders as well, including the current governor, Susana Martinez, and the former congressman Manuel Lujan Jr., who represented New Mexico for twenty years.

20. Democrats lost control of the state senate in 1996 and lost every other statewide race in 1998. By 2002, Republicans had also gained control of the state House.

References

Aarts, Kees, and Holli Semetko. 2003. "The Divided Electorate: Effects of Media Use on Political Involvement." *Journal of Politics* 65, no. 3: 759–84.

Abrajano, Marisa A., and R. Michael Alvarez. 2010. *New Faces, New Voices: The Hispanic Electorate in America*. Princeton, NJ: Princeton University Press.

Allen, Oliver E. 1993. *The Tiger: The Rise and Fall of Tammany Hall*. New York: Addison-Wesley.

Alvarez, Michael R., and Tara L. Butterfield. 1998. "Citizenship and Political Representation in Contemporary California." California Institute of Technology Social Science Working Paper 1041. Pasadena.

Alvarez, Michael R., and Jonathan Nagler. 1999. "Is the Sleeping Giant Awakening? Latinos and California Politics in the 1990's." Paper presented and the Annual Meeting of the Midwest Political Science Association, Chicago.

Andersen, Kristi. 1979. *The Creation of a Democratic Majority, 1928–1936*. Chicago: University of Chicago Press.

Aneshensel, Carol S., Rosina M. Becerra, Eve P. Fielder, and Roberleigh H. Schuler. 1990. "Onset of Fertility-Related Events during Adolescence: A Prospective Comparison of Mexican American and Non-Hispanic White Females." *American Journal of Public Health* 80, no. 8: 959–63.

Arbitron. 2007. *Arbitron Report: Hispanic Radio Today: How America Listens to Radio, 2007 Edition*.

———. 2010. *Arbitron Report: Hispanic Radio Today: How America Listens to Radio, 2010 Edition*.

———. 2011. *Arbitron Report: Hispanic Radio Today: How America Listens to Radio, 2011 Edition*.

Associated Press. 2006. "Marching Orders Issued in Spanish." March 29, 2006.

Bada, Xóchitl, Jonathan Fox, and Andrew Selee, eds. 2006. "Invisible No More: Mexican Migrant Civic Participation in the United States." Woodrow Wilson International Center for Scholars. www.wilsoncenter.org/mexico.

Bahadur, Gaiutra. 2006. "Workers Step from Shadows." *Philadelphia Inquirer*, February 15, A1.

Bai, Matt. 2004. "The Multilevel Marketing of the President." *New York Times Magazine*, April 25.

Baines, Paul R. 1999. "Voter Segmentation and Candidate Positioning." In *Handbook of Political Marketing*, edited by Bruce I. Newman. Thousand Oaks, CA: Sage.

Balistreri, Kelly, and Jennifer Van Hook. 2004. "The More Things Change the More They

Stay the Same: Mexican Naturalization before and after Welfare Reform." *International Migration Review* 38: 113–30.

Banfield, Edward C., and James Q. Wilson. 1963. *City Politics*. Cambridge: Harvard University Press.

Barlow, William. 1998. *Voice Over: The Making of Black Radio*. Philadelphia: Temple University Press.

Barreto, Matt. 2005. "Latino Immigrants at the Polls: Foreign-born Voter Turnout in the 2002 Election." *Political Research Quarterly* 58: 79–86.

———. 2012. "Why Pollsters Missed the Latino Vote––2012 Edition." *Latino Decisions*. October 23. www.latinodecisions.com/blog/2012/10/23/why-pollsters-missed-the-latino-vote-2012-edition/.

Barreto, Matt A., Loren Collingwood, and Sylvia Manzano. 2010. "Measuring Latino Political Influence in National Elections." *Political Research Quarterly* 63: 4.

Barreto, Matt A., Sylvia Manzano, Ricardo Ramírez, and Kathy Rim. 2009. "Mobilization, Participation, and Solidaridad: Latinos during the 2006 Immigration Protest Rallies." *Urban Affairs Review* 44, no. 5: 736–64.

Barreto, Matt A., Ricardo Ramírez, Luis Fraga, and Fernando Guerra. 2010. "Why California Matters: How California Latinos Influence Presidential Elections." In *Beyond the Barrio: Latinos in the 2004 Elections,* edited by Rodolfo de la Garza, Louis DeSipio, and David Leal. Notre Dame: University of Notre Dame Press.

Barreto, Matt A., Ricardo Ramírez, and Nathan D. Woods. 2005. "Are Naturalized Voters Driving the California Electorate? Measuring the Effect of IRCA Citizens on Latino Voting." *Social Science Quarterly* 86, no. 4: 792–811.

Barreto, Matt A., Gary M. Segura, and Nathan D. Woods. 2009. "The Mobilizing Effect of Majority-Minority Districts on Latino Turnout." *American Political Science Review* 98, no. 1: 65–75.

Barreto, Matt A., and Nathan Woods. 2005. "The Anti-Latino Political Context and Its Impact on GOP Detachment and Increasing Latino Voter Turnout in Los Angeles County." In *Diversity in Democracy: Minority Representation in the United States,* edited by Gary Segura and Shawn Bowler. Charlottesville: University of Virginia Press.

Bass, Loretta E., and Lynne M. Casper. 1999. "Are There Differences in Registration and Voting Behavior between Naturalized and Native-born Americans?" U.S. Census Bureau, Population Division Working Paper No. 28. www.census.gov/population/www/documentation/twps0028/twps0028.html.

Beck, Paul Allen, and M. Kent Jennings. 1979. "Political Periods and Political Participation." *American Political Science Review* 73, no. 3: 737–50.

———. 1982. "Pathways to Participation." *American Political Science Review* 76, no. 1: 94–108.

Beltrán, Cristina. 2010. *The Trouble with Unity: Latino Politics and the Creation of Identity*. New York: Oxford University Press.

Bennion, Elizabeth A. 2005. "Caught in the Ground Wars: Mobilizing Voters during a Competitive Congressional Campaign." *Annals of the American Academy of Political and Social Science* 601: 123–41.

Bouvier, Leon. 1996. *Embracing America: A Look at Which Immigrants Become Citizens*. Washington, DC: Center for Immigration Studies.

Bowler, Shaun, and David M. Farrell. 1992. *Electoral Strategies and Political Marketing*. New York: St. Martin's.

Bowler, Shaun, Stephen P. Nicholson, and Gary Segura. 2006. "Earthquakes and Aftershocks: Tracking Partisan Identification amid California's Changing Political Environment." *American Journal of Political Science* 50, no. 1: 146–59.

Bowler, Shaun, and Gary Segura. 2011. *The Future Is Ours: Minority Politics, Political Behavior, and the Multiracial Era of American Politics.* Washington, DC: Congressional Quarterly Press.

Braungart, Richard G., and Margaret M. Braungart. 1986. "Life-Course and Generational Politics." *Annual Review of Sociology* 12: 205–31.

Bravender, Robin. 2012. "Obama Spanish Language Ad Blitz Aims to Wrap up Latino Vote." *Politico.* July 1. www.politico.com/news/stories/0612/78036.html.

Browning, Rufus P., Dales Rogers Marshall, and David H. Tabb. 1984. *Protest Is Not Enough: The Struggle of Blacks and Hispanics for Equality in Urban Politics.* Berkeley: University of California Press.

Brulliard, Karin. 2006. "'A True Believer in Immigration': The Rev. José E. Hoyos." *Washington Post,* September 20.

Butler, David, and Austin Ranney, eds. 1992. *Electioneering: A Comparative Study of Continuity and Change.* New York: Oxford University Press.

Caldeira, Gregory A., Aage R. Clausen, and Samuel C. Patterson. 1990. "Partisan Mobilization and Electoral Participation." *Electoral Studies* 9: 191–204.

Caldeira, Gregory A., Samuel C. Patterson, and Gregory A. Markko. 1985. "The Mobilization of Voters in Congressional Elections." *Journal of Politics* 47: 490–509.

Calvo, Maria Antonia, and Steven J. Rosenstone. 1989. *Hispanic Political Participation.* San Antonio, TX: Southwest Voter Research Institute.

Campbell, James E. 1985. "Sources of the New Deal Realignment: The Contributions of Conversion and Mobilization to Partisan Change." *Western Political Quarterly* 38: 357–76.

Carlton, Jim. 2008. "Clinton Courts Hispanics for Crucial Super Tuesday." *Wall Street Journal,* March 11.

Carsey, Thomas M., and Geoffrey C. Layman. 2004. "Policy Balancing and Preferences for Party Control of Government." *Political Research Quarterly* 57, no. 4: 541–50.

Casper, Lynne M., and Loretta E. Bass. 1998. "Current Population Reports," pp. 20–504, Voting and Registration in the Election of November 1996. Census Bureau, U.S. Department of Commerce, Economics and Statistics Administration.

Carmines, Edward G., and James A. Stimson. 1989. *Issue Evolution: Race and the Transformation of American Politics.* Princeton, NJ: Princeton University Press.

Castañeda Paredes, Mari. 2003. "The Transformation of Spanish-Language Radio in the U.S." *Journal of Radio Studies* 10: 5–16.

Center for the Study of Immigrant Integration (CSII), University of Southern California. 2011. LPR Status and Naturalization Data (raw data originally provided by the Office of Immigration Statistics, Citizenship and Immigration Services).

Challet, Anna. 2012. "Ethnic Voters to Determine California's Political Course." *New American Media.* November 3. www.newamericamedia.org/2012/11/field-poll-ethnic-voters-to-determine-californias-political-course.php.

Cohen, Cathy. 1999. *The Boundaries of Blackness: AIDS and the Breakdown of Black Politics.* Chicago: University of Chicago Press.

Crotty, William J. 1971. "Party Effort and Its Impact on the Vote." *American Political Science Review* 65: 439–50.

Dahl, Robert A. 1961. *Who Governs? Power and Democracy in an American City.* New Haven: Yale University Press.

Davila, Arlene. 2000. "Mapping Latinidad: Language and Culture in the Spanish TV Battlefront." *Television New Media* 1, no. 1: 75–94.

Dawson, Michael C. 1995. *Behind the Mule: Race and Class in African-American Politics.* Princeton, NJ: Princeton University Press.

De Genova, Nicholas. 2004. "The Legal Production of Mexican/Migrant 'Illegality.'" *Latino Studies* 2, no. 2: 160–85.

de la Garza, Rodolfo, and Louis DeSipio. 1992. *From Rhetoric to Reality: Latino Politics in the 1988 Elections.* Boulder, CO: Westview.

———. 1996. *Ethnic Ironies: Latino Politics in the 1992 Elections.* Boulder, CO: Westview.

———. 1999. *Awash in the Mainstream: Latino Politics in the 1996 Elections.* Boulder, CO: Westview.

———. 2005. *Muted Voices: Latinos and the 2000 Elections.* Lanham, MD: Rowman and Littlefield.

de la Garza, Rodolfo O., Louis DeSipio, and David L. Leal, eds. 2010. *Beyond the Barrio: Latinos in the 2004 Election.* Notre Dame, IN: University of Notre Dame Press.

de la Garza, Rodolfo O., Carolyn Dunlap, Jongho Lee, and Jaesung Ryu. 2002. "Latino Voter Mobilization in 2000: Campaign Characteristics and Effectiveness." Tomás Rivera Policy Institute.

de la Garza, Rodolfo, Angelo Falcon, and F. Chris Garcia. 1996. "Will the Real Americans Please Stand Up? Anglo and Mexican-American Support of Core American Political Values." *American Journal of Political Science* 40, no. 2: 335–51.

DeSipio Louis. 1996. *Counting on the Latino Vote: Latinos as a New Electorate.* Charlottesville: University Press of Virginia.

———. 2001. "Building America, One Person at a Time: Naturalization and Political Behavior of the Naturalized in Contemporary American Politics." In *E pluribus unum? Contemporary and Historical Perspectives on Immigrant Political Incorporation,* edited by Gary Gerstle and John H. Mollenkopf, 67–106. New York: Russell Sage Foundation.

Diaz, Joy. 2013. "Group Says It Can Turn Texas Blue." Radio report. KUT, January 25. www.kut.org/2013/01/group-says-it-can-turn-texas-blue/#.

Edsall, Thomas B. 2012 "Let the Nanotargeting Begin." *New York Times,* April 15.

Elazar, Daniel J. 1984. *American Federalism: A View from the States.* 3rd ed. New York: Harper and Row.

Eldersveld, Samuel J. 1956. "Experimental Propaganda Techniques and Voting Behavior." *American Political Science Review* 50: 154–65.

Erie, Steven P. 1988. *Rainbow's End: Irish-Americans and the Dilemmas of Urban Machine Politics, 1840–1985.* Berkeley: University of California Press.

Erikson, Robert S., and Kent L. Tedin. 1981. "The 1928–1936 Partisan Realignment: The Case for the Conversion Hypothesis." *American Political Science Review* 75: 951–62.

———. 1986. "Voter Conversion and the New Deal Realignment: A Response to Campbell." *Western Political Quarterly* 39, no. 4: 729–32.

Félix, Adrián. 2008. "New Americans or Diasporic Nationalists? Mexican Migrant Responses to Naturalization and Implications for Political Participation." *American Quarterly* 60, no. 3: 601–24.

Félix, Adrián, Carmen González, and Ricardo Ramírez. 2008. "Political Protest, Ethnic Media, and Latino Naturalization." *American Behavioral Scientist* 52, no. 4: 618–34.

Field Institute. 2000. *A Digest Examining California's Expanding Latino Electorate.* San Francisco: Field Institute.

Fix, Michael, Jeffrey S. Passel, and Kenneth Sucher. 2003. "Trends in Naturalization." In *Immigrant Families and Workers: Facts and Perspectives.* Immigration Studies Program. Washington, DC: Urban Institute.

Fox, Jonathan, and Xóchitl Bada. 2011. "Migrant Civic Engagement." In *Rallying for Immigrant Rights: The Fights for Inclusion in 21st Century America,* edited by Kim Voss and Irene Bloemraad. Berkeley: University of California.

Fraga, Luis R., John A. Garcia, Rodney Hero, Michael Jones-Correa, Valerie Martinez-Ebers, and Gary M. Segura. 2006. Latino National Survey (LNS) [Computer file]. ICPSR20862-v4. Ann Arbor, MI: Inter-university Consortium for Political and Social Research [distributor], 2010-05-26. doi:10.3886/ICPSR20862.v4.

———. 2010. *Latino Lives in America: Making It Home*. Philadelphia: Temple University Press.

Fraga, Luis R., and Ricardo Ramírez. 2004. "Demography and Political Influence: Disentangling the Latino Vote." *Harvard Journal of Hispanic Policy* 16: 69–96.

Franke-Ruta, Garance, and Harold Meyerson. 2004. "The GOP Deploys." *American Prospect*, February 1.

Frymer, Paul. 1999. *Uneasy Alliances: Race and Party Competition in America*. Princeton, NJ: Princeton University Press.

Gandy, Oscar H., Jr. 2000. "Race, Ethnicity and the Segmentation of Media Markets." In *Mass Media and Society*, 3rd. ed., edited by James Curran and Michael Gurevitch, 44–69. New York: Arnold; and Oxford University Press.

Garland, Phyl. 1982. "The Black Press: Down but Not Out." *Columbia Journalism Review* 21, no. 3: 43–50.

Gerber, Alan. S., and Donald Green. 2000. "The Effects of Canvassing, Telephone Calls, and Direct Mail on Voter Turnout: A Field Experiment." *American Political Science Review*, 94, no. 3: 653–63.

Gershtenson, Joseph. 2003. "Mobilization Strategies of the Democrats and Republicans, 1956–2000." *Political Research Quarterly* 56: 293–308.

Gibson, Campbell J., and Emily Lennon. 1999. "Historical Census Statistics on the Foreign-Born Population of the United States: 1850–1990." Population Division Working Paper No. 29. Washington, DC: U.S. Bureau of the Census.

Ginsberg, Steve. 1994. "Ex-Field Hands Score as Deejays on Hispanic Radio (Juan Carlos Hidalgo and Jesus Garcia)." *Los Angeles Business Journal*, February 21, 1994. www.encyclopedia.com/doc/1G1-15198620.html.

Ginsberg, Thomas, and Deborah Bolling. 2001. "The Changing Face of Who We Are." *Philadelphia Inquirer*, March 25, B1.

Glazer, Nathan, and Daniel Patrick Moynihan. 1963. *Beyond the Melting Pot: The Negroes, Puerto Ricans, Jews, Italians, and the Irish of New York City*. Cambridge: MIT Press and Harvard University Press.

Gonzales, Alfonso. 2009. "The 2006 Mega Marchas in Greater Los Angeles: Counter-Hegemonic Moment and the Future of El Migrante Struggle." *Latino Studies* 7: 30–59.

Gonzalez, Daniel, and Yvonne Wingett. 2006. "Power of Pulpit Inspired Immigrants to Protest." *Arizona Republic*, March 29.

Gonzalez, Emilio T. 2008. "Naturalization Delays: Causes, Consequences And Solutions." Written testimony prepared for Emilio T. Gonazalez, director, U.S. Citizen and Immigration Services, for the January 17, 2008, hearing "Naturalization Delays: Causes, Consequences, and Solutions." House Judiciary Committee: Subcommittee on Immigration, Citizenship, Refugees, Border Security, and International Law.

Gorman, Anna, and Tami Abdollah. 2007. "Turnout Is Low at Immigration Rallies." *Los Angeles Times*, March 26.

Gorman, Anna, and Jennifer Delson. 2007. "Citizenship Requests Soar before Big Changes: A Stiffer Test, Higher Fees and Perhaps New Laws Are on the Horizon." *Los Angeles Times*, February 25.

Gosnell, Harold F. 1926. "An Experiment in the Stimulation of Voting." *American Political Science Review* 20: 869–74.

—. 1927. *Getting Out the Vote.* Chicago: University of Chicago Press.

Green, Donald P., and Alan S. Gerber. 2001. "Getting Out the Youth Vote: Results from Randomized Field Experiments." Institution for Social and Policy Studies, Yale University. www.yale.edu/isps/publications/Youthvote.pdf.

—. 2004. *Get Out the Vote!* Washington, DC: Brookings Institution.

Guerra, Fernando J., and Luis R. Fraga. 1996. "Theory, Reality, and Perpetual Potential: Latinos in the 1992 California Elections." In *Ethnic Ironies: Latino Politics in the 1992 Elections,* edited by Rodolfo O. de la Garza and Louis DeSipio. Boulder, CO: Westview Press.

Gutiérrez, David G. 1999. "Migration, Emergent Ethnicity, and the "Third Space": The Shifting Politics of Nationalism in Greater Mexico." *Journal of American History* 86, no. 2: 481–517.

Gutiérrez, Felix. 2006. Interview by Bob Garfield. *On the Media.* National Public Radio. WNYC, New York City. March 31.

Gutiérrez, Félix F., and Jorge Reina Schement. 1979. "Spanish-Language Radio in the Southwestern United States." Monograph No. 5. Center for Mexican American Studies, University of Texas at Austin.

Hajnal, Zoltan L. 2009 "Who Loses in American Democracy? A Count Of Votes Demonstrates the Limited Representation of African Americans." *American Political Science Review* 103, no. 1: 37–57.

Hamilton, James. 2000. "Alternative Media: Conceptual Difficulties, Critical Possibilities." *Journal of Communication Inquiry* 24: 357–78.

Hernandez, Daniel. 2006. "Stirring the Other L.A.: How the Media and Immigrant Advocates Got 500,000 People to Protest." *LA Weekly,* March 27, 2006.

—. 2007. "Year One of the Immigrant Rights Movement: Washington Drags Its Feet While the Rest of Society Adapts to a New Reality." *Los Angeles Times,* March 25, 2007.

Hero, Rodney E. 1992. *Latinos and the U.S. Political System: Two-Tiered Pluralism.* Philadelphia: Temple University Press.

—. 1998. *Faces of Inequality: Social Diversity in American Politics.* New York: Oxford University Press.

Hero, Rodney, and Patricia A. Jaramillo. 2005. "Latinos and the 2000 Elections in Colorado: More Real than Apparent, More Apparent than Real?" In *Muted Voices: Latino Politics in the 2000 Elections,* edited by Rodolfo O. de la Garza and Louis DeSipio. Lanham, MD: Rowman and Littlefield.

Highton, Benjamin, and Arthur L. Burris. 2002. "New Perspectives on Latino Voter Turnout in the United States." *American Politics Research* 30: 285–306.

Hoefer, Michael, Bryan C. Baker, and Nancy F. Rytina. 2012. "Estimates of the Unauthorized Immigrant Population Residing in the United States, January 2011." Office of Immigration Statistics, Policy Directorate, U.S. Department of Homeland Security (DHS). www.dhs.gov/xlibrary/assets/statistics/publications/ois_ill_pe_2011.pdf.

Huckfeldt, Robert, and John Sprague. 1992. "Political Parties and Electoral Mobilization: Political Structure, Social Structure, and the Party Canvass." *American Political Science Review,* 86, no. 1: 70–86.

Huntington, Samuel P. 2004. *Who Are We? The Challenges to America's National Identity.* New York: Simon and Schuster.

Iyengar, Shanto. 1991. *Is Anyone Responsible? How Television Frames Political Issues.* Chicago: University of Chicago Press.

Iyengar, Shanto, and Donald R. Kinder. 1987. *News That Matters: Television and American Opinion.* Chicago: University of Chicago Press.

Jasso, Guillermina, and Mark R. Rosenzweig. 1990. *The New Chosen People: Immigrants in the United States.* New York: Russell Sage Foundation.

Jennings, M. Kent. 1979. "Another Look at the Life Cycle and Political Participation." *American Journal of Political Science* 23, no. 4: 755–71.

———. 1987. "Residues of a Movement: The Aging of the American Protest Generation." *American Political Science Review* 81, no. 2: 367–82.

Johnson, Hans P., Belinda I. Reyes, Laura Mameesh, and Elisa Barbour. 1999. *Taking the Oath: An Analysis of Naturalization in California and the United States.* San Francisco: Public Policy Institute of California.

Johnson, Mark, and Linda Spice. 2006. "Thousands Marched for Immigrants." *Milwaukee Journal Sentinel,* March 23.

Johnson, Martin, Robert M. Stein, and Robert D. Wrinkle. 2003. "Language, Residential Stability, and Voting among Latino-Americans." *Social Science Quarterly* 84, no. 2: 412–24.

Johnson, Phylis. 2004. "Black Radio Politically Defined: Communicating Community and Political Empowerment through Stevie Wonder's KJLH-FM, 1992–2002." *Political Communication* 21, no. 3: 353–67.

Jones-Correa, Michael. 1998. *Between Two Nations: The Political Predicament of Latinos in New York City.* Ithaca, NY: Cornell University Press.

Juenke, Eric Gonzalez, and Robert R. Preuhs. 2012. "Irreplaceable Legislators? Rethinking Minority Representatives in the New Century." *American Journal of Political Science* 56, no. 3: 705–15.

Kandel, William A. 2011. "US Foreign-Born Population: Trends and Selected Characteristics." *Congressional Research Service.* www.fas.org/sgp/crs/misc/R41592.pdf.

Kim, Thomas P. 2007. *The Racial Logic of Politics: Asian Americans and Party Competition.* Philadelphia: Temple University Press.

Kopicki, Allison, and Will Irving. 2012. "Assessing How Pivotal the Hispanic Vote Was to Obama's Victory." *New York Times,* November 20.

Lazos, Sylvia R. 2007. The Immigrant Rights Marches (Las Marchas): Did the "Gigante" (Giant) Wake Up or Does It Still Sleep Tonight? *Nevada Law Journal* 7: 202–52.

Leal, David. 2002. "Political Participation by Latino Non-Citizens in the United States." *British Journal of Political Science* 32: 353–70.

Lees-Marshment, Jennifer. 2001. *Political Marketing and British Political Parties: The Party's Just Begun.* Manchester: Manchester University Press.

Leighley, Jan E. 2001. *Strength in Numbers? The Political Mobilization of Racial and Ethnic Minorities.* Princeton, NJ: Princeton University Press.

Leighley, Jan E., and Arnold Vedlitz. 1999. "Race, Ethnicity, and Political Participation: Competing Models and Contrasting Explanations." *Journal of Politics* 61, no. 4: 1092–114.

Lien, Pei-te. 1994. "Ethnicity and Political Participation: A Comparison between Asian and Mexican Americans." *Political Behavior* 16: 237–64.

Llenas, Bryan. 2012. "Obama Win Fueled by Latino Voter Muscle, FOX Exit Polls Show." *FOX News Latino.* November 8, www.latino.foxnews.com/latino/politics/2012/11/08/obama-win-fueled-by-latino-voter-muscle-fox-exit-polls-show/.

Logan, John, Jennifer Darra, and Sookhee Oh. 2012. "The Impact of Race and Ethnicity, Immigration and Political Context on Participation in American Electoral Politics." *Social Forces* 90, no. 3: 993–1022.

Lopez, Mark Hugo, and Ana Gonzalez-Barrera. 2012. "Latino Voters Support Obama by 3–1 Ratio, but Are Less Certain Than Others about Voting." Washington, DC: Pew

Hispanic Center. www.pewhispanic.org/2012/10/11/latino-voters-supportobama-by -3-1-ratio-but-are-less-certain-than-others-about-voting.

MacManus, Susan A., and Carol A. Cassell. 1982. "Mexican-Americans in City Politics: Participation, Representation, and Policy Preferences." *Urban Interest* 4, no. 1: 57–69.

Mancini, Paolo, and David L. Swanson, eds. 1996. *Politics, Media, and Modern Democracy: An International Study of Innovations in Electoral Campaigning and Their Consequences.* Westport, CT: Praeger.

Matsubayashi, Tetsuya, and Rene R. Rocha. 2012. "Racial Diversity and Public Policy in the States." *Political Research Quarterly* 65, no. 3: 600–614.

Mauser, Gary A. 1983. *Political Marketing: An Approach to Campaign Strategy.* New York: Praeger.

Medina, Olga, and Marisabel Torres. 2009. "Citizenship beyond Reach." *National Council of La Raza.* Washington, DC.

Michelson, Melissa R. 2005. "Meeting the Challenge of Latino Voter Mobilization." *Annals of the American Academy of Political and Social Science* 601: 85–101.

Moctezuma, Miguel. 2004. "La experiencia política binacional de los zacatecanos residentes en Estados Unidos. El caso del Frente Cívico Zacatecano." In *Nuevas Tendencias y Desafíos de la Migración Internacional México-Estados,* edited by Raúl Delgado Wise and Margarita Favela. Zacatecas: Universidad Autónoma de Zacatecas.

Mora, G. Cristina. 2009. "De muchos, uno: The Institutionalization of Latino Panethnicity 1960–1990." Ph.D diss., Princeton University.

Morain, Dan. 1994. "California Elections; the Propositions; Funds Fuel Prop. 187 Fight; Tobacco Gives Millions to Prop. 188." *Los Angeles Times,* October 29, 23.

Motel, Seth, and Eileen Patten. 2012. *Latinos in the 2012 Election: New Mexico.* Washington, DC: Pew Hispanic Center. www.pewhispanic.org/files/2012/10/NM-election-factsheet .pdf.

Mutz, Diana C., and Joe Soss. 1997. "Reading Public Opinion: The Influence of News Coverage on Perceptions of Public Sentiment." *Public Opinion Quarterly* 61: 431–51

NALEO Educational Fund. 2012. "The 2012 Latino Vote—Turning Numbers into Clout." Los Angeles: NALEO.

Newton, Kenneth. 1999. "Mass Media Effects: Mobilization or Media Malaise?" *British Journal of Political Science* 29, no. 4: 577–99.

Nickerson, David W. 2006. "Hunting the Elusive Young Voter." *Journal of Political Marketing* 5, no. 3: 47–69.

Nie, Norman H, Sidney Verba, and John R Petrocik. 1976. *The Changing American Voter.* Cambridge: Harvard University Press.

Oboler, Suzanne. 1995. *Ethnic Labels, Latino Lives: Identity and the Politics of (Re)Presentation in the United States.* Minneapolis: University of Minnesota Press.

Ong, Paul. 2011. "Defensive Naturalization and Anti-Immigrant Sentiment: Chinese Immigrants in Three Primate Metropolises." *Asian American Policy Review* 21: 39–55.

Osborn, Tracy, Scott D. McClurg, and Benjamin Knoll. 2010. "Voter Mobilization and the Obama Victory." *American Politics Research* 38, no. 2: 211–32.

Owen, Bruce M., and Steven S. Wildman. 1992. *Video Economics.* Cambridge: Harvard University Press.

Pachon, Harry. 1991. "U.S. Citizenship and Latino Participation in California Politics." In *Racial and Ethnic Politics in California,* edited by Bryan O. Jackson and Michael B. Prestson. Berkeley, CA: Institute of Governmental Studies.

Pachon, Harry, and Rodolfo de la Garza. 1998. "Why Pollsters Missed the Latino Vote— Again!" *Policy Note.* Claremont, CA: Tomás Rivera Policy Institute. July.

Pan, Philip P. 2000 "Naturalization: An Unnatural Process." *Washington Post,* July 4, A1.

Pantoja, Adrian, Ricardo Ramírez, and Gary M Segura. 2001. "Citizens by Choice, Voters by Necessity: Patterns of Political Mobilization by Naturalized Latinos." *Political Research Quarterly* 54, no. 4: 729–50.

Passel, Jeffrey S., and D'Vera Cohn. 2008. *A Portrait of Unauthorized Immigrants in the United States.* Washington, DC: Pew Hispanic Center.

Passel, Jeffrey S., and Roberto Suro. 2003. *The Rise of the Second Generation: Changing Patterns in Hispanic Population Growth.* Washington, DC: Pew Hispanic Center. October.

Pastor, Manuel, and Jared Sanchez. 2012. "Rock the (Naturalized) Vote: The Size and Location of the Recently Naturalized Voting Age Citizen Population." Los Angeles: Center for the Study of Immigrant Integration. www.csii.usc.edu/documents/Naturalization_and_Voting_Age_Population_web.pdf.

Peter, Jochen. 2004. "Our Long 'Return to the Concept of Powerful Mass Media'—A Cross-National Comparative Investigation of the Effects of Consonant Media Coverage." *International Journal of Public Opinion Research* 16, no. 2: 144–68.

Pilkington, Ed. 2012. "Latino Voter Eligibility at All-Time High in US but Turnout Likely to Remain Low." *Guardian,* October 1.

Plascencia, Luis. 2012. *Disenchanting Citizenship: Mexican Migrants and the Boundaries of Belonging.* New Brunswick, NJ: Rutgers University Press.

Portes, Alejandro, and John Curtis. 1987. "Changing Flags: Naturalization and its Determinants among Mexican Immigrants." *International Migration Review* 21, no. 2: 352–71.

Portes, Alejandro, and Rafael Mozo. 1985. "Naturalization, Registration, and Voting Patterns of Cubans and Other Ethnic Minorities: A Preliminary Analysis." In *Proceedings of the First National Conference on Citizenship and the Hispanic Community,* edited by NALEO Educational Fund. Washington, DC: NALEO Educational Fund.

Portes, Alejandro, and Min Zhou. 1993. "The New Second Generation: Segmented Assimilation and Its Variants." *Annals of the American Academy of Political and Social Science* 530: 74–96.

Presser, Stanley, and Michael W. Traugott. 1992. "Little White Lies and Social Science Models: Correlated Response Errors in a Panel Study of Voting." *Public Opinion Quarterly* 56, no. 1: 77–86.

Preuhs, Robert R. 2005. "Descriptive Representation, Legislative Leadership, and Direct Democracy: Latino Influence on English Only Laws in the States, 1984–2002." *State Politics and Policy Quarterly* 5, no. 3: 203–24.

———. 2007. "Descriptive Representation as a Mechanism to Mitigate Policy Backlash Latino Incorporation and Welfare Policy in the American States." *Political Research Quarterly* 60, no. 2: 277–92.

Preuhs, Robert R., and Eric Gonzalez Juenke. 2011. "Latino US State Legislators in the 1990s Majority-Minority Districts, Minority Incorporation, and Institutional Position." *State Politics and Policy Quarterly* 11, no. 1: 48–75.

Prengaman, Peter. 2006. "Immigration Rally in LA Attracts 200 Demonstrators." *Washington Post,* September 6.

Preston, Julia, and Fernanda Santos. 2012. "A Record Latino Turnout, Solidly Backing Obama." *New York Times,* November 7.

Prior, Markus. 2007. *Post-Broadcast Democracy: How Media Choice Increases Inequality in Political Involvement and Polarizes Elections.* New York: Cambridge University Press.

Radionotas. 2006. "Entrevista con el Peladillo" (interview with El Peladillo). Radionotas.com.

Ramakrishnan, Karthick. 2005. *Democracy in Immigrant America: Changing Demographics and Political Participation.* Stanford: Stanford University Press.

Ramírez, Ricardo. 2002. "The Changing Landscape Of California Politics, 1990–2000." Ph.D. diss., Stanford University.

———. 2005. "Giving Voice to Latino Voters: A Field Experiment on the Effectiveness of a National Non-Partisan Mobilization Effort." *Annals of the American Academy of Political and Social Science* 601, no. 1: 66–84.

———. 2007. "Segmented Mobilization: Latino Nonpartisan Get-Out-the-Vote Efforts in the 2000 General Election." *American Politics Research* 35, no. 3: 155–75.

———. 2011. "Mobilization en Español: Spanish-Language Radio and the Activation of Political Identities." In *Rallying for Immigrant Rights: The Fights for Inclusion in 21st Century America*, edited by Kim Voss and Irene Bloemraad. Berkeley: University of California.

Ramírez, Ricardo, and Luis Fraga. 2008. "Continuity and Change: Latino Political Incorporation in California since 1990." In *Racial and Ethnic Politics in California: Continuity and Change,* edited by Bruce E. Cain and Sandra Bass. Berkeley: Berkeley Public Policy Press, Institute of Governmental Studies.

Rodriguez, Cindy Y. 2012. "Latino Vote Key to Obama's Re-Election." CNN. November 9. www.cnn.com/2012/11/09/politics/latino-vote-key-election.

Rojas, Guillermo. 1975. "Chicano/Raza Newspaper and Periodical Serials Listing." *Hispania* 58, no. 4: 851–63.

Roscigno, Vincent J., and William F. Danaher. 2001. "Media and Mobilization." *American Sociological Review* 66: 21–48.

Rosenstone, Steven J., and John Mark Hansen. 1993. *Mobilization, Participation, and Democracy in America.* New York: Macmillan.

Rytina, Nancy. 2002. "IRCA Legalization Effects: Lawful Permanent Residence and Naturalization through 2001." Office of Policy and Planning, Statistics Division, U.S. Immigration and Naturalization Service. www.dhs.gov/xlibrary/assets/statistics/publications/ irca0114int.pdf.

———. 2009. "Estimates of the Legal Permanent Resident Population in 2007." U.S. Department of Homeland Security. www.dhs.gov/xlibrary/assets/statistics/publications/ lpr_pe_2007.pdf.

Schmitt, Eric. 2001. "Census Figures Show Hispanics Pulling Even with Blacks." *New York Times,* March 8, A1.

Sears, David O., and Nicholas A. Valentino. 1997. "Politics Matters: Political Events as Catalysts for Preadult Socialization." *American Political Science Review* 91, no. 1: 45–65.

Segura, Gary M., Denis Falcon, and Harry Pachon. 1997. "Dynamics of Latino Partisanship in California: Immigration, Issue Salience, and Their Implications." *Harvard Journal of Hispanic Policy* 10: 62–80.

Shaw, Daron, Rodolfo de la Garza, and Jongho Lee. 2000. "Examining Latino Turnout in 1996: A Three-State, Validated Survey Approach." *American Journal of Political Science* 44: 338–46.

Simonett, Helena. 2000. "Popular Music and the Politics of Identity: The Empowering Sound of Technobanda." *Popular Music and Society* 24, no. 2: 1–24.

Smith, Gareth, and Andy Hirst. 2001. "Strategic Political Segmentation—A New Approach for a New Era of Political Marketing." *European Journal of Marketing* 35, no. 9/10: 1058–73.

Smith, Michael Peter, and Bernadette Tarallo. 1995. "Proposition 187: Global Trend or Local Narrative? Explaining Anti-Immigrant Politics in California, Arizona and Texas." *International Journal of Urban and Regional Research* 19: 664–76.

Squires, Catherine R. 2000. "Black Talk Radio: Defining Community Needs and Identity." *Harvard International Journal of Press/Politics* 5, no. 2: 73–93.

Starr, Alexandra. 2006. "The Spanish-Language DJs behind the New Wave of Latino Activism." *Slate Magazine,* May 3. www.slate.com/id/2141008/.

Stein, Robert M., Jan Leighley, and Christopher Owens. 2005. *Who Votes, Who Doesn't, Why and, What Can Be Done?* Report to the Federal Commission on Electoral Reform. www.american.edu/spa/cdem/upload/4-stein.pdf.

Stoker, Laura, and M. Kent Jennings. 1995. "Life-Cycle Transitions and Political Participation: The Case of Marriage." *American Political Science Review* 89, no. 2: 421–33.

Suro, Roberto, and Gabriel Escobar. 2006. *2006 National Survey of Latinos: The Immigration Debate.* Washington, DC: Pew Hispanic Center. www.pewhispanic.org.

Tactaquin, Catherine. 2004. "Voting Rights for Immigrants." *Poverty and Race* 13: 5–7.

Tam Cho, Wendy, K. 1999. "Naturalization, Socialization, Participation: Immigrants and (Non-)Voting." *Journal of Politics* 61, no. 4: 1140–55.

Taylor, Paul, Ana Gonzalez-Barrera, Jeffrey S. Passel, and Mark Hugo Lopez. 2012. "An Awakened Giant: The Hispanic Electorate Is Likely to Double by 2030." Washington, DC: Pew Hispanic Center. www.pewhispanic.org/files/2012/11/hispanic_vote_likely _to_double_by_2030_11–14–12.pdf.

Teixiera, Ruy A. 1992. *The Disappearing American Voter.* Washington, DC: Brookings Institution.

Thomas, Evan, ed. 2010. *A Long Time Coming: The Inspiring, Combative 2008 Campaign and the Historic Election of Barack Obama.* New York: Public Affairs.

Tichenor, Daniel J. 2002. *Dividing Lines: The Politics of Immigration Control in America.* Princeton, NJ: Princeton University Press.

Tomás Rivera Policy Institute. 1996 Survey of Latinos in California.

Uhlaner, Carole, J. 1996. "Latinos and Ethnic Politics in California: Participation and Preferences." In *Latino Politics in California,* edited by Anibal Yanez-Chavez. San Diego: Center for U.S.-Mexican Studies, University of San Diego.

Uhlaner, Carole J., Bruce E. Cain, and D. Roderick Kiewiet. 1989. "Political Participation of Ethnic Minorities in the 1980s." *Political Behavior* 11: 195–221.

Uranga, Rachel. 2006. "March against Immigrant Bill Expected to Attract Thousands." *Los Angeles Daily News,* March 24.

U.S. Immigration and Naturalization Service. 1997. *Statistical Yearbook of the Immigration and Naturalization Service, 1996.* Washington, DC: U.S. Government Printing Office.

———. 1998. *Monthly Statistical Report, September FY 1998 Year End Report.* Washington, DC: U.S. Government Printing Office.

United States Bureau of the Census. 2001. "Population Projections of the United States by Age, Sex, Race, Hispanic Origin, and Nativity: 1999 to 2100." Population Division, Population Projections Branch. www.census.gov/population/projections/nation/sum mary/np-t5–b.pdf.

United States Department of Homeland Security. 2004. *Yearbook of Immigration Statistics: 2003.* Washington, DC: U.S. Government Printing Office.

———. 2006. *Yearbook of Immigration Statistics: 2004.* Washington, DC: U.S. Department of Homeland Security, Office of Immigration Statistics.

———. 2006. *Yearbook of Immigration Statistics: 2005.* Washington, DC: U.S. Department of Homeland Security, Office of Immigration Statistics.

———. 2007. *Yearbook of Immigration Statistics: 2006.* Washington, DC: U.S. Department of Homeland Security, Office of Immigration Statistics.

————. 2008. *Yearbook of Immigration Statistics: 2007.* Washington, DC: U.S. Department of Homeland Security, Office of Immigration Statistics.

————. 2009. *Yearbook of Immigration Statistics: 2008.* Washington, DC: U.S. Department of Homeland Security, Office of Immigration Statistics.

Verba, Sidney, Kay Lehman Schlozman, and Henry Brady. 1993. "Race, Ethnicity, and Political Resources: Participation in the United States." *British Journal of Political Science* 23: 453–97.

————. 1995. *Voice and Equality: Civic Voluntarism in American Politics.* Cambridge: Harvard University Press.

Verba, Sidney, and Norman H. Nie. 1972. *Participation in America: Social Equality and Political Democracy.* New York: Harper and Row.

Wang, Andrew L. 2005. "Protesters Decry Lipinski's Vote on Immigration Bill." *Chicago Tribune,* December 29, 2005.

Wang, Ted, and Robert C. Winn. 2011. "Groundswell Meets Groundwork: Building on the Mobilizations to Empower Immigrant Communities." In *Rallying for Immigrant Rights: The Fights for Inclusion in 21st Century America,* edited by Kim Voss and Irene Bloemraad. Berkeley: University of California.

Ward, Brian. 2004. *Radio and the Struggle for Civil Rights in the South.* Gainesville: University Press of Florida.

Waslin, Michele. 2005. "Latino Naturalization and the Federal Government's Response." Manuscript. Director of Immigration Policy Research. National Council of La Raza.

Watanabe, Teresa, and Hector Becerra. 2006. "500,000 Pack Streets to Protest Immigration Bills." *Los Angeles Times,* March 6.

Watkins, Mel. 1994. *On the Real Side: Laughing, Lying, and Signifying: The Underground Tradition of African-American Humor That Transformed American Culture, from Slavery to Richard Pryor.* New York: Simon and Schuster.

Weintraub, Daniel M. 1994. "Crime, Immigration Issues Helped Wilson, Poll Finds." *Los Angeles Times,* November 9, A1.

Wielhouwer, Peter W. 2002. "Releasing the Fetters: Parties and the Mobilization of the African-American Electorate." *Journal of Politics,* 62: 206–22.

Wolfinger, Raymond E., and Steven J. Rosenstone. 1980. *Who Votes?* New Haven: Yale University Press.

Wong, Janelle. 2005. "Mobilizing Asian American Voters: A Field Experiment." *Annals of the American Academy of Political and Social Science* 601: 102–4.

————. 2006. *Democracy's Promise: Immigrants and American Civic Institutions.* Ann Arbor: University of Michigan Press.

Zaller, John. 1992. *The Nature and Origins of Mass Opinion.* New York: Cambridge University Press.

————. 1996. "The Myth of Massive Media Impact Revived: New support for a Discredited Idea. In *Political Persuasion and Attitude Change,* edited by Diana C. Mutz, Paul M. Sniderman, and Richard M. Brody, 17–78. Chicago: Chicago University Press.

Zepeda-Millán, Chris. 2011. "Dignity's Revolt: Threat, Identity, and Immigrant Mass Mobilization." Ph.D. diss., Cornell University.

Index

Abrajano, Marisa A., 79

affirmative action, Proposition 209 (California) and, 77, 149n20

African Americans: California demographics and, 147–48n3; electoral capture of, 126; as homogeneous, 5; political campaigns and, 102–3; political marginalization of, 28; racial category in voter registration and, 144n20; in Texas, 138, 139

Almendárez Coello, Renán "El Cucuy," 38, 47–48, 52, 144n2, 145n10

Alvarez, R. Michael, 79, 149–50n26

Angle, Sharron, 134

Arbitron, 42, 44, 45–46, 51, 145n17

Arizona: changing composition of Latino population in, 6; Chicano identity in, 153n16; demographics of, 132–33; demography as destiny in, 71; as epicenter of reactive mobilization, 130–31; expectations for Latino electorate in, 130–33; Latino organizations in, 131–32, 153n16; level of Latino presence in, 13, 14–15; Mexican American studies in, 131; proactive mobilization in, 131; registration parity ratio in, 16–17; SB 1070 and, 130–31; Spanish-language media in, 131–32, 153n17; ten states with most Latinos and, 11; two-party system in, 132

Asian Americans: California demographics and, 147–48n3; historical immigration patterns and, 122; as politically ignored, 28, 152n10;

as politically isolated minority, 126; U.S. population growth and, 152n4

Baines, Paul R., 99

Barlow, William, 47

Barrera, Colo, 144n2

Barreto, Matt: on Latino voter registration cohorts, 82, 112, 149n19; literature on Latino political participation and, 148n10; on native-born versus naturalized Latino voters, 112; on pollsters missing Latino vote, 143n3

Bass, Loretta E., 80

battleground states, 67

Battleground Texas, 139

Beck, Paul Allen, 81

Beltrán, Cristina, 4, 5

Bendixen, Sergio, 1

Bennion, Elizabeth A., 101

Berenice, Mayra, 144n2

bilingual education, 77, 135, 149n20

black media: community-building capacity and, 46; community through identity and, 40; versus corporate mass media, 48; early 1990s civic activism in Los Angeles and, 49; endogenous forces affecting, 48; public scrutiny of, 47; radio and community mobilization and, 39–41, 47–48; Rodney King verdict and, 40; Spanish-language radio and, 46–49, 128; target audience and goals of, 47; voice and racial identity in, 47

Border Protection, Anti-terrorism, and
Illegal Immigration Control Act
(2005). *See* HR 4437 protests
Bowler, Shaun, 7, 15, 126
Bracero Program, 143n6
Brady, Henry, 53
Braungart, Margaret M., 81
Braungart, Richard G., 81
British immigrants, 57
Brody, Richard M., 149n25
Brown, Kathleen, 77
Browning, Rufus P., 54
Burris, Arthur L., 80–81, 150n33
Bush, George H. W., 19
Bush, George W., 103, 138

Cadelago, Hugo, 144n2
Cain, Bruce E., 34
California: affirmative action in, 77; age
distribution in, 74; bilingual education
in, 77; changes in demographic
composition of, 73–74, 147–48nn2–3;
choice of for case study, 148n5; context
of Latino mobilization and, 27, 144n18;
demography as destiny in, 71, 74;
growth in Latino electorate in, 23;
higher naturalization rates in, 59–61;
historical Latino political activation in,
23; Latino organizations in, 131; Latino
participation puzzle in, 83–85, 149n25;
Latino population concentration
and, 97; Latinos as sleeping giant in,
78; Latino share of electorate of, 83;
Latinos in labor unions of, 151n39;
Latino voter turnout in, 78–82; legal
permanent residents in, 20; legislative
supermajorities in, 127, 152nn7–8;
level of Latino presence in, 13, 15;
majority-minority population in, 22,
73; Mexican-origin population in,
80; native-born versus naturalized
Latino citizens in, 75, 85–95; nativity of
Latinos in, 83, 149n23; naturalization
in, 27, 83; party affiliation of Latinos
in, 86; party politics in, 148nn7–9;
party realignment in, 128–29, 152n11;
political socialization of Latinos in,
112; radio and politics in the 1990s
in, 45; registration parity ratio in, 17;

ten states with most Latinos and, 11;
unauthorized immigrants in, 143n11;
voter turnout among registration
cohorts in, 85–95; voting records in,
150n28. *See also* California ballot
initiatives
California ballot initiatives: campaign
for Proposition 187 and, 76–77;
contentious political context and,
146n7; defensive naturalization and,
60–61; electoral effects of, 77–78,
84–85, 94–95, 112, 149–50n26; money
spent for and against Proposition 187
and, 148n6; party realignment and,
128–29; Pete Wilson effect and, 124,
152n6; provisions of Proposition 187
and, 60, 149n20, 152n11; provisions of
Proposition 209 and, 149n20, 152n11;
reactive mobilization and, 9–10, 74,
124, 127; registration cohort effect
and, 115; Spanish-language radio and,
45; voters' receptivity to mobilization
requests and, 114–15
California Teachers Association, 148n6
Canadian Americans and Canadian
immigrants, 57, 149n24
Casper, Lynne M., 80
Center for Community Change, 109
Century Freeway protest (Los Angeles),
45
Cesar Chavez Foundation, 132
Chicano identity, 5, 153n16
Cho, Tam, 79–80
citizenship. *See* naturalization
citizen voting age population (CVAP):
in Arizona, 132; in Colorado, 134–35;
composition of, 67, 69; mobilization
needs and, 9; in Nevada, 133; rates of
growth in, 18; unregistered voters in, 20
civil rights movements of 1960s:
alternative media and, 37; black media
and, 128; political socialization and,
111; radio and politics in the 1960s in,
37, 39
Clear Channel, 52
Clinton, Bill, 40, 121
Clinton, Hillary, 1
Collaborative Multiracial Political Study,
102

Colorado: citizen voting age population (CVAP) in, 134–35; expectations for Latino electorate in, 134–35; foreign-born population of, 9; Latino electoral presence in, 144n15; Latino organizations in, 9; Latino voter registration in, 9; level of Latino presence in, 12–13, 14–15; low naturalization and voter registration rates in, 135; registration parity ratio in, 17; ten states with most Latinos and, 11

comprehensive immigration reform, 19, 65, 124

Contreras, Miguel, 151n39

Cuban Americans: endorsement of Obama by, 153n13; ethnic approach to Latino electorate and, 3–4; naturalization and, 146n4; political affiliation of, 130, 152n15; proportion of in Latino population, 6; rates of registration and voter turnout among, 148n14

Current Population Survey, 18–19, 80

CVAP (citizen voting age population). *See* citizen voting age population (CVAP)

Danaher, William F., 37

Davila, Arlene, 43

de la Garza, Rodolfo, 110, 143n3

DeLay, Tom, 30

Democratic Party: growing Latino preference for, 130; Latino elected officials and, 153n19; reliance of on minority voters, 126

DeSipio, Louis: on barriers to naturalization, 149n24; on Latino electoral participation, 79–80, 152n9; on new electorates, 18–19, 20; on politically salient ethnicity, 4

DiCamillo, Mark, 127

Elazar, Daniel J., 23

El Cucuy (radio DJ). *See* Almendárez Coello, Renán "El Cucuy"

"El Cucuy" Foundation, 47

election of 1996, 121

election of 2000, 40, 100, 104–6, 151n2, 151n37

election of 2002, 106–7, 116

election of 2004, 103, 104, 107–8

election of 2006, 108–9

election of 2008: Clinton and Latinos in primaries and, 1; Democratic realignment and, 7; get-out-the-vote campaigns in, 103–4, 109, 116–17; Latino voting patterns in, 129; media's focus regarding Latinos and, 29; mobilization of Latinos in, 104; Obama and Latinos in general election and, 1; turnout effect in, 151n4

election of 2010, 110, 116–17, 134

election of 2012: exit poll results in, 152n5; Latinos' importance in outcome of, 119–20; Latino voting patterns in, 129; media's focus regarding Latinos and, 29; Obama and Latinos in, 2; pollsters and Latino vote and, 143n3; predictions about Latino vote in, 1–2, 152nn1–2; Spanish-language campaign ads and, 102; voting patterns by race and ethnicity in, 122–23

election of 2016, 153n18

Electoral College, 12

El Mandril (radio DJ). *See* Sanchez, Ricardo "El Mandril"

El Peladillo (radio DJ). *See* Garcia, Jesus "El Peladillo"

El Pistolero (radio DJ). *See* Pulido, Rafael "El Pistolero"

English-language media, 31–35. *See also* black media; mass media; Spanish-language media

Entravision Communications Corporation, 51, 69, 109, 146n15

Erie, Stephen P., 79

Estefan, Gloria, 153n13

Félix, Adrián, 143n9

Field Institute, 83

Flores, Anitere, 130

Florida: changing Latino population in, 2, 6; demography as destiny in, 71; expectations for Latino electorate in, 129–30; Latino organizations in, 131, 152n14; Latino political influence in, 114n15; Latinos' political affiliation in, 129–30; Latino voter turnout in,

King, Martin Luther, Jr., 39, 40
King, Rodney, 40
KJLH (radio station), 40
KLAX (radio station), 44–46, 47, 52
KLVE (radio station), 44, 46
KNAI (radio station), 132, 153n17
Knoll, Benjamin, 151n4
Kopicki, Allison, 120, 152n2
KSCA (radio station), 52
KXOL (radio station), 145n21

labor activism, radio and, 36–37
labor unions, 9, 133, 151n39
language: antecedents to Latino electoral presence and, 25; get-out-the-vote campaigns and, 28; political participation and, 33, 34, 35, 53; polls and, 143n3. *See also* Spanish-language media
La Opinión, 69
La Peligrosa (radio DJ). *See* Sandoval, Rocio "La Peligrosa"
La Preciosa network, 52
La Raza. *See* National Council of La Raza
Latino electorate: in Arizona, 130–32; in California, 153n12; campaigning versus mobilization and, 102–3; changing composition of, 19, 67, 69; changing political landscape and, 21–25; demography is destiny approach and, 3, 7–8, 11–12, 15–16, 71, 74, 121, 126, 138; dynamics beyond the ballot box and, 120–21; ethnic approach to understanding, 3–5, 11; evolutionary change in, 119; exogenous versus endogenous thresholds for electoral strength and, 7, 143n7; in Florida, 129–30, 153n12; four antecedents to Latino electoral presence and, 25; growth and growing influence of, 14–15, 119–21, 140–41; health of American democracy and, 141; as inactive, 113; increasing complexity of, 84; ineligibility to vote and, 18–20; journalistic and scholarly perceptions of, 119–21; versus Latino population, 13–14, 15, 16; legislative representation and, 125–26; low-propensity voters and, 104, 128, 152n10; multiple Latino electorates and,

143n5; versus non-Latino electorate, 14; pan-ethnic identity and, 130; particularized mobilization of, 104; partisan transformation of, 144n17; party neglect of, 144n19; pivotal vote thesis and, 3, 6–8, 11, 21, 120, 130; potential size of, 20–21; pre-voting age Latinos and, 20; primary versus general elections and, 6–7; rates of naturalization and, 54; reasons for growth in, 6–7; receptivity of to mobilization requests, 114–15; redefinition of American democracy by, 123–24; responsive capacity of, 8; reticents, reluctants, and recruits and, 19, 20, 152n9; scope, size, and consistency of growth in, 126–27; size of, 96, 121; state-centered and process-driven approach to understanding, 6–11, 23–25, 127, 140–41, 143n5; two-party system and, 125–27; uneven expansion of across states, 97. *See also* citizen voting age population (CVAP); Latino organizations; Latinos
Latino National Political Survey, 5, 19, 62–63, 80, 148n10
Latino organizations: collaboration of with Spanish-language media, 54, 69–70, 109, 127–28, 131–32, 146n15; collaborations after 2006 immigrant protests and, 109, 110; in Florida, 130, 152n14; lack of in Arizona, 131, 153n16; mobilizing opportunities and, 140; naturalization and, 68–69, 70, 71–72, 124, 125; in Nevada, 133–34; in New Mexico, 136; nonpartisan electoral work and, 104, 105; in Texas, 139. *See also specific organizations*
Latinos: age and educational attainment among, 148n11; assimilation of immigrants and, 110; binders full of, 2; commodification of identity of, 51–52; contexts driving political influence of, 3; heterogeneity of, 3, 143n5; historical immigration patterns and, 122; levels of population presence and, 12–15; national-origin differences among, 5, 6; pan-ethnic identity and, 4–5, 11, 14, 43–44, 51–52; political importance

Latinos (*continued*)
of, 11–15; political marginalization of,
99, 100, 152n10; population presence
versus electoral presence of, 13–14,
15, 16; as sleeping giant, 2, 78; states
where most live, 11–12; state- versus
national-level importance of, 11–12;
U.S. population growth and, 152n4. *See
also* Latino electorate
Leading Edge Data Services, 105
Leal, David, 34
legal permanent residents: geographical
distribution of, 20; green cards and,
59, 94–95, 146n6; Latinos versus non-
Latinos as, 57; naturalization and,
57–58, 68–69, 146n9; number of, 20
Liberman Broadcasting, 51
Lipinski, Daniel, 31
López-Cantera, Carlos, 130
Lorenz, Gerardo, 144n2
LPRs. *See* legal permanent residents
Luevanos, Marcela, 52, 144n2
Lujan, Manuel, Jr., 153n19
Luna, Humberto, 48, 52, 144n2, 145n10

Manzano, Sylvia, 139
Marshall, Dales Rogers, 54
Martinez, Susana, 136–37, 153n19
mass media: alternative media and,
37, 145n12; antecedents to Latino
electoral presence and, 25; business of
broadcasting and, 50, 52; civil rights
movements of 1960s and, 37, 39; ethnic
media for immigrant communities
and, 40–41; historical mobilizing role
of, 39–41; legitimization of protest and,
39; literature on political effects of,
36–37. *See also* black media; English-
language media; Spanish-language
media
McClurg, Scott D., 151n4
Mean Mauri (radio DJ). *See* Reinoso,
Mauricio "Mean Mauri"
media. *See* black media; English-language
media; mass media; Spanish-language
media
Mexican Americans and Mexican
immigrants: ethnic approach to Latino
electorate and, 3–4; Immigration

Act (1965) and, 152n3; Immigration
Reform and Control Act (1986)
and, 146n3; naturalization rates and,
149n24; naturalization rates of, 57;
proportion of in Latino population, 6;
raza studies and, 131
Michelson, Melissa R., 114, 152n13
Mi Familia Vota, 109, 131, 146n15
mobilization: antecedents to Latino
electoral presence and, 25; biases
in, 103; coethnic appeals and,
114; corporatization of radio and,
51–53; electoral and nonelectoral
participation and, 8; elites'
mobilization activities and, 97–99,
103, 105; as good business for
Spanish-language media, 50–51;
growth in Latino electorate and,
23; for high- versus low-propensity
voters, 27–28, 104–5; historical
Latino political activation and,
25; how change happens and, 22;
identification of Latino voters and,
144n20; Latino organizations' role
in, 144n19; of Latinos in presidential
campaigns, 97; multiplier effect of,
147n23; organizational resources
and, 8–9; particularized, 151n1;
personal characteristics and, 98–99;
personalized, 118; versus political
campaigning, 102–3; political
machines and, 118; registration parity
ratio and, 16; segmented, 110–18;
studies of get-out-the-vote efforts
and, 100–101; voter segmentation
and, 99–100, 103–5, 107, 109–11. *See
also* proactive mobilization; reactive
mobilization
Mora, Cristina, 44
Mountjoy, Richard, 76
music, banda, 44, 145n16

Nagler, Jonathan, 149–50n26
NALEO. *See* National Association of
Latino Elected and Appointed Officials
National Association of Black-Owned
Broadcasters, 40
National Association of Latino Elected
and Appointed Officials: education

fund of, 146n15; field experiments of, 113, 152n12; get-out-the-vote efforts of, 105–10, 115–18; low-propensity voters and, 107, 110, 116, 152n10; We Are America Alliance and, 109

National Council of La Raza, 40, 109, 146n15

National Latino Immigrant Survey, 19

naturalization: antecedents to Latino electoral presence and, 25; application fees and, 61, 66, 146n10, 147n24; in Arizona, 132; backlog of applications for, 61, 146n12; barriers to, 9, 61, 67, 71, 124–25, 147n24, 149n24; California anti-immigrant propositions and, 77; catalysts for change in rates of, 54–55, 65–70; changing pool of Latino immigrants and, 57; citizenship test and, 61, 146n11; cost-benefit analysis and, 59, 146n6; defensive, 26, 60, 65, 69–70; denial of benefits to immigrants and, 59; denied applications for, 61, 146n13; electoral participation and, 27, 54, 70, 79–80; fee waiver process and, 147n24; HR 4437 protests and, 26, 61, 62–65, 69–70, 124; Latino organizations and, 68–69, 70, 71–72, 124; of Latinos versus non-Latinos, 56, 67–68, 71; legal permanent residents and, 57–58; multiplier effect and, 147n23; number of Latino new citizens and, 21; potential versus actual rates of, 57, 143n8; predictors of intention to, 63–65, 70; proactive mobilization and, 8–9; proximity to home country and, 149n24; rates of by country of origin, 57, 146n4; rates of by metropolitan area, 147nn21–22; rates of by region of origin, 59; rates of in California, 83; research methods and, 150nn32–33; scholarship lacking on reasons for increases in, 61–62; slogans in 2006 immigrant protests and, 55; Spanish-language media and, 53, 68, 69, 70, 71; spikes in rates of, 58–59, 66–67, 86; time required for, 147n19; voter registration and, 70, 85; voter turnout and, 70, 81–82, 85, 150nn32–33; Ya Es Hora ¡Ciudadania! campaign and, 65–69

Nevada: expectations for Latino electorate in, 133–34; foreign-born population of, 9; Latino civic organizations in, 9; Latino voter registration in, 9; level of Latino presence in, 12–13, 14–15; registration parity ratio in, 17; ten states with most Latinos and, 11

New Jersey: changing composition of Latino population in, 6; level of Latino presence in, 12–13, 14–15; registration parity ratio in, 16–17; ten states with most Latinos and, 11

New Mexico: citizen voting age population in, 18; expectations for Latino electorate in, 135–37; Hispanos as term in, 144n16; Latinos' long-term political presence in, 23; Latino state and federal representatives in, 135–37; level of Latino presence in, 12–13, 14–15; majority-minority population in, 22, 73; registration parity ratio in, 16–17; voter registration rates in, 136

New York: changing composition of Latino population in, 6; citizen voting age population in, 18; Latino electoral presence in, 144n15; Latino organizations in, 131; Latino population concentration and, 97; Latino voter turnout in, 80; level of Latino presence in, 12–13, 14–15; registration parity ratio in, 16–17; state and federal legislative delegations of, 133; ten states with most Latinos and, 11

Nickerson, David W., 101

Nie, Norman H., 82

Obama, Barack, and Obama campaigns: Battleground Texas and, 139; election of 2008 and, 1, 103, 129; election of 2012 and, 119–21, 129; electoral coalition of, 7; Florida Latinos and, 2, 130, 153n13; Spanish-language campaign ads and, 102

Ong, Paul, 60

Osborn, Tracy, 151n4

Osterman, Rachel, 145n20

Owen, Bruce, 50

Pacheco, Paul, 137

Pacheco, Rod, 148n9

Pachon, Harry, 143n3

Pantoja, Adrian: on changing California voter, 95; on fluctuations in Latino voter turnout, 111–12, 148–49n17; on Latino electoral participation, 81–82; on naturalization and turnout, 150n32; on reactive mobilization, 60, 149–50n26

participation, political: among native-born versus naturalized Latino citizens, 75, 79–80; barriers to, 8; electoral, 54, 96; English-language ability and, 33, 34, 35, 53; generational and cohort effects on, 74–75, 81–82; individual characteristics versus political context and, 74–76; literature on Latinos', 79, 148n10, 148n13; mass media and, 36–37; political incorporation and, 151n38; recruitment for, 34

party affiliation: Arizona two-party competition and, 132; consequences of partisan integration and, 137–38; of Cuban Americans, 130, 152n15; engines of transformation of, 144n17; growing Latino electorate and two-party system and, 125–26; immigrant block voting and, 122–23; of Latinos in California, 112; New Mexico two-party competition and, 135–36; partisan realignment and, 111, 112, 128–29; race and two-party system in history and, 126; split in non-Latino voter preferences and, 14; Texas two-party system and, 137–39

party system. *See* party affiliation

Pastor, Manuel, 143n8

Perry, Rick, 138

Personal Responsibility and Work Opportunity Reconciliation Act (1996), 59

Petrocik, John R., 82

Piolin (radio DJ). *See* Sotelo, Eduardo "Piolin"

Piolin por la mañana (radio show), 51, 52

polls: 2012 Latino vote and, 1–2; undersampling of Latino voters and, 143n3

Portes, Alejandro, 110

PPIC. *See* Public Policy Institute of California (PPIC)

proactive mobilization: as change from within, 123; in Colorado, 135; critical changes in, 127–28; election of 2016 and, 153n18; elite-sponsored activities and, 8–9; in Florida, 130; later start of in Arizona, 131; naturalization and electoral participation in, 143n8; in Nevada, 134; in New Mexico, 136; political context of, 96–97; reactive mobilization and, 24–27, 70–72, 114, 124, 127–28, 131, 140; in Texas, 138–39

Proposition 187 (California). *See* California ballot initiatives

Proposition 209 (California). *See* California ballot initiatives

Proposition 227 (California). *See* California ballot initiatives

public policy: political incorporation and, 151n38; state context and Latino incorporation and, 23–24

Public Policy Institute of California (PPIC), 83, 95

Puerto Ricans, 3–4, 6, 130

Pulido, Rafael "El Pistolero," 38–39, 48, 51–52

Ramírez, Ricardo: on changing California voter, 95; field experiments by, 114, 152n13; on fluctuations in Latino voter turnout, 81–82, 111–12, 148–49n17; on naturalization and turnout, 150n32; on reactive mobilization, 60, 149–50n26; registration parity ratio and, 16

reactive mobilization: of 1960s and 1970s, 131; Arizona anti-immigrant legislation and, 130–31; California anti-immigrant propositions and, 77, 112, 149–50n26; as change from without, 123; in Colorado, 135; defensive naturalization as, 26, 60; elimination of raza studies and, 131; as essential but not sufficient for electoral transformation, 131; Florida anti-immigrant legislation and, 130; growth of Latino electorate, 140; Latino political agency and, 123; in Nevada, 134; in New Mexico, 137; as panacea, 144n18; Pete Wilson effect and, 124; political context of, 96–97; political threat and, 9–10; proactive mobilization and, 24–27, 70–72, 114, 124, 127–28, 131, 140; among Republicans, 139; short- and long-term effects of, 27, 124–25, 144n18; in Texas, 138–39; voter ID laws and, 130

redistricting, 144n14

registration parity ratio, 16–17, 20, 21–22

Reid, Harry, 134

Reinoso, Mauricio "Mean Mauri," 145n9

Republican Party: Contract with America and, 148n6; Latino elected officials and, 153n19; Proposition 187 and, 76–78; voter ID laws and, 130

Richards, Ann, 138

Rocha, Nestor Pato, 144n2

Romney, Mitt, 143n2

Roscigno, Vincent J., 37

Rosenstone, Steven J., 99

Rytina, Nancy, 58

Sanchez, Jared, 143n8

Sanchez, Ricardo "El Mandril," 48, 52, 144n2, 145n10

Sandoval, Rocio "La Peligrosa," 52, 144n2

Saralegui, Christina, 153n13

SB 1070 (Arizona), 130–31

Schlozman, Kay Lehman, 53

Seacrest, Ryan, 48

Segura, Gary: on changing California voter, 95; demography is destiny approach and, 7, 15; on fluctuations in Latino voter turnout, 81–82, 111–12, 148–49n17; literature on Latino political participation and, 148n10; on naturalization and turnout, 150n32; on political consequences of demographic changes, 126; on reactive mobilization, 60, 149–50n26

Sensenbrenner, Jim, 144n1

Sensenbrenner Bill. See HR 4437 protests

September 11, 2001, attacks, 146n13

Service Employees International Union, 102, 146n15

Simonett, Helen, 45

Sotelo, Eduardo "Piolin," 38, 47–48, 51–52, 144n2, 145n10

South, American, as homogeneous, 4–5

Southwest Voter Registration and Education Project, 104

Spanish Broadcasting System, 51

Spanish-language media: 2006 immigrant protest marches and, 25–26, 31–35, 37–39, 48–49, 51, 145nn9–10; after 2006 immigrant protest marches, 41, 49, 51, 145n13; in Arizona, 131–32, 153n17; audience segmentation and, 42; bilingualism in, 145, 145n9, 145n15; black media and, 46–49, 128; campaign ads in, 102, 104; collaboration of with Latino organizations, 54, 69–70, 109, 127–28, 131–32, 146n15; collective Latino identity and, 36, 38; consequences of political activism of, 145n5; cooperation among media outlets and, 48–49, 128; as corporate mass media, 48, 50–53; criticism of politicians by, 45; decisions about civic activism in, 46; disaster relief and, 47; endogenous forces affecting, 48; English dominant radio listeners and, 42; English-language media on, 34–35; Florida anti-immigration bills and, 130; growing advocacy role of, 127; growth of Spanish-language radio and, 41–46; lack of scholarly attention to, 53; Latino civic leaders and, 33–34; limitations of for mobilization, 51–52; linguistic isolation of, 47–49; market share and rankings and, 48–50, 51–52, 145n14, 145nn19–20; as mobilizer versus instrument of mobilizers, 34–35, 37–39; mobilizing capacity of, 26, 36, 53; mobilizing opportunities and, 140; national audience expansion and, 52–53; naturalization and, 26–27, 53, 68–71; pan-ethnic identity and, 52–53; radio formats and, 145n18; radio listening habits and, 42–43; Spanish radio as medium of choice and, 46; sub-ethnic versus pan-ethnic marketing and, 43–44; syndication of radio morning shows and, 51; target audience and goals of, 47; in Texas, 139; unifying effect of, 38; volatility among radio DJs and, 52; voter registration and, 53; voter turnout and, 145n7; women

Spanish-language media (*continued*)
in, 52. *See also* black media; English-language media; mass media
Squires, Catherine, 40
Stein, Robert, 35
Stern, Howard, 48
super PACs, 102

Tabb, David H., 54
Tancredo, Tom, 135
Texas: Battleground Texas and, 139; changing composition of Latino population in, 6; demography and destiny in, 71, 138; expectations for Latino electorate in, 137–39; John F. Kennedy's presidential win and, 104; Latino descriptive representation in, 23, 144n14; Latino organizations in, 131; Latino population of, 23, 97; Latino voter turnout in, 80, 82; level of Latino presence in, 13, 14–15; majority-minority population in, 22, 138; Mexican-origin population in, 80; registration parity ratio in, 17; Republican moderation on immigration in, 138–39; size of Latino electorate in, 23; ten states with most Latinos and, 11; two-party system in, 137–38, 153n20
Thomas, Evan, 103
Tomás Rivera Policy Institute: on Latino voter-mobilization efforts in 2000, 105, 151n2; Survey of Latinos in California, 27, 75, 85–90, 150n29
Treaty of Guadalupe Hidalgo (1848), 4

Uhlaner, Carole, 34
unauthorized immigration: driver's licenses and, 136–37; Immigration Act (1965) and, 152n3; mobilization and, 19; number of immigrants and, 19, 143n11
undocumented immigrants. *See* unauthorized immigration
United States Citizen and Immigration Services, 27, 61, 66, 147n24
Univision, 51–52, 69, 132, 146n15, 148n6
USCIS. *See* United States Citizen and Immigration Services

Velasco, Omar, 144n2
Verba, Sidney, 53, 82

Voces del Pueblo, 106–9, 116, 151n7
Voice of the People. *See* Voces del Pueblo
voter ID laws, reactive mobilization and, 130
voter registration: black radio and, 40; California anti-immigrant propositions and, 77; history of among Latinos, 104; naturalization and, 70; political baptism and, 86, 112–13, 114; racial category data in, 144n20; rates of, 9, 20; registration cohorts and, 82, 86–95, 112, 115, 149n19; slogans in 2006 immigrant protests and, 55; Spanish-language media and, 53. *See also* registration parity ratio
voter turnout: age and, 101, 116–17, 150n36; California ballot initiatives and, 77–78, 84–85, 94–95, 112, 149–50n26; California participation puzzle and, 83–85; election of 2012 versus 1996 and, 121; factors affecting, 22, 87–95, 149n21; general and Latino-specific determinants of, 78–82; generational and cohort effects on, 81–82, 85–95, 111, 112, 149n19; individual voter characteristics and, 110–11, 118; native-born versus naturalized Latino citizens and, 75–76, 85–95, 111–12; naturalization and, 54, 70, 79–80, 81–82, 150nn32–33; perceived political threat and, 27, 144n18; political socialization and, 111, 112; proactive mobilization and, 8–9; reasons for nonvoting and, 19, 20; socioeconomic status and, 98–99; Spanish-language media and, 145n7; studies of voter mobilization efforts and, 99–101; super-voters and, 88–90, 150n30; among Texas Latinos, 80; underestimates of Latinos', 2. *See also* get-out-the-vote campaigns

Walmart, 144–45n4
Ward, Brian, 39
Washington, Harold, 40
We Are America Alliance, 65, 109
welfare reform, naturalization and, 94–95
whites, political campaigns and, 102–3
Wildman, Steven S., 50
Wilson, Pete: Pete Wilson effect, 124,

152n6; Proposition 187 and, 9, 76–77; reactive mobilization and, 74, 124; Spanish-language radio and, 45

women: binders full of, 143n2; in Spanish-language radio, 52

Wong, Janelle, 79, 80–81

Woods, Nathan D., 82, 112, 148n10, 149n19

Wrinkle, Robert D., 35

Ya Es Hora: collaborating organizations and, 146n15; get-out-the-vote efforts of, 109, 110; naturalization and, 27, 65–69, 70, 71–72; organizational and media presence of, 68, 147n20; survey of citizens receiving assistance from, 67, 147n17; We Are America Alliance and, 109

Yearbook of Immigration Statistics, 67, 147n18

Youth Vote 2000 coalition, 100

Zhou, Min, 110

Race, Ethnicity, and Politics

CPSIA information can be obtained at www.ICGtesting.com
Printed in the USA
BVOW05s1021220815

414530BV00001B/25/P

9 780813 938110